D0205264

DAILY LIFE IN

COLONIAL LATIN AMERICA

Recent Titles in
The Greenwood Press Daily Life Through History Series

DAILY LIFE IN

COLONIAL LATIN AMERICA

ANN JEFFERSON AND
PAUL LOKKEN

The Greenwood Press Daily Life Through History Series

AN IMPRINT OF ABC-CLIO, LLC
Santa Barbara, California • Denver, Colorado • Oxford, England

Copyright 2011 by Ann Jefferson and Paul Lokken

All rights reserved. No part of this publication may be reproduced, stored in a retrieval system, or transmitted, in any form or by any means, electronic, mechanical, photocopying, recording, or otherwise, except for the inclusion of brief quotations in a review, without prior permission in writing from the publisher.

Library of Congress Cataloging-in-Publication Data

Jefferson, Ann, 1944–
  Daily life in colonial Latin America / Ann Jefferson and Paul Lokken.
        p. cm. — (The Greenwood press daily life through history series)
  Includes index.
  ISBN 978-0-313-34070-3 (hardback) — ISBN 978-1-57356-744-2 (ebook)   1. Latin America—Social life and customs.   2. Latin America—Social conditions.   3. Latin America—Civilization.
4. Latin America—History—To 1830.   I. Lokken, Paul.   II. Title.
  F1408.3.J44   2011
  980—dc23   2011015567

ISBN: 978-0-313-34070-3
EISBN: 978-1-57356-744-2

15 14 13 12 11   1 2 3 4 5

This book is also available on the World Wide Web as an eBook.
Visit www.abc-clio.com for details.

Greenwood
An Imprint of ABC-CLIO, LLC

ABC-CLIO, LLC
130 Cremona Drive, P.O. Box 1911
Santa Barbara, California 93116-1911

This book is printed on acid-free paper ∞

Manufactured in the United States of America

R0445233171

CONTENTS

PREFACE

Two pivotal moments sparked my interest in and approach to this study. The first happened when I went to Guatemala to do the research for my dissertation. My topic was a rebellion of the peasantry, the *campesinos,* of a rural area of eastern Guatemala in 1837. I wanted to find out why they had put down their hoes and picked up anything that could serve as a weapon for several years, finally marching on Guatemala City where their young leader Rafael Carrera, known as *"el indio,"* formed the alliances that enabled him to threaten and later destroy the Republic of Central America. As I read documents of all sorts from that period, I began to notice that the true leaders of the rebellion were the men of several large extended families that owned many acres in cattle ranches. I searched for these men and their wives in court records, land surveys, purchase and sale agreements, wills, and baptismal and marital records, and I saw that many of them were categorized as *mulato libre.* Ethnicity in this part of Latin America in the early 19th century was mostly a matter of observation or phenotype, and various scholars have discussed the unreliability of these ethnic appellations in defining a person's true ethnicity. Since Rafael Carrera became the first president of an independent Guatemala after the breakup of the United Provinces of Central America, there are pictures of him available, and, in spite of his nickname, his features appear at least as much

African as Indian. One aspect of these racial categories that scholars seem to agree on is that the word *mulato* was applied to people who appeared to be at least partly of African descent and who came from a non-Indian village. The word was *not* applied to children who had been born in an Indian village or who appeared to be *mestizos,* a combination of Europeans and indigenous people. Taking this standard as my guide, I realized that the primary leaders of this important rebellion were men of African descent. This was a surprise. Although historians had noted that most of the people living between Guatemala City and San Salvador were *ladinos,* a catchall category still used in Guatemala to mean "non-Indian," the ethnicity of these people had been treated as irrelevant to their role in history. As I read more and more documents, the ethnicity of these people began to seem far from irrelevant. It seemed to me that their ethnicity was at the core of what they did and why they did it. And I began to wonder how many other people of African descent had been hidden from history by this assumption that their ethnicity was unimportant in motivating their actions.

The other moment came when I began teaching Latin American survey courses. I always begin with a precontact sketch of the peoples of three continents who blended to create the Latin Americans of today: the indigenous people of the Western Hemisphere, the European invaders, and the Africans who were brought against their will as laborers. And I always stress the nearly insurmountable odds that the Africans and their descendants faced in the Americas, and the way they refused to be crushed by the inhospitable conditions of their new home. I did not, however, find a colonial textbook that gave these people an equal share in the construction of the Latin America we know today. This is changing, largely because of the well-researched monographs that have been coming out over the past 20 years, and on which we relied in writing this book. Before long, the influence of people from Africa will be recognized in the standard survey text, and I wanted to play a part in that historiography. When the opportunity came up to do this study of daily life in the colonial period, it seemed like the perfect chance to bring some of this recent research to a wider audience. I hope we have not unbalanced this study too heavily in the direction of the Africans, but we intentionally drew many of our examples from the experience of Africans and people of African descent in Latin America, and we have focused on the institutions, like slavery, that affected them most. I hope we have shown how these people shaped Latin American history while they made their lives as best they could within the parameters of a heartless coerced-labor system and how at times they even claimed that most revolutionary right of working people: to laugh and enjoy life.

Ann Jefferson

* * *

Like Ann, my own historical research has focused extensively on Guatemala. Also like her, I discovered in the course of conducting archival research for my doctorate that people of African ancestry had played a more important role there than I or nearly anyone else had realized. In my own doctoral dissertation I decided to explore the history of Africans and their descendants in an earlier era, the 17th century, and in the course of the research process expanded my geographic scope to include what is now El Salvador as well. My interest was in understanding the significance of the African presence in that time and place and, in addition, those aspects of colonial society that may have contributed along with modern racism to the gradual disappearance of that presence from historical memory in northwestern Central America. What I found in the records was a whole world of people, some enslaved and others free, who did everything from producing sugar under the terrible conditions in which that fateful crop was grown everywhere in the Americas, to escaping from enslavement to carve out independent lives in the remote bush, to fighting in the king's militias against foreign invaders and then using their records of military service to bargain for relief from the discriminatory tax burdens the same king levied on people of African ancestry. I also encountered many, many individuals who forged bonds of love and family across the boundaries of a legal system of racial hierarchy by which colonial authorities hoped to keep indigenous peoples, Africans, and Europeans divided into separate spheres.

As Ann has already noted, a great deal of similar research has been carried out recently for much of the vast region of the Americas over which Spain ruled for three centuries, and we have relied extensively on some of it to incorporate a fresh, deeper understanding of the colonial African experience into our discussion of daily life throughout Spanish America. Due to the importance of the sugar economy in Portuguese-ruled Brazil, that place has sometimes been treated as the only area of Latin America to be profoundly influenced by centuries of forced African immigration.

But recent research has revealed the broader impact of this forced immigration. A quick way to make this point is by referring the reader to the statistical tables included in the exhaustive, online Transatlantic Slave Trade Database, which includes records of some 35,000 of the voyages that transported more than 10 million Africans across the Atlantic against their will between the early 16th and mid-19th centuries. Fully 60 percent of those forced migrants went to Iberian-ruled areas of the Americas, most to Brazil but well over a million either to the Spanish Caribbean or to mainland Spanish America.[1] Beyond the numbers, of course, are individual lives, which have been the subject of much other recent research into the African experience in the Americas. When taken together with the findings of a longer-running effort by scholars to give proper attention to the native peoples who met the newcomers from across the Atlantic and who still constitute the majority of the population in some parts of Spanish America, this new research on the lives of Africans and their descendants has allowed us to see Latin American colonial societies in a far richer light. Thanks to the painstaking work of dozens of historians, experiences that were for a long time either slighted or ignored entirely, whether those of Africans or of native peoples, are at the forefront of the history we tell here.

Paul Lokken

NOTE

1. http://www.slavevoyages.org/tast/assessment/estimates.faces (accessed February 10, 2009).

ACKNOWLEDGMENTS

As indicated in the preface, we owe a profound scholarly debt to the individuals whose work appears in the chapter notes and annotated bibliography. Their research, in turn, was built upon a foundation laid by many other historians of colonial Latin America. We also express our profound gratitude to Mariah Gumpert of Greenwood Press for her editorial advice, direction, and patience. Each of us also wishes to thank a few people who have provided some balance to our own daily lives, although many others will go unnamed.

* * *

First and foremost, I want to thank the person without whom this book would quite literally never have seen the light of day, my coauthor Paul Lokken whose knowledge of colonial Latin America is wide and deep, and who turned out to be a meticulous scholar, a generous collaborator, and a gentle critic. I am also grateful to Catherine Komisaruk who enlivened the time we shared in the Archivo General de Centroamérica and who has continued to show an enthusiastic interest in my work. Thanks also to John Higginson and Mariana Leal Ferreira who contributed their scholarly talents to parts of the project. Finally, and from the bottom of my heart, I thank my colleagues in the History Department at the University of Tennessee who welcomed me and provided the only academic home I have found in a decade of teaching at several universities. For making my daily life worth living, I thank my son Brooke, my niece Liz, my mother, and my sisters and brothers.

Ann Jefferson

I'd like to thank Ann for creating this project, allowing me to share her vision, and making me a better writer in spite of myself. For daily mercies, my deepest gratitude to Paula, another generous and astute critic among all else, and to Annelise and Martine. I also express profound appreciation to my mother and my parents-in-law for their support. And for keeping me up-to-date on our own popular culture in all its wondrous manifestations, many thanks to Thom Oleksiuk, Doug Tompson, and Jeff Ponting.

Paul Lokken

INTRODUCTION: RACE AND FAMILY, KEYS TO THE COLONIAL PERIOD

PATRIARCHY AND RACE: AN EXAMPLE

In 1782, José de Alfaro, husband of Josefa Cadena, a pregnant *chocolatera,* or chocolate vendor, brought charges against Teresa Bravo, Teresa's husband Diego Fernández, and three members of their household for beating Josefa in the street after Mass on Sunday. The court ordered an examination of Josefa by the two doctors of the town, San Juan Teotihuacán, outside Mexico City. They found that she had indeed suffered bruises over much of her body and a scratch above the eye. Since the doctors were unable to stop the hemorrhage that had begun after the beating, one of them testified to the likelihood of a miscarriage, while the other was of the opinion that she might not lose the baby in spite of the heavy bleeding. Various witnesses confirmed the attack by Teresa and her companions, although at least one witness, a friend or acquaintance of Teresa's husband Diego, testified that Josefa started the fight. The record is incomplete and does not show any determination by a judge. It may be that a settlement was made out of court and the case dropped, especially since various facts about the life of Teresa and Diego indicate that they occupied a higher rung of the social ladder than a chocolate vender and her husband, whom the record shows to have been illiterate.

Although we can only speculate as to the outcome, the details of the incident provide important clues to the nature of colonial society in New Spain (Mexico).[1]

For one thing, witnesses testified that before attacking Josefa, Teresa called her a "black whore," a slur Josefa's husband found important to answer in his complaint. He defended his wife's honor and noted that charging a married woman with infidelity was the worst insult she could receive. In addition, he stated that his wife was not "black" but a *castiza,* one of the numerous labels created by Spaniards in their efforts to draw legal distinctions among racially mixed individuals in colonial society on the basis of actual or perceived degrees of non-European ancestry. One witness testified that the charge of "whore" was leveled at Teresa by Josefa as well, suggesting that this insult was a powerful one. The fact that José de Alfaro took pains to assert his wife's mixed-race status shows that at least in a late colonial town near Mexico City, it was considered more desirable to belong to the category *castiza,* which connoted a significant proportion of European ancestry, than to be black. By hurling the term *black* at her opponent, Teresa established her own superior position in the racialized social structure of the colonies. There is no indication that Josefa used a racial slur against Teresa, probably because Teresa, married to a functionary of the Spanish crown, was likely to have been white, although the document does not specify.

The term *whore* insulted not only the reputations of these two wives, but also that of their husbands, since patriarchal society held husbands responsible for the behavior of their wives, especially their sexual behavior. This may be one reason Josefa's husband considered the incident serious enough to warrant a court suit, although the probable loss of the anticipated child may have been the primary reason. The need to defend the family honor, considered the responsibility of the man of the household, and to assign blame for the likely miscarriage, provide clues to the workings of the patriarchal family, an institution that undergirded colonial Latin American society.

A surprising aspect of this case is that a woman of the highest social rank exchanged insults with a woman clearly below her in the social structure and even lowered herself to engaging in a catfight—complete with scratching and hair pulling, *after Mass,* no less, in full view of the Sunday morning churchgoers, who must have been highly entertained—with a woman who was six months pregnant and visibly preparing to enter the sacred institution of motherhood. If Josefa lost her child, her attackers might be considered murderers. What could provoke such an attack?

Since the record is incomplete, the causes remain a matter of speculation. Doña Teresa alleged that Josefa had brushed against her, but Josefa's husband denied this. What seems clear is that the two women had had some previous unpleasant experience with each other, and it may be that one of the women had information damaging to the reputation of the other. Or, since attacking a pregnant woman in such a way as to jeopardize the life of the baby suggests that causing a miscarriage may have been the goal, could it be that Teresa suspected that her own husband Diego was responsible for Josefa's pregnancy? The record is silent on the real causes of the fight, as well as whether José and Josefa received satisfaction, but in spite of its failure to resolve all our questions, the document provides a window on the Latin American colonial period and some of the underlying assumptions shared by the people who lived there. The chapters to come will examine in more detail the patriarchal family system and the race-based social structure, of which fleeting glimpses appear in the record of the fight between Josefa Cadena and Teresa Bravo in 1782.

OBJECTIVE OF THE BOOK

The purpose of this book is to investigate how people lived their daily lives in the American colonies of the Spanish and Portuguese crowns from the late 16th to the beginning of the 19th centuries, and how their everyday lives shaped the history of the region. In the past few decades, the historiographical focus has shifted from the traditional emphasis on momentous events and the lives of "great" men to the daily lives of everyday people, and to their beliefs and values, their hopes and fears, and especially to the relationship between these and their actions. While daily life may be intrinsically interesting, its importance as a historical category lies in its relationship to the events that rate a spot on history's timeline. These major events that touch, and in some cases shape, many lives are made by large groups of people engaged in living their lives in an ever-changing world and, in so doing, both enacting big changes and reacting to them. The major events historians struggle to interpret cannot be understood apart from people's everyday lives.

The book's temporal focus is the mature colonial era, a designation given to the second and third centuries of rule by the Iberian monarchs over nearly all of the central and southern part of the Western Hemisphere. This era witnessed the consolidation of colonial institutions first imposed in the decades following the arrival of Spanish and Portuguese adventurers, who initiated the process of bringing new territories and peoples under Iberian control. An understanding of the three centuries of Iberian colonial rule is fundamental to an understanding of Latin America today, since the period before independence lasted longer than the 200 years that have followed. The political, social, and economic institutions developed during this lengthy era of colonial domination constitute the foundations of the structures that organize the daily lives of Latin Americans in our time.

In addition to investigating daily life in the colonial period, an additional goal of this work is to broaden and deepen the North American student's grasp of Latin American life and culture. Perhaps because we share the Western Hemisphere, or because there are some similarities between the pre-Columbian peoples of the northern and southern parts of this hemisphere and some parallels in the way they experienced European colonization, there is a tendency for students in the United States to look southward and judge the success or, as they often see it, failure of Latin American economies, societies, cultures, and polities according to standards that are deeply ingrained in the North American experience. Often these measures are almost totally unrelated to the real day-to-day lives of Latin Americans and to their historical experience. Understanding the early centuries of European colonization is the key to grasping the subsequent divergence of the paths on which the northern and southern continents of the Western Hemisphere set out. Looked at in this way, the fact that these paths have led our two regions to very different places in today's world is not surprising.

Talking about Latin America as one region is inevitably misleading, of course; the geographic scope for our study includes all territories under at least the nominal control of the Spanish and Portuguese crowns. At its largest extent, this Iberian-ruled section of the Western Hemisphere stretched from what are now the U.S. Southeast and Southwest to the tip of Patagonia, including the Spanish Caribbean. We will emphasize regional distinctions within Latin America from time to time, especially between Spanish realms and Portuguese-dominated Brazil, and these should be kept in mind as a counterweight to an overly rigid notion of Latin America's social and cultural commonalities. These commonalities were evident, however, and underpin the book's topical focus:

what people living in this time and place did every day and—to the extent that we can catch glimpses of or make an educated guess about these intangibles—what they thought and felt about themselves and their societies.

Ultimately, this study is designed as an exercise in both analysis and empathy, as the best historiography always is. We will visit the past, meet the people who live there, and interrogate them—or the traces they have left—regarding what mattered to them, how they lived, what they did, and why they did it. We will explore the boundaries of people's lives and the lives people constructed inside these boundaries, or in some cases across them, as they negotiated space for their lives within legal structures and social norms.

DEFINING TERMS

A book on daily life in colonial Latin America must begin by defining some of the central concepts of the region and the period. While terms like *Latin America, colonial, race,* and *Indian,* probably convey some general meaning to all readers, there are debates within the discipline on their meanings and their usefulness.

Colonial Latin America

The term *Latin America* refers to the Spanish-speaking countries of North, Central, and South America plus Portuguese-speaking Brazil. Haiti is sometimes included because, although a colony of France, it shares a history with the Spanish-speaking Dominican Republic, the other country of the island of Hispaniola. *Latin* is a reference to the Romance languages spoken in these countries that have their roots in Latin, the language of the Romans.

As noted earlier, this volume covers the mature colonial period, the 200 years that followed the initial conquest years of the 16th century. The period ends with the successful expulsion of the last Spanish troops from Peru in 1826, the victory that brought independence to all the former Spanish colonies on the American mainland. Brazil, following a very different path to the same goal, declared independence in 1822. Unlike Africa and parts of Asia, the Americas were thoroughly colonized by Europeans soon after their arrival, with the Spanish conquests preceding by nearly 40 years the settlement of Brazil by the Portuguese. Some historians dispute the accuracy of the term *conquest* because of the importance of the native peoples in shaping life in the Americas even after the arrival of the

Europeans. These historians argue that if the indigenous peoples had been thoroughly defeated, as the term *conquest* implies, they would not have been in a position to play as large a role as they did in constructing Latin American history. It would be accurate, however, to state that the Spanish and Portuguese crowns succeeded in delineating administrative areas, sending agents to manage them, and imposing systems of social control over the native population. Since these are characteristics of colonization, it is useful and reasonable to refer to this span of just over 300 years, from the European invasion to the independence era, as a *colonial* period, a time during which the two Iberian crowns managed to establish judicial and political authority; extract resources, including labor, from the territory and the people under their rule; and play a large role, although certainly not the only role, in making daily life what it was.

Colonies exist for the benefit of the mother country. Therefore, the goals and motives of the Europeans who went to the Americas to serve the crowns' interests were frequently at odds with those of the native peoples. Nevertheless, there were indigenous people, generally from the upper levels of pre-Columbian society, who found ways to benefit from working with the Europeans. Therefore, a strict binary system that places Europeans and Indians at opposite poles would not be an accurate schematic of social relations. Some who came from Europe to make their fortune ended up falling down several rungs on the social ladder because of poor health, an unlucky accident, or simply an inability to find a niche in the societies under construction. Some among the indigenous groups, generally those who had occupied high positions in pre-Columbian society, exercised their ingenuity by collaborating with the new rulers to secure a fairly cozy place for themselves and their families in the new social, political, and economic systems.

Indians

Another term that presents some problems is *Indian*. The application of this misnomer to the native peoples reflects the misunderstanding on the part of Columbus and his navigators of world geography and their landfall. Since they thought they were in the Indies, they referred to the people they met there as Indians. This study will use the term, but not to refer to specific nations of indigenous people and not before the arrival of the Europeans. During the colonial period, because of the Iberian crowns' success in establishing systems of law and administration, the widely varying peoples of the First Nations of the region were lumped together under the single heading *Indian*. This appellation was used in legal documents to refer to anyone who held this legal status in society and so is unavoidable, even accurate, since the Spanish and Portuguese were in a position to define the terms. So while referring to the native peoples as Indians before the arrival of the Europeans would be inaccurate, since neither they nor anyone else in the world used this term to refer to them, during the colonial period we are left with no other option. Indians they were called, and Indians they became. Indeed the emergence of indigenous movements in the late 20th century has led to the adoption of that term by various groups that have joined together to make demands on local and international governing bodies specifically as *Indians*, a term that underlines their commonalities, many of which are rooted in the colonial period, rather than their differences.

A *New World* or the *Americas?*

Another term that has often come in for criticism is *New World*. The attacks on this way of characterizing the Western Hemisphere are well founded, given that this part of the world was no newer than the so-called Old World in a geological sense and that it was certainly not new to the great variety of peoples who had been living in it and using it for thousands of years. Is there a better, more accurate term though? The *Americas* is no better, since that name was applied by the Europeans in honor of an early Italian navigator named Amerigo Vespucci, a fact, incidentally, that also makes the widespread substitution of *Native American* for *Indian* less than satisfying. Even the term *Western Hemisphere*, probably the most neutral term used, is based on a Eurocentric pole from which east and west are then measured. Since at times it is necessary to distinguish between the landmass new to the Europeans who began setting out on the open sea during the 15th century and the world they already knew that stretched from the Atlantic Ocean to Asia, some term is necessary. The term *New World* was used by the Europeans in writing about what was for them a discovery, certainly, so it will be used here at times when our concern is the point of view of the Europeans. Given their important role in defining the terms of this new situation, and the fact that the written records on which history relies so heavily are nearly all of European origin and refer to the *New World*, use of the term is at times unavoidable.

Race

Perhaps the most problematic of the terms employed in this study is *race*, a concept essential to any understanding of Latin American history. In the early 21st century, most historians, supported by geneticists, would agree that it is impossible to distinguish among groups of human beings on the basis of immutable "racial" characteristics. This does not, however, make *race* insignificant or, unfortunately, an outdated or irrelevant concept. At this point in human development, when we know that all members of the human species share the same origins, basic characteristics, and potential, most of us have arrived at an understanding of race as important but not natural in any biological sense. That is, a person's *race* is important because humans have made it important. Because human beings have used race to define positions in the social hierarchy and to restrict access to scarce resources, it has *become* an important determinant in a person's life, an important indicator of what kind of life a person can expect to have. However, this fact is based on social, rather than biological, factors. Biologically, we are all members of one race, the human race, but socially we divide ourselves, or we are divided by others, into groups based on phenotype (i.e., characteristics of pigmentation, hair, and the shape of physical features). The inaccuracy of such judgments is underscored by the fact that all of the characteristics just mentioned can change dramatically from one generation to the next in a family where a genetically related parent and child, such as U.S. president Barack Obama and his mother, are not seen to share the same race.

Latin America is a fine example of how racial divisions can be employed to structure society, and the race-based social structure of the region is discussed below at some length. It must be noted right at the beginning, however, that modern ideas about race emerged out of the misplaced zeal for biological classification displayed by (white) scientists of the late 19th century whose interests lay in finding a "natural" justification for the creation of social hierarchies based on phenotypic differences. In contrast to these relatively recent ideas of race, Catholic Iberians of the 15th century were working with ideas of human difference rooted in the notion of *limpieza de sangre,* or blood purity. This concept was first employed to marginalize Jews and Muslims during the consolidation of the Catholic nation states and then carried to the New World where it was applied to peoples of non-European ancestry. Thus, the concept of *impurity* carried in the blood long predated 19th-century notions of race as natural, although earlier proponents of what look a lot like racial concepts to us did not employ the methods or terminology of 19th-century scientists.

In addition to distinctions among and between Iberians, Africans, and Indians, there was another important division employed during the colonial period, this one between whites born in the mother countries and those born in the colonies. People born in Spain but living in the colonies, frequently as agents of the Spanish crown, were *peninsulares*, a term referring to their origin in the Iberian Peninsula. The equivalent term in Brazil is *reinois*, from *reino* meaning "kingdom" (i.e., people from the kingdom of Portugal). In Spanish America, white people born in the Americas were labeled *criollos* (creoles), while whites born in the Portuguese colony of Brazil were known as *mazombos*. While all these terms refer to white people who generally occupied the top socioeconomic levels of these colonial societies, those who came from the mother countries and those who were born in the Americas had interests that sometimes diverged widely. As the forces that led to independence developed, the rift between these two groups widened as creoles and mazombos grew increasingly restless under the colonial system administered by the peninsulares and reinois. The independence movements that would be successful in most of Latin America and bring the colonial period to an end in 1826 emerged primarily out of creole/mazombo dissatisfaction with the colonial system and their place in it.

Daily Life

Finally, a word on the meaning of *daily life*. While even kings and high statesmen have a daily life, when that concept is used in history it refers to the lives of the majority, the ordinary people who became the protagonists of much historiography in the late 20th century, partly as a result of the rise of a feminist analysis of history and the application of gender as a key analytical tool. When the focus of historical study is, as it often has been, the study of great events and those who led large groups of people during these events, we normally encounter few women. In a study of daily life, not only do we find women playing a starring role, we also find other formerly excluded groups—peasants and other working people, people engaged in buying and selling, lawbreakers, children and young people, churchgoers, sinners, craftspeople—in short, we find people like most of us. So the history of daily life is the history of women, men, and children; its focus is what most people did every day, their work, what they ate and wore, what they built, how and what they worshipped, what they celebrated, and, to the extent that we can find or guess this, what they hoped and feared. The task of this study will be to condense the research done on these topics over the past 20 years or so and bring to life the daily pleasures and struggles of the people who made colonial Latin America.

TWO DIFFERING COLONIES

Latin America is made up of a wide range of natural geographic and climatic features that led to very different societies and cultures in the pre-Columbian period, but the arrival of Europeans from two different kingdoms also created social and political differences in the region. Some of the important differences that existed between the colonies of the Spanish crown and the colony of the Portuguese still shape the Latin American experience.

Early Portuguese Colonialism

The major difference between the Spanish and Portuguese crowns in the late 15th century lies in the direction of their expansionist projects. After expelling the Muslims from the southernmost part of the kingdom of Portugal in the middle of the 13th century, the Portuguese had achieved the social and political unity that allowed them to look outward. Early in the 15th century, they conquered Ceuta in northern Africa and then began heading down the coast of West Africa. Prince Henry's seafaring research center focused on trade with Africans and rounding the continent to find a sea route to the spice trade in the Far East that would allow the Portuguese to break the hold of the Muslim merchants of the eastern Mediterranean on trade between Asia and Europe. Four years before Columbus first landed in the Caribbean, the Portuguese navigator Bartolomeu Días reached the southern tip of Africa, achieving one of the goals of the Portuguese and setting the stage for their entry into the commercial network of the Indian Ocean. Once there, the Portuguese made war on the Muslim and Chinese traders who had plowed the Indian Ocean for hundreds of years. Following Vasco da Gama's return from India itself in 1499, other Portuguese navigators began setting out for Asia. One of these, Pedro Alvares Cabral, made a detour on his way east and reached Brazil. He made his landfall there in 1500 and claimed the territory for the Portuguese crown. For several decades thereafter, the primary interest of the Portuguese in their newly claimed territories would be in trading with various subgroups of Tupi, mainly for brazilwood, which produced a red dye in great demand for textile production in Europe.

The Portuguese focused most of their energy on building a seafaring empire dedicated to trade between Europe and the East, and they had considerable success in this endeavor. Wealthy citizens of Portugal who were interested in investing in agriculture could, and did, go to islands off the western coast of Africa where they mainly grew sugarcane, relying on the labor of captured Africans. In the early days, they showed little interest in traveling across the ocean to an untamed land inhabited by, as they must have seen it, primitive tribes of cannibals, where the huge profits that could be made in the spice trade were nowhere in evidence. Brazil would turn out to be rich in gold, not to mention its suitability for the production of sugar and coffee, but all that lay in the future. In the early 16th century, Brazil could not compete with the Indian Ocean for the attention of either the Portuguese investor or the crown.

Early Spanish Colonialism

The Spanish crown, on the other hand, aspired to control a region of its own for trade and colonization, partly in order to compete with the Portuguese and Italians who controlled the bulk of European trade, and partly as a source of resources—especially precious metals. So Spanish investors looked to the Western Hemisphere and were rewarded by their discovery of two complex hierarchical empires known to us as the Aztec, in Central Mexico, and Inca, in the South American Andes. In both of these imperial polities, organized systems of tribute and labor founded on intensive agricultural production of corn, potatoes, and other Western Hemisphere crops maintained an urban class of nobles living in luxury. It was not long before the Spanish removed the native elites and placed themselves at the top of the tribute system that continued functioning much as it had before.

RACE AND SOCIAL STRUCTURE IN THE COLONIES

The life of everyone who migrated to or was born in the Spanish and Portuguese colonies of Latin America was shaped by two tremendously powerful institutions established by the Europeans and still very much in evidence today. They are the patriarchal extended family and the race-based social structure; together they provide twin keys to understanding daily life during the period.

Religious and Cultural Conflict in the Iberian Peninsula

Catholic rulers in the Iberian Peninsula had been engaged for centuries in religious campaigns of varying intensity against the Muslims they considered *infidels*. Portuguese Catholics drove Muslim forces out of southern Portugal in the middle of the 13th century, and in 1492, the rulers of the main Spanish kingdoms captured Granada, the last outpost of Muslim rule in the Iberian Peninsula, making it, at least nominally, completely Christian. The Catholic monarchs who defeated Granada, Isabella of Castile and Ferdinand of Aragon, advanced the unification of Spain as an explicitly Christian nation-state. The crown expelled Jews who did not convert and began a campaign against Islam, burning books and decreeing conversion for Muslims who wished to remain on the peninsula. The relative religious tolerance of the Muslims on the Iberian Peninsula was a thing of the past, and, when Martin Luther inadvertently started a theological revolution among Western European Christians 30 years later, the response by the Roman Catholic Church made it clear that there could be only one true religion, that it was Christianity as defined by the pope in Rome, and that the souls of those who did not share this belief were in extreme peril.

The attitudes born in this project of military conquest, territorial expansion, commercial growth, and Christian zealotry fueled the age of European discovery and certainly accompanied the Iberians on their arrival in the rest of the world. The religious tolerance and cultural relativism that receive at least lip service in our own "postmodern" period of Western history were not even on the horizon of the 15th-century Catholic kingdoms of the Iberian Peninsula. The Christians, as they called themselves in their chronicles of the conquests, showed no signs of doubt concerning their mission from God, who they believed was aiding them in winning the conquest wars so that the eternal souls of these barbaric peoples might be saved—and possibly so the Spanish crown could have enough gold to fund its military mission as the primary defender of Christianity. Conquest of the New World was the extension of the project of Reconquest that they viewed as carrying out God's work in the world.

Religion, Culture, and Race in the Americas

The Iberian Christian sense of religious and cultural superiority set the tone for the colonial systems that the Spanish and Portuguese would construct. It may be impossible to colonize a group one sees as equal, but be that as it may, when the Europeans came to the Western Hemisphere and met peoples who engaged in human sacrifice or ritual cannibalism, drew pictographs or had no form of writing at all, and relied on human energy to carry heavy objects long distances, they did not pause to debate their own superiority. In their view, their role was clear: it was to take control of these lands, resources, and peoples and to put all to "good" use, meaning a use that would promote the projects in which Europeans were already engaged in Europe. Collectively, this meant state building and the extension of Catholicism; for individuals, it meant accumulating wealth and securing a place among the Iberian nobility.

In the scenario envisioned by the Europeans, the native peoples were to serve as workers, as indeed most of them had in the pre-Columbian period, so the Europeans organized systems of labor to control the population and employ their labor in the extraction of the natural resources of the newly acquired territories. This is the origin of the racial hierarchy that would play a fundamental role in structuring Latin America during the colonial period, as the physical appearance of the native populations and the laborers brought from Africa served to identify them and tie them to their status as laborers. Anyone who looked like an Indian or an African was therefore assumed to be part of the laboring population and tracked accordingly. Given this assumption, the burden of proof fell on any person of Indian or African appearance who was *not* a tribute-paying village laborer or an enslaved worker to prove his status as a free person.

Nothing about daily life can be understood outside of the racial and ethnic boundaries that defined everyone's roles, responsibilities, rights, and opportunities in colonial Latin America. Whether the discussion focuses on material culture (i.e., clothing, personal possessions, houses and their contents), choice of a marital partner, occupation, or social life, one's racial category was the key determinant. While individuals did sometimes escape their category and rise in the social structure, the structure was set up to be a rigid system that would have a place for everyone and keep everyone in his or her place.

This race-based social structure made Latin America paradoxically both the region of greatest mixing of peoples of diverse origins in the world and a region in which a person's color, or phenotype, defined his or her life to an extremely high degree. This racialized social structure is best seen as a construction by dominant groups determined to restrict access to resources and political power in the

face of challenges by subaltern groups. The Europeans, both colonists and crowns, were organizing these newly discovered territories for the extraction of wealth. In a period before the invention
of machines when work was performed by human energy, labor
had to be coerced or coaxed from people, lots of them. Race was
the primary tool used to distinguish those in control from those
to be controlled. This is not to say that those in the groups to be
controlled meekly trooped off to meet their fate . . . far from it. In
fact, their rejection of the rules presents us with some of the most
interesting and inspiring stories in Latin American history. But that
comes later.

The Multiplication of Racial Categories

In the beginning, the racial division was clear and straightforward because there were just two groups: those who came across
the ocean from Europe and the people who met them. While a few
African servants came with the Iberians, their numbers were small,
and they were not differentiated from the others who came from
Europe. Unfortunately for the neatness of this system, conditions on
the ground soon changed. People lost no time in muddling the categories by producing offspring that were the result of sexual encounters across ethnic boundaries. There were several reasons for this:
women of the conquered peoples were treated as part of the booty
of conquest, taken by or given to the Christians. In Christian societies, where sex was cast as sinful outside of marriage, men's access
to women was limited by law and custom. So although women
from Europe began to arrive in the American colonies shortly after
the first conquerors, their numbers were low, and they were not
necessarily available as sexual partners for European men. The
women of the conquered peoples were part of what was won in the
wars of conquest, as workers and sex objects or, in some cases, willing sexual partners and, if not always legal wives, mothers of the
next generation.

In addition, as recent research on the Puebloans of New Mexico
shows, some very different meanings could be attached to sexual
intercourse and its function in the universe. This Pueblo perspective
sheds new light on stories of indigenous women throwing themselves at the conquerors. It suggests that while there was surely
some, possibly substantial, degree of rape and exploitation of women's bodies against their will, as there is in any military invasion,
if we can step outside Christian teachings that associate sex with

sin and shame, we encounter the possibility, at least in the earliest days of the colonial period, of women willingly engaging in sexual relations with the new arrivals. According to one scholar, in some cultures of the First Nations, this was done as a way for women to empower themselves and their communities, and to divest the invaders of power to do harm.

The offspring of alliances between indigenous people and those who had arrived from across the seas merged previously isolated populations of Africans, Europeans, and native people and created a society of *castas,* a generic term applied by Spaniards to racially mixed peoples. These *mestizos, mulatos,* and *zambos,* to give only the three most common labels dreamed up by Spaniards to distinguish among various "types" of castas, began to appear quite early in the colonial period, and their place in colonial society was not as rigidly fixed as that of Indians and whites. Seeking to meet their

During the 18th century, artworks known as casta paintings, depicting family groupings, generally father, mother, and one child, became popular collectors' items in Europe. The point of these paintings was to show and label the results of racial and ethnic mixtures occurring in New Spain. In this casta family of fruit sellers, the child is learning the family business. (The Art Archive / Museo de America Madrid)

daily needs for food, shelter, clothing, love, and good times, these racially mixed people challenged the rigidity of the social structure and found ways to exploit its interstices, sometimes rising into the dominant groups.

Another factor that confused the racial hierarchy was that some whites did not fall into the category of elites, either because they came from marginalized economic groups in Europe and were not able to raise their status in the New World, or because they lost status for reasons of luck, health, or vice. Thus not all whites were at the top of the social structure, although in general they had a better chance of getting there.

In any case, the Europeans found phenotype a useful tool in their project of organizing a colonial society for the extraction of wealth from what was to them a new world, and race would continue to play a crucial role in the lives of Latin Americans long after the colonial period had ended. Many would argue it still does.

THE PATRIARCHAL EXTENDED FAMILY

The other key to understanding Latin American history is the patriarchal extended family. Even today, many, it might even be fair to say most, Latin Americans gain access to resources, meaning a place to live, employment, or a marriage partner, through exploiting family relationships. What might be seen as nepotism in another region of the world is often viewed in Latin America as simply the best way to get things done. When there is a job opening, who is more to be trusted, a person who comes in off the street—even if he has good credentials—or the relative of a long-term, reliable employee? Many Latin Americans would choose the latter on the assumption that the older worker will make sure the new worker, her relative, measures up to the standards of the company. Often this assumption is born out, because of the strength of reciprocal responsibilities within the extended family. Therefore, this study will devote considerable attention to the formation of the extended family structure in Latin America.

The Elite Family

Family structure among elites has been called patriarchal, meaning dominated by a *patriarch*, the man of the household and official holder/manager of the family property. This patriarch, whose income in colonial Latin America was generally based on a hacienda, plantation, or mine, established the social position of the family. His effectiveness in controlling his dependents—meaning his children, whether born of his wife or of another woman; the women of his household (i.e. wife, sisters, sisters-in-law, mother, mother-in-law, and possibly granddaughters); poor relatives; and domestic servants, slaves, or tributary Indians—was a matter of utmost importance since his reputation as an *hombre de bien* (honorable member of the community) was at stake. Frequently, the eldest son of the patriarch succeeded him in that position, to reap the rewards and shoulder the responsibilities implied by this position of chief executive officer of the family.

Nonelite Families

For families lower on the social scale, the family might not be organized around the man of the house. Indeed, in the lower ranks of society, the family could often be said to be matriarchal, led by a widow, single mother, or eldest sister. This did not, however, diminish the strength of family ties and may even have fostered greater reliance on the extended family as a source of the necessary contacts that would lead to work, a home, or a partner.

OUTLINE OF THE BOOK

What follows will show how colonial institutions structured daily life and were in turn structured by people's daily lives over 200 years of Latin American history. The discussion is divided into chapters on marriage and home life; sexual mores and affective life; childhood and education; the material aspects of daily existence; work and economic relationships; popular art, entertainment, and religious life; and political systems and resistance to them. The conclusion will summarize the key features of colonial life since 1600 after briefly sketching the achievement of independence in most of Latin America early in the 19th century. Perhaps not surprisingly, despite this achievement the colonial period came to its official end without bringing much change to the daily lives of the majority of Latin Americans.

NOTES

In addition to the work cited separately as a source of direct quotations, the following source has been drawn on for specific examples in this chapter: Ramón Gutiérrez, *When Jesus Came the Corn Mothers Went Away.* For full citation and other useful readings, see the annotated bibliography.

1. For an English translation of the surviving documents in the case and an analysis of their significance, see Sonya Lipsett-Rivera, "Scandal at the Church: José de Alfaro Accuses Doña Theresa Bravo and Others of Insulting and Beating His *Castiza* Wife, Josefa Cadena (Mexico, 1782)," in *Colonial Lives: Documents on Latin American History, 1550–1850,* ed. Richard Boyer and Geoffrey Spurling (New York: Oxford University Press, 2000), pp. 216–23.

TIMELINE

1492	Mexica-dominated Aztec Empire midway through reign of Ahuitzotl.
	Reign of Tupa Inca Yupanqui over Tawantinsuyu nears its end.
	Death of Sonni Ali, ruler of expanding Songhay Empire in West African interior; a new dynasty emerges under Askia Muhammad.
	Catholic religious influence spreads in Kingdom of Kongo with approval of ruler following arrival of Portuguese traders in 1480s.
	Sugar production based on labor of enslaved Africans expands on Madeira and other Iberian-ruled islands off Africa's northwest coast.
	Isabella of Castile and Ferdinand of Aragon decree the expulsion of Jews from their kingdoms.
	Spanish Catholic forces conquer Granada, the last Muslim-ruled kingdom in the Iberian Peninsula.
	First transatlantic voyage of Christopher Columbus.
1500	Pedro Alvares Cabral lands on northeastern coast of Brazil, claiming it for Portugal.

1502 Earliest documented arrival in the Americas of enslaved individuals of African ancestry; in accordance with Spanish law, all have already experienced Iberian society and adapted to Iberian culture before being transported to the Caribbean island of Hispaniola.

1503 Earliest documented rebellion in the Americas by enslaved individuals of African origins, in alliance with members of Hispaniola's native population.

1505 Laws of Toro guarantee inheritance rights for women in Spain.

1512 Laws of Burgos aim with little success to address Spanish abuses of native labor in the Caribbean by regulating more closely the *encomienda*, a grant of native laborers to individual Spaniards.

1518 Spanish crown drops a ban on the transportation of enslaved Africans directly across the Atlantic to the Americas and is soon selling licenses to encourage such transportation by Portuguese, Genoese, and other European merchants.

1521 Earliest documented rebellion in the Americas by enslaved migrants brought directly from Africa, Wolofs from Senegambia, on Hispaniola sugar plantation owned by Diego Columbus, son of the explorer.

On a second attempt, Hernán Cortés and his Spanish forces, assisted by thousands of Tlaxcalan and other indigenous allies, seize control of the Aztec capital of Tenochtitlán and found Mexico City on its ruins.

1524 Franciscan order establishes a presence in Mexico.

1532 Forces led by Francisco Pizarro conquer the Inca capital at Cuzco.

1542 Charles I of Spain decrees the New Laws in order to end the worst forms of exploitation of native labor in the Americas and assert greater royal control over the distribution and use of that labor; outright enslavement of native peoples is soon outlawed, with a few exceptions such as capture in frontier wars, while the encomienda is further restricted; forced labor continues, however, by means of the village labor draft known as *repartimiento* or *mita*.

1545–1563 Council of Trent of the Roman Catholic Church produces a formal, wide-ranging response to the Protestant Reformation launched by Martin Luther in 1517 in the interest of reasserting and strengthening clerical control over the lives of parishioners in Catholic lands.

1549   Portugal establishes royal government in Brazil at Salvador da Bahía, replacing a system that placed large tracts of territory under the control of favored private individuals; members of Jesuit order accompany new royal governor to Brazil.

1550   Debate at Valladolid in Spain over the nature and proper administration of the native peoples of the Americas between the Dominican friar Bartolomé de las Casas, famed "Defender of the Indians," and Juan Ginés de Sepúlveda, who employs Aristotle's theory of natural slavery to advocate Spanish dominance; Las Casas' writings on Spanish abuses will later be cited by other Europeans as proof of both Spanish cruelty (the so-called Black Legend) and their own superiority as colonial rulers.

1569–1571   Holy Office of the Inquisition established in Lima and Mexico City.

1573   Arrival at Potosí silver mine of first contingent of native workers drafted in accordance with revised mita system organized by Viceroy Toledo.

1575   Portuguese establish port of Luanda on the coast of Angola, which is soon transformed into the leading source of enslaved labor bound for the Americas.

1580–1640   Portugal ruled by Spanish crown.

1595–1640   Portuguese merchants make a series of contracts known as *asientos* with the Spanish crown, enabling them to transport tens of thousands of Africans to key Spanish American ports for sale as slaves.

ca. 1618   Town of San Lorenzo de los Negros formally established on Mexico's Gulf Coast by rebel slaves following peace treaty with royal authorities.

ca. 1630   Repartimiento begins to be phased out as means of labor supply to northern Mexican silver mines and agricultural enterprises; importance of wage labor and debt peonage correspondingly on the increase.

1630–1654   The Dutch rule parts of northeastern Brazil, briefly controlling the world's major sugar-producing territories.

1631   Free militiamen of African ancestry in Lima gain temporary relief from race-based tribute payments, citing their role in defending the city from the Dutch in 1624.

ca. 1640   Sharp decline in African arrivals to Mexico and Peru, in part as a result of Spain's loss of control over Portugal; the number of Africans transported to Brazil continues to rise.

Native populations begin to recover in Mexico and Central America from devastating losses following European invasions, later in the Andes.

1679   African-born nun Juana Esperanza de San Alberto dies in a convent in Puebla, New Spain.

1692   Major riot in Mexico City following unprecedented food shortages.

1693   *Bandeirantes* from São Paulo discover gold in the Brazilian interior north of Rio de Janeiro, setting off 18th-century gold and diamond rush in Minas Gerais.

1694   *Quilombo* of Palmares defeated by Portuguese forces in northeastern Brazil nearly a century after escaped slaves first establish it.

ca. 1740   Mexican city of Guanajuato replaces Potosí as most important silver-mining center in Spanish America.

ca. 1750   Era of the Bourbon reforms begins in Spanish America, raising tensions between the Spanish crown and its American subjects.

1780–1783   Massive indigenous rebellion in the southern Andes led initially by Túpac Amaru II in the Peruvian highlands and the Katari brothers in the Bolivian highlands.

1781   *Comunero* revolt against Spanish officials in New Granada (Colombia).

1786   New regulations introduced for Mexico City's main theater in order to eliminate "disorderly" conduct both on stage and in the audience.

1789   Nearly 2,000 *cofradías* in existence in the Archdiocese of Guatemala alone.

1791–1804   Haitian Revolution leads to establishment of world's first independent black republic and the second independent nation-state in the Americas.

1794   Mexican theater director María Ordóñez released from confinement in a *casa de recogimiento*, where she has been imprisoned for years for transgressing the bounds of female propriety.

1795 Short-lived rebellion by free people of color and slaves in Venezuelan port town of Coro.

1798 Tailors' Rebellion in Bahia, Brazil, led by free *mulatos*.

1808–1825 Independence era in mainland Spanish America and Brazil.

1

MARRIAGE, HOME, AND FAMILY

INTRODUCTION

Nothing in colonial Latin America, and especially not the formation of the couple, can be separated from the race-based social structure of society. It would therefore be a mistake to discuss the "typical" home and family as being white and upper class, relegating all other types to some lesser status or category. Colonial families living within established norms can be found at every level of society, just as there were families at every level that differed from those norms. As far as formal marriage goes, however, that institution was more common among elites and Indians, for reasons that will be explained. Married or not, the couple and their children formed the fundamental building block of society.

Colonial society was based on the patriarchal extended family. Not necessarily in the sense that couples and their children all lived together in the house of the patriarch, but in the sense that families tended to be made up of several generations of couples with their children/grandchildren, frequently living on the same or adjoining lands, sharing domestic tasks, and supporting each other in various ways. This family structure emerged in the colonial period and, somewhat modified, remains important in Latin America today, generally more important in less modernized areas.

The family has been called "the locus of moral and political socialization."[1] It is in the institution of the family that customs and traditions are transferred from the older to the younger generation. This social function lends the family a communal significance that extends beyond the personal level. Marriage is of importance not only to the married couple. It establishes a bond between extended families and thereby cements or jeopardizes the honor and interests of two, sometimes large, groups of people. As the basic social unit and the institution through which social standards were maintained and property was passed on, marriage and marital practices were of deep interest to both church and state. Because of its centrality to human life and relationships, marriage provides all kinds of information on the organization of colonial society, political life, and the economy. One study of marriage and the family points out, "When people marry they create social alliances, establish a new social unit, change residence, exchange property, and gain rights to sexual service."[2]

The patriarchal family was reflected in monarchy, the form of government in which the king is the omniscient and omnipotent father of society. So the patriarchal state reflects the patriarchal family and vice versa. The family has been termed the "fundamental expression" of patriarchal society, with monarchy growing out of the patriarchal family only to supersede it and become the model for it.[3]

Recently though, historians have begun to ask whether the patriarchal family was as pervasive, and as orderly, as formerly believed. It may be that a bit of wishful thinking has entered into descriptions of the unquestioned rule of the patriarch, an attempt perhaps by men of the 20th century experiencing diminishing control over their own families to find a past in which men held unquestioned sway over family members who lent them blind obedience. Recent research on the colonial era in Mexico finds a system of male dominance that is pervasive but porous. That is, both men and women accepted the idea of patriarchy, but in practice, wives linked their obedience to the measure of respect accorded them by their husbands and found sometimes sneaky ways to disobey orders.

This standard family model based on marriage, was probably more often violated than observed, however. Many couples were not formally married, especially if they occupied positions below the elite but above the Indians in the social structure. Sometimes the household was headed by a woman, possibly a single mother who had never married, a widow, or an eldest sister. If the family controlled little or no property, the "patriarch" had marginal control over other family members as a result of having few consequences to dole out for their misbehavior.

This chapter will show the centrality of the family to social life and the expectations of the church for maintaining social order through the promotion of marriage and male-defined standards of women's honor. It will also examine the normative standard of the patriarchal extended family and deviations from this norm.

FAMILIES, THE SOCIAL BUILDING BLOCK

Although the pervasiveness and power of the patriarchal family has lately become a matter of debate, it still makes sense to begin with this model of the elite colonial family because it defines the norm to which church, state, and creole colonists aspired. In this model, the nucleus of colonial society was the white couple married by the church. This family was run by the patriarch, an *hombre de bien* (good man), who managed his wife, his legitimate children, possibly several daughters-in-law, a widowed mother, any poor relatives or "natural" (i.e. illegitimate) children who had become part of the household, domestic servants, and other laborers. He was to be, above all, an honest and honorable person in affairs of business, in the home, in his political alliances, and as a subject of the king. Since everything from employment to social opportunities and marital partners depended on the family's reputation, maintaining a high standard of honor was essential to the future success of all its members.

It was the business of this father figure to maintain order in the home, not only for his own benefit, but also for the good of every member of the extended family. As the person responsible, the patriarch received the credit or the blame for the behavior of all members of the household. One of his responsibilities was to arrange the marriages of everyone in the extended family, including any servants. Marriage was a contract between families, and of such great importance that it was nothing to be left to the capriciousness of the young folks who might not recognize the ramifications of their decision on other family members.

Since people in all societies generally marry others of the same social rank, marriage is a good indicator of social class position. A noted historian of colonial New Mexico finds that "[m]arriage in Spanish society was strictly supervised to assure the perpetuation of social inequalities."[4] That is, marriage was the primary institution through which hierarchical social structure was maintained and strengthened. This helps to explain the close supervision of the institution by the Roman Catholic Church, which used its moral and legal authority to protect wealthy and powerful families from self-destructing through poorly chosen marriages even as it sought in many cases to defend a contradictory principle favoring the free will of couples. One result of the self-destruction of important families might be the loss to the church of the legacies of the wealthy who traditionally bequeathed money and land to the church in their last will and testament. In addition, since the family was the basic social building block, the destruction of these model patriarchal families would, in the view of the authorities, have wreaked havoc on the social order. Marriage was the contract that established this normative couple and the rite of passage to adulthood for both men and women. This family created the environment in which procreation occurred and children were socialized.

Patriarchal Control of Marriage

As lord of the household, the master had the right and the responsibility to arrange the marriages of his dependents, not only his children but also his younger siblings and the household servants. Any dependent in the house who wished to marry needed his permission and was subject to his will in the matter. When 16-year-old Gómez de León exchanged marriage vows with his girlfriend, younger than he by a year, he considered himself married even though the ceremony consisted of a simple statement of intent by the couple as they held hands in the girl's home, with the bride's sister and a household servant as witnesses. Gómez's new father-in-law, a Mexico City merchant, did not agree and took his entire family back to Spain, their place of origin. It seems Gómez was known for his gambling, and it is likely the merchant had loftier goals for his young daughter.

In another story of young love nearly thwarted by parental opposition, a Spanish mule train owner in early 17-century New Spain (Mexico) refused to give permission for his 22-year-old daughter to marry her suitor. In this case, the father, not content with scoldings and beatings loud enough for the neighbors to hear, was finally reduced to ejecting his daughter from his house while pelting her with rocks and then disowning her. Undeterred, the couple went through all the steps and was formally married by a priest. In this case, the church's official policy in support of the right of marital choice against the interests of a parent was upheld, in part, perhaps, because of the aggrieved father's relatively modest social status.

The patriarch was also responsible for making a marital match for his servants. A wealthy and powerful patriarch could even marry a servant to a partner of his choice without regard for any previous commitments made by the hapless servant. In a case from 16th-century Mexico City, Catalina de Vega, originally of Spain, had come to America with her widowed father in 1561 and had been placed by him with a wealthy family of Mexico City as a servant to the lady of the house. Two years later, when she was 13, she secretly married her boyfriend, Pedro de Ribero, while her master was out of town. Her employer refused to permit the young couple to take up married life, placing Catalina in the custody of the church. Catalina's father went a step further, threatening Pedro's life. Under these circumstances, Pedro left for Peru in a hurry, but he did not forget about his bride. Two years later, now an *encomendero*, he wrote to Catalina, her father, her employer, and the supervisor of the *colegio* where Catalina had been held for a year. By that time, the church had decided the matter in Catalina's favor, but Pedro of course was long gone. And because he sent all his letters through the local parish priest, he was dependent on the cleric's good will. Father Jorge would later claim that he could not find the parties to whom the letters were addressed; in any case, they were never delivered. Catalina married someone else, only to face bigamy charges by the Inquisition after 10 years of married life with Alonso, her second husband. After the Inquisition labeled her a bigamist and separated her from Alonso, she was alone for 16 years before what must have been a long-lost hope materialized: Pedro showed up to claim her as his wife. She was by then 46 years old, having been separated for more than 30 years by the good offices of those responsible for her best interests from a man who in the end risked everything to return to her.

Women and Family

It was the church, itself a rigidly hierarchical organization, that promoted the idea of the patriarch as the keeper of his women. The church constantly reminded its flock of the norms of good behavior and the duties of all parties in the family hierarchy. As descendants of Eve, women were seen by the Roman Catholic Church as slaves to passion who had caused the fall from paradise. Therefore, women required the constant vigilance of the patriarch to keep them on the straight and narrow path of righteousness, for if they strayed, not only their own honor was jeopardized, but also that of the whole extended family. Since women were worldly, rather than spiritual, beings, they would not stay on this path of their own accord, making the honorable woman proof positive of a well-managed household under the careful eye of a responsible man. Since the most visible proof of an honorable family was the behavior of its women, elite wives and daughters were kept under strict surveillance, generally in *recogimiento*, seclusion in the home. If they did go out, they never went alone but were closely supervised by an appropriate chaperone.

The woman's age at the time she began to engage in sexual relations was the most important determinant of family size, since without reliable birth control methods, children were the frequent result of sex. About half of all children born reached adulthood, with indigenous women having higher rates of both fertility and mortality than whites and *castas* (racially-mixed people). Family size was also affected by the nature of the husband's employment. Many men worked at occupations that required travel, either across the sea to Europe or as muleteers, peddlers, or soldiers/sailors. The husband's absence led to lower birth rates, possibly somewhat balanced by the nonmonogamy or bigamy of men who were away from home for long periods or at frequent intervals.

The family was one knot in a web of social relations, and it was through this web of relationships that individuals found respectable, well-remunerated employment and a good marriage. The honor of an individual depended on the honor of this family. According to a prominent historian of women in the colonial era, "Eighteenth-century society was organized around the family, its social position, and the preservation of its honor."[5] One dishonorable marriage was a stain on the honor of the whole extended family, passing both horizontally to cousins and more distant relatives, and vertically to future generations. An unfavorable marriage would call into question a family's social and racial status, presenting an obstacle to favorable marriages for succeeding generations.

Thus a man's home was viewed as his sacred space, and women were his most closely guarded property. An elite family line was continued through the womb of the female who therefore had to be pure at marriage. While young men served the family by continuing the work of their father, or entering the clergy or the military, virgin daughters played the part of pawns in the family's efforts to maintain its social position.

Where is romantic love in this picture? It was suspect. Youthful love and passion were conducive to social disruption and therefore treated by the church and the community elders as threatening to an orderly society. Affective life also threatened a family's strategies for maintaining its social position and, as such, was an unwelcome intruder in the business of making an advantageous match. Parents and the authorities were therefore allied against youth and romance in the battle to preserve social order and maintain a strict hierarchical social structure. We have already seen where insisting on the right to choose one's partner led Catalina de Vega and Pedro de Ribero, as well as Gómez de León and his bride.

Lately, new research has suggested that the patriarchal family may not have incarcerated its members quite as neatly as this picture suggests, certainly not in the middle and lower classes. While it was a model, and one held up by the church as an example for all, some people found ways to open the cage doors so they could come and go and exercise a higher degree of control over their lives. Recent research on families low on the social ladder in colonial New Spain has uncovered various contested areas. Marriage among the common people was viewed as a reciprocal contract in which the husband was responsible for maintaining his partner, while she was responsible for carrying out the domestic tasks and obeying her husband. A wife often based her cooperation on her husband's faithfulness in fulfilling his side of the marital bargain. Women employed subterfuge to get what they wanted out of their lives, to some extent; they dallied with friends when going to fetch water, they stretched out a visit to mother, they delayed meal preparation, and they organized the housework in their own way. Some women, as we shall see, even engaged in sexual relationships outside marriage. While some of these women paid with their lives, the ultimate price, others got away with breaking the patriarchal sexual rules. In any case, the stereotype of the patriarchal household run by an iron-willed male to whom all females and subordinate males were submissive does not tell the whole story.

THE ROLE OF THE AUTHORITIES

The colonial institution most concerned with maintaining the official family, and through it, an orderly society, was the Roman Catholic Church. The church viewed all activities of daily life through the lens of its central mission, that of saving the individual soul. In pursuit of this mission, the church intruded deeply into personal life in a variety of ways, as subsequent chapters will demonstrate. Here the focus is on its intense interest in enforcing Christian precepts of marriage and sexuality. Further, as the arm of the government charged with stabilizing society and maintaining social order, a subject also discussed at greater length later in the book, the church sought to restrict individuals to alliances within their social rank.

It was during the 12th century that the church began to play its role of organizing society by controlling marriage. The three players in marriage arrangements were the couple, their families, and the church. Through marriage, the church legitimized the couple, the basic nucleus of society, keeping these unions public and acknowledged by the whole community. In prenuptial interviews with the couple, the priest gathered the information that would protect society from incestuous relationships as defined by canon law, and he made sure both parties were willing. The church became both mediator and judge at times when the couple and the parents did not agree.

In the mid-16th century, just as the conquest period was ending and the colonial system was being set up, the Council of Trent (see chapter 6) codified marriage, declaring that a priest had to witness the couple willingly consenting to marry. Previously, following a practice inherited from Roman law, the church had recognized marriage carried out in secret based solely on the consent of both members of the couple. The Romans had two classes of marriage, an older one that ignored the will of the couple and simply required the legal transfer of the woman from her father's to her husband's household, and one that developed later recognizing consent as the key component of marriage. The latter form even recognized sexual union as marriage, on the assumption that engaging in sexual relations proved consent. In general, like the concept of common-law marriage still recognized in parts of the Western world, a couple was considered married if they behaved willingly and publicly as husband and wife. The clandestine marriages that took place during the colonial period in Latin America were rooted in these ancient Roman practices, but the Counter-Reformation, discussed later in the book, tightened church control over marriage. In an effort to put an end to the wrangling that sometimes resulted from clandestine marriages based solely on consent and to impose greater order over social relations, canon law after the Council of Trent recognized only marriages overseen by the church.

Canon law also defined the coerced marriage as invalid. Marriage was a holy sacrament overseen by God, undertaken "to serve

God better," as many marriage applications state. According to canon law, this union served God's plan only if the free will of both parties was the basis of their decision to marry. In this matter of free will, however, the church played a contradictory role. Priests sometimes took the side of the family to force a marriage on a resisting child or servant, but there are examples of priests standing firm in defense of the freewill provision of canon law and refusing to marry couples in which one party was unwilling, regardless of the wishes of the parents. At times the church denied its support to parents who opposed unions that crossed boundaries of social class or ethnicity. This probably happened infrequently, however, since most priests were closely linked to powerful families of the parish, through blood or financial dependency, and therefore had to think twice about jeopardizing their own situation. In addition, the church was no more enthusiastic about cross-class marriages than were the parents.

In one case, the priest himself was the one who forced marriage on an unwilling party in early 17th-century Peru. Ysabel Allay Suyo, after a little more than a year of marriage to Diego Andrés de Arenas, spoke with a Spanish inspector who was making the rounds in 1618, telling him that she had been forced to marry Diego against her will. The inspector encouraged her to bring an annulment suit. In the suit, she attested that the person who had forced the marriage was a priest, Diego's master. According to her own testimony and that of several witnesses, Ysabel practically had to be dragged to the ceremony, and two or three times during the ceremony, when asked if she was willing to marry Diego, said no, in spite of various attempts to persuade her. Apparently, she had been crying before the ceremony and continued to cry while it took place, after which she ran away and had to be brought back and ordered to embrace her husband. Although several witnesses impugned the testimony of Ysabel's witnesses, in the end the court agreed with her and the marriage was annulled. There is no mention of any reprimand for the priest who forced the marriage in clear violation of his legal and spiritual obligation to ensure the free will of both parties.

The Spanish crown considered canon law to extend to slave and Indian marriages as well and in the 16th century issued edicts protecting free will as the basis of their marriages. Given the slight control servants and laborers had over their choice of a partner, as well as over whether or not that choice was legitimized in formal marriage, these edicts may have been ineffectual, but there are some examples of priests defending free will between partners from the lower social ranks. In a complicated case from New Mexico in the mid-18th century, an Indian slave named Cipriano appealed for permission to marry Isabel, the Indian slave of another landowner, in spite of the fact that he had had relations with a different Indian slave that resulted in the birth of a child. After a beating sufficiently severe to cause Cipriano to lose some of the sheep in his care, the church intervened and supported the right of Indian slaves to marry whomever they wished. Since Isabel and Cipriano wished to marry each other, the marriage took place, under the protection of the church, but against the will of both masters.

Impediments to Marriage

Although the church considered the spiritual path of the chaste and celibate life superior to married life, Christian teachings established marriage as a sort of second-best state to that of celibacy. Through marriage, man controlled his lustful, sinful nature and served God by producing and socializing children. So serious was the church about the procreative function of sex that anything blocking the possibility of having children, impotence for instance, was considered an impediment to marriage. If a complaint was brought to the priest within one month after marriage and proved to his satisfaction, the marriage could be invalidated and the couple freed to marry other people.

Marital plans could be interrupted by other impediments under canon law. The priest interrogated the prospective couple to find out if any impediments existed, in which case a waiver or *dispensa* was required from the diocese. The most common impediment was a blood relationship between the couple, *consanguinidad*, because this impediment applied to family relationships up to the fourth generation. Many people, especially those living in villages founded by two or three settler families, shared a great-grandparent, and this was an impediment to their marriage. However, applications for the waiver of these impediments were regularly approved by the archdiocese, and the marriage of first cousins was quite common. Another obstacle to marriage was the age of the couple since those under age could not, by law, possess free will, the assumption being that they could not appreciate the seriousness of the life they were undertaking. In addition, a marriage application could be invalidated by giving false information for name, marital status, or social rank.

Marriage and the Bourbon Reforms

Until the late 18th century, church and secular administration were simply two closely linked arms of a government that viewed official marriage as crucial to the maintenance of social order. The church was the wing of government that most concerned itself with supervising morality and managing social relations. In the Bourbon reforms that began in the 1770s, cracks between church and state widened. The secular arm of the state began to exert more power over the church and its social functions. Primarily interested in the stabilization of society through marriage as the nucleus of social life, the state strengthened the parental hand, most especially that of the head of the patriarchal household. Secular authority began to restrict the power of the church over marriage because the state viewed the church's emphasis on the free will of both parties as detrimental to the creation of a stable, well-ordered society. Beginning where stability mattered most, the administrative reforms of 1778 specified that white American couples under age 25 needed parents' permission to marry; the racially mixed were exempt. Also, under Charles III, economic differences joined canon law impediments as legitimate cause to prevent a marriage. So much for love and free will.

The Decree of 1778 was followed in the 1780s by other measures that strengthened the hand of the father. A wife was prohibited from willing her property to a child who had effected a marriage without paternal approval. Also, in violation of more than 200 years of emphasis on the free will of the couple, parental consent, meaning primarily that of the father, was made a necessary prerequisite to marriage. These measures had the effect of limiting the power of the church to define marriage as a sacrament and emphasizing the civil role of legitimate families. In addition, the regulations were extended to people of mixed race.

The Spanish crown's concern in tightening restrictions on marriage was that unions not approved by parents created social disorder and friction in families. The new legislation was based on the view that children owed their parents respect, in accordance with one of the Ten Commandments, and the church's support of free will rather than parental consent as the basis of marriage was destroying family values. These provisions can also be assumed to have supported a more rigid social structure, since parents generally opposed marriages that were considered unfavorable and could lower the family's station in life and its future prospects.

THE MARRIAGE NORM

The two social groups most likely to be formally married were colonial elites and indigenous people, both for reasons having to do with the Roman Catholic Church. In 17th-century Guadalajara, Mexico, for example, whites represented just over half of all marriage cases, but less than one-third of the population. The church had great power over elites because a violation of church protocol could ruin a family's good name, and thereby its economic viability. The church also exercised tight control over the lives of the indigenous people who needed, from the European point of view, Christianization and civilization, meaning Europeanization. Because formal marriage was most frequent among these two groups, we will first turn our attention to each of them and then go on to examine marriage among people of African descent and the racially mixed middle groups of colonial society.

Formal marriage under the auspices of the church involved several steps. The first was the *palabra de casamiento,* or betrothal; followed by an interview with the parish priest recorded in the *expediente matrimonial*; then the marriage banns, which were read on Sunday for three successive weeks; and finally, the marriage itself conducted by the priest. The Council of Trent in the mid-16th century established the minimum age requirements for marriage: 14 for boys and 12 for girls. Average ages at marriage were frequently higher, however, with males normally marrying after age 25 and females between the ages of 14 and 21. In some areas and periods, the average age of brides was about 25; this average probably reflects many second marriages of women whose previous husbands had died.

Elite Marriage

Formal marriage among elites was more a rite of passage to adulthood for men than for women. Women simply went from dependency on their fathers to dependency on their husbands, but young men gained control over one of the prerequisites of home life: women's labor. Marriage was an essential step toward male independence. As for women, since a spinster's life was generally seen as no life at all, they also had a powerful motivation for finding a husband, regardless of the inegalitarian nature of the bargain. Another option for avoiding spinsterhood, of course, was entering a convent, a subject to be addressed later in the book.

While the church might have seen reproduction as the primary purpose of marriage, families generally treated the institution as a way to climb the social ladder. What elites sought in formal marriage was not simply the joining together of two people in a socially approved relationship for the purpose of producing heirs to the family property, but the securing of an alliance between patriarchal extended families. These alliances were of great importance to a family's standing in the community and therefore to the family economy, as well as to the appeal of other sons and daughters as future marital partners. As a result, parents arranged marriages with an eye toward improving their economic position and their access to the politically powerful. A favorable marriage served to secure the place of two families in the top echelon of society.

In a race-based social structure like that of colonial Latin America, white families evaluated possible marital partners for their potential to protect the family from charges of racial mixing. Formal marriage was a way to control the racial characteristics of offspring, or to attempt this control, although people frequently formed alliances outside formal marriage and racially mixed children were sometimes the result.

Among property-holding families, the most important marriage was that of the first male child. After 1505, and far in advance of similar legislation in the English-speaking world, Spanish inheritance laws were clear in specifying that one-half of the property of the male head of household was to go to his wife upon his death, and the other half to be divided among the legitimate children both male and female. However, the father would frequently try to arrange matters so that the bulk of his property, especially land, remained intact under the management of his eldest son, by means of a legal process known as entailment that was intended primarily to prevent the dissolution of great noble estates. In addition, the advantageous marriage of the eldest son raised the prospects of his younger brothers and all his sisters. The son who inherited most of the property would also probably be responsible for maintaining other family members and dependents, so for this reason too, his favorable, honorable marriage was important. Not surprisingly, since the eldest son stood a good chance of receiving the bulk of the inheritance, statistics show he was the child most likely to agree to his father's wishes respecting the choice of a marital partner.

At times, disagreements arose between parents and their children over the choice of a marital partner. Research on matrimonial documents from the Río de la Plata area in the late 18th century finds that the church consistently defended the rights of the couple, and that most of the parental appeals originated among the urban families of Buenos Aires. These parents were more likely to oppose sons' marriages than those of daughters, possibly because daughters lived a more protected life while sons got out more, thereby finding more opportunities to meet inappropriate partners. It may also be, though, that parents put up less opposition to a borderline choice by daughters if the main inheritance would go to their sons, and they might employ the dowry to exert some control over their daughters. Legal cases were expensive for the parents, costing on average more than 100 pesos, a sum well beyond the means of the vast majority of the population at the time, so this was clearly a recourse only for those with substantial resources.

Cousin marriage was common among some elite groups, especially where small populations restricted the availability of marriage partners of the same *calidad*, an informal but powerful understanding of social status based largely on a combination of ancestry and economic well-being. Some who married their cousins in colonial New Mexico stated their reasons as follows: protection and maintenance of family honor, status, purity of the bloodline, and protection of the family patrimony. The key thing was not to lose control over the family's property.

If the role of the eldest son was to protect the family property by making a favorable marriage, the role of the daughters was to maintain their virginity, a valuable commodity among elites. Virginity was a sign that daughters had been protected by a vigilant patriarch, and it was a mark of high social status. Among the common people, women who were not virgins could marry and retain their honor, at least in the estimation of their social peers, but the property-holding classes, who believed that honor was the exclusive property of the social elite, left no stone unturned in their efforts to protect the virginity of daughters, and thereby the honor of the family.

Other than her virginity and the status of her family, what made an elite woman appealing as a marriage partner was the size of her dowry. Dowries of wealthy brides were normally made up of semiliquid assets that could be moved easily, things like clothing and jewelry, family furniture and art, a few slaves, cash, or some farm animals. In 1623, the parents of doña Inés de Guzmán of San Salvador, capital of present-day El Salvador, sent an enslaved woman, Isabel, and Isabel's three children along with their daughter to Guatemala, where the four slaves formed a valuable portion of the substantial dowry accepted by their new son-in-law, Juan de León. Generally, brothers got the family business, often either the plantation or the mine, along with the family home, but at times these too were part of a dowry. The dowry was seen as advance payment of the inheritance that would come to a daughter eventually, but paid to her early in order for her to enter into a favorable marriage. A woman's dowry remained her property, to be passed on to her children upon her death or to revert to her family if there were no children. In some cases, women won court suits that removed their property from the management of a careless husband.

In 16th-century Brazil, it was quite common to favor daughters by granting them large dowries that would allow them to marry well and maintain elite status. This forced their less-fortunate brothers to find their own way in the economy, perhaps by entering into the business of capturing the native people of the area for sale in the slave market, or by finding a place in the agricultural or commercial economy.

The dowry was not absolutely necessary for a favorable marriage, and by the 1750s, it was falling out of use. In some areas of Spanish America, the bride or her family might receive a reciprocal gift from the bridegroom known as *arras*, frequently amounting to 10 percent of the bridegroom's net worth.

Indigenous Marriage

Marriage rites prior to the arrival of the Europeans varied as widely as the First Nations themselves. Just to give one example, among the pre-Columbian Pueblo groups of New Mexico, girls married at about age 17, boys around 19. Marriage was initiated by the boy, who asked his parents for permission to marry the chosen girl. His parents and extended family then collected gifts for the girl's family and presented them along with the proposal of marriage. Those of the girl's family who accepted a gift were expected to reciprocate with a gift of equal value four days later.

When the Europeans came and the Roman Catholic Church took up the project of civilizing and Christianizing the indigenous people, part of it was to get the indigenous people formally and legally married. Some pre-Columbian cultures had practiced polygamy and approved of premarital relations and cohabitation. One bridegroom in the Andes even expressed the opinion that his bride's virginity indicated that she was not attractive to other men. These practices were anathema to the Christians, of course. The church was committed to eradicating anything viewed as pagan and therefore kept a close eye on the sex lives of the Indians who were strongly encouraged, or in some cases even forced, to marry according to Christian rites. This was done in part because the Indian nuclear family was responsible for paying tribute, so the religious arm of the government took on the responsibility of getting these familial units organized. Beyond this purely practical reason, however, the fact remains that the church taught indigenous populations the notion of Christian sin, including sex outside marriage or any form of nonprocreative sex within marriage, as a way of bringing these peoples to European systems of belief. In pre-Columbian societies, the community's moral code took as its starting point the good of the whole community and the perpetuation of all life, whereas the concern of the Roman Catholic Church with the individual soul posed a challenge to the Indians' communal values.

Relationships between indigenous couples were usually stable in spite of the fact that some sources indicate that wife beating was a common, and commonly accepted, part of the couple's daily life. Shortly after the end of the colonial period, a notary for the archdiocese of Guatemala commented as follows on a common-law marriage between two middle-aged indigenous people: ". . . it is common for these women . . . to seek the protection of the man wherever he may be, and although he may repeatedly mistreat her, these women are long-suffering toward the end of preserving their relationship, thus in this type of long-term lascivious relationship only the death of one of the partners is sufficient to separate them."[6]

Marriage among the Enslaved

While the church pressured, even forced, indigenous people to marry, it generally ignored the cohabitation of enslaved Africans and their descendants. Formal marriage for enslaved laborers was inconvenient for masters, who constituted the primary source of funds for the church. So for many enslaved workers, the norm was cohabitation, and legal marriage was relatively uncommon. In addition to the opposition or lack of concern of masters, another factor was the cost of Christian marriage; who would pay the fee and host the party?

Family formation, though, was central to both the physical and emotional survival of the enslaved, the only refuge in the storm. It was a common occurrence for a young woman to have a first child as the result of a liaison shortly after puberty and then form a monogamous relationship, possibly with a different partner who would be the father of subsequent children. While some slaves lived in large collective quarters called *barracoons,* it was common in many areas of Latin America for slaves to form relatively stable couple relationships in family huts grouped together in one area of the estate with a plot of land on which to grow their food. However, the short life expectancy of enslaved laborers and the nearly total lack of control they had over their futures was the source of great instability in family life, especially in plantation areas where the demands of sugar production in particular took a heavy toll on workers. Even in nonplantation regions, where the lives of enslaved Africans and their descendants were often very different, the whim or the fortunes of the master often led to the separation of family members. Since the children would stay with the mother unless sold away from her, stepfathers were a frequent occurrence.

In at least one area of Brazil, it appears that official Christian marriage was common among the enslaved, but the documents also show that these families were subject to the whim of the slaveholder. In the probate proceedings at the death of Mariana Dias, wife of a slaveholder in late 18th-century Paraíba, the inventory of property held jointly with her husband showed that of their 17 enslaved laborers, 6 of them were married, 3 were unmarried adults, and 8 were children. Three of these children were labeled *mulatos,* indicating that they were not the offspring of black couples. When Mariana's husband Antonio died six years later, all property either went to pay off debts or was distributed among the heirs. Antonio's will manumitted the three young mixed-race slaves, suggesting that they may have been his own children, and all the others either went to the auction block to pay the couple's debts or were distributed among the heirs without any regard for their marriages or their parent-child relationships. None of the three married families remained together after the death of Antonio.

This distribution of the property of Mariana and Antonio demonstrates the key feature of families in the slave community: an external force—the hand of the slaveholder—was decisive. Since slaves were property, that status generally, although not always, trumped the rights they were explicitly accorded as married couples or parents under medieval law codes like the Spanish *Siete Partidas.* So in a situation in which there was precious little warmth or protection, what little there was turned out to be as precariously balanced as a house of cards. We can only dimly grasp the

MARIAGE DE NÈGRES D'UNE MAISON RICHE.

Original in the John Carter Brown Library at Brown University

Mariage de nègres d'une maison riche (marriage of slaves belonging to a wealthy household) by Jean Baptiste Debret dated 1835. Although Brazil was no longer a colony at this time, slavery would remain firmly in place for several more decades. This drawing shows several black couples being formally married by a priest in a chapel. (Courtesy of the John Carter Brown Library at Brown University)

importance of family relationships in a coerced labor system in which there were few oases, and it is probably impossible for us to imagine the pain and loneliness these separations caused the enslaved Africans and their descendants. We can, however, recognize the centrality of family relationships to the survival of the enslaved. Family formation in this situation became almost a form of resistance, a way for people whose lives were defined by their role as workers to insist on having a life with some pleasure and humanity in it. In addition, African and African American culture was passed from one generation to the next through their families, which makes the family an important institution to examine in order to understand the development of black culture in the Americas.

On the large estate where there might be hundreds of field hands, the male to female ratio of two to one did not favor family formation. Where the nature of the work made male workers preferable to female, new workers from Africa were constantly introduced. Often they lived in primitive communal dormitories known as *barracoons* and were marched out to the fields every day like prisoners on a chain gang. In those cases, their chances of forming a family were very slim. At work sites that remained stable over several generations, workers reproduced, and the ratio of males to females naturally adjusted itself somewhat. In that situation, couples formed, and they might obtain a hut with a bit of land to grow food.

Many census records make it difficult to identify families in the enslaved community because slaves were categorized according to their age or work assignments rather than as families. Some estate records do identify slave families, however. On one 18th-century Brazilian estate of 110 enslaved workers, nearly all of them were living in families, with just over 50 percent living in nuclear families of a couple with their children. And in early 17th-century Guatemala, one of many areas of Spanish America where enslaved Africans and their descendants played a more important role in colonial society than is often recognized, all 54 children listed in an inventory of the largest sugar plantation in the region had at least one parent among the resident adult workforce of 98 men and 39 women. While families were the norm for slaves on the larger estates, at least to the extent possible given the frequent imbalance between women and men, domestic workers who lived in urban areas might have just a few other African people in their place of residence and work, making family formation with other people of African ancestry more difficult. As Africans in the Americas had children, more of the enslaved population was born into a network of family relationships; this, of course, was not usually the case for workers newly arrived from Africa.

Although polygyny, the practice of one man having more than one wife at the same time, was practiced in Africa by those men who could maintain more than one wife and the resulting children, there is little evidence of this family form in the Americas. There were several circumstances that mitigated against polygyny, primarily the unfavorable male/female ratio of Africans and the difficulty of acquiring the necessary wealth as an enslaved laborer. Certainly, the Christian slaveholders' belief in monogamous marriage also played a role in preventing the taking of several wives.

In a frontier region of Brazil, 18th-century church records show that priests performed 400 marriages of enslaved people in about a 100-year period spanning the 18th and 19th centuries. Most of these people married while in their 20s. More than 90 percent of them married a person belonging to the same owner. Enslaved workers also married free people at times. Of all marriages involving at least one slave in this region, just over 20 percent included a free person as well, usually a person who worked for the same owner. Children of the union followed the status of the mother, so a free mother gave birth to free children, while a free father might find a way to buy the freedom of his children. Whether the wife or the husband was the free party, marrying a free person opened up options for one's offspring.

Given legal realities, an enslaved man was far more able to take advantage of this possibility than an enslaved woman, since her status passed automatically to her children, making her unattractive as a formal partner. Outside plantation zones in places like Central America, a decided majority of enslaved men who married found a free spouse, often an indigenous woman, and thereby secured free birth for their children. Meanwhile, enslaved women almost always married men who shared their own inferior legal status if they married at all. But among people of African ancestry, it was those who were already free who were most likely to marry, at least in the frontier area of Brazil mentioned above. This is an interesting finding because they themselves would have had to pay the fee and any costs related to their marriage, suggesting that formal marriage was important to them. They might have seen marriage as the path to legitimacy in the eyes of society and a means of strengthening their hold, and that of their children, on any property they had managed to accumulate.

Not surprisingly, families headed by women were frequent among the enslaved population. Often these families were the result of the accessibility of black women to white men, whether these men were their owners and the owners' sons or overseers and other white men on the plantation. Although we can assume that many of these relationships were unwelcome to the woman, there were advantages to having a child fathered by a white man. In one case, an enslaved woman with five *mulato* children, all fathered by different men, managed to get their fathers to buy their freedom. She purchased her own freedom as well, so that in the end she had managed to free the whole family. Various events might cause the breakup of a nuclear family unit; the father could die or be sold away from the house, leaving his wife and children as a female-headed household. Later, if a stepfather entered the picture, the family would regain its status as a nuclear unit. So a family might pass through a cycle of female headed to nuclear, back to female headed, and then back once again to nuclear.

The institution of godparenting shows the enslaved workers' attempts to connect their offspring to the community in ways that would be helpful in the children's future. Often slaves chose members of their owner's family, which linked the children vertically to powerful people in the community. Another common choice was other members of the community of slaves, connecting the children horizontally to other people of African descent. Nuclear families usually chose godparents from among other slaves, while single mothers chose godparents from the planter class or the free peasantry, presumably the fathers of their children or members of the father's family.

The event most threatening to a slave family was the death of an owner and the distribution of his property. It was at this point that slave families were broken up, couples separated, and children divided among the heirs or sold to liquidate assets. At the death of one slave owner in the mid-18th century in Paraíba, Brazil, most of the 25 married couples were kept together, but many lost their children, or some of them. Even very young children were separated from their parents in this case. A baby of one year was sold on the auction block, a widow was separated from all three of her children, and a female-headed family was completely separated with some of the children distributed among the heirs and others sold at auction. Perhaps there can be no greater clue to the dehumanizing nature of the system of slavery than these dry facts. It is tempting to conclude that the slave-owning population believed men to be better workers if they had a wife to care for them and for that reason kept slave couples together. In addition, family ties tended to discourage running off. For the estate owners, though, slave family stability occupied a place that was a distant second to maintaining the productivity of the laboring population. These statistics seem to say that a woman can always have more children and adults can find new partners so they will not long feel the loss of those who have been taken away. Respecting the humanity of the African people would have forced the slaveholders to admit to causing them enormous grief by separating their families.

Casta Families

Among the non-Indian lower social groups, Christian marriage was uncommon. The norm was cohabitation. One reason was the prohibitive cost of marriage. Another was the lack of property to pass on. The landless population, those living and working on haciendas, found little reason for Christian marriage since there was no property to protect for future generations. Without this hold over their children, parents had little control over young people's freedom to choose their partners and settle down without benefit of marriage. The main reason to marry formally was to climb the social ladder by practicing this most important rite of Christianity and European values. Peasants who did choose to marry might do so after setting up a household and acquiring some property. Or their reasoning might be to lift their children out of the stigmatized category of illegitimacy. Frequently, marriage applications state that the young woman is pregnant or that the couple already has one or more children, indicating a connection even in this marriage-shy population between having children and seeking formal marriage.

The church did not succeed in exerting the same control over these families that it had over the highest and lowest social groups. In urban areas, the church was more concerned with ministering to elite families than to the racially mixed working population, and in rural areas, villages were scattered widely across the land and priests were few and far between, and thus very overworked. Although they struggled to bring their wayward sheep into the marriage fold, it was an uphill battle, given the broad acceptance of common-law marriage among the casta population.

The primary limitation on finding a partner was the small number of families living on the hacienda or in the village. Marriage between first cousins—a frequent occurrence among the elite, as discussed above—was also fairly common in the casta population, although for different reasons. In the latter case, cousins married not to protect family property and social status, but because of the difficulty of finding a partner of the right age in a small community where most of the population was related.

Among peasants who owned their own land or had rights to common village lands, the patriarchal family might exert as much control over the choice of their child's marital partner as did elite parents. When he married, the young man received his portion of his father's land and space in his father's house, generally part of the common space, although an addition might be added later; the bride went to live with her new husband's extended family. Some peasant families even employed the dowry as a symbol of their upcoming contract, although its size would not reach that of the lavish dowries provided to daughters of the elite.

This engraving of a casta family by Juan de la Cruz from 1784 depicts a family of the French Caribbean. Casta paintings, many of them produced in 18th-century Mexico, were prized by European collectors fascinated with the exotic racial categories depicted by artists interested less in representing colonial reality than in conveying messages about the supposed social consequences of racial mixing. (The Art Archive / Bibliothèque des Arts Décoratifs Paris / Gianni Dagli Orti)

BIGAMY

What are we to make of the fact that statistically the casta population was least likely to marry and also the most likely to marry twice? Once again, the answer probably lies in the relative lack of control the church exercised over the lives of these people and, of course, the growing size of this population during the colonial period. In addition, the frequency of bigamy in this group may be simply an indication of its more freewheeling lifestyle and lack of enthusiasm for monogamous, lifelong Christian marriage.

The Inquisition devoted considerable energy to investigating bigamy. Although the main business of the Inquisition in the American colonies was to ferret out "New Christians" who might be secretly practicing Jewish rituals, a phenomenon discussed more fully in chapter 6, the institution concerned itself with a wide variety of violations of Christian principles. Bigamy ranked high on the list of infractions. While Islam permitted polygamy, the Roman Catholic Church treated bigamy as both immoral and heretical. One way that Catholics differentiated themselves from the Muslim culture that had dominated the Iberian Peninsula for hundreds of years was by establishing marriage as an exclusive relationship between one man and one woman.

Nevertheless, some people of the lower social groups committed bigamy, and since the punishments doled out were severe, it makes sense to ask why they did it. Usually they were men, many of whom had found it necessary to leave one area and take up residence in another. This might happen because a man found himself on the wrong side of the law, but more often simply for employment. The assumption under the colonial patron-client system—the traditional form being a plantation owner, or *hacendado,* with a large household of dependents and servants, as well as many laborers who relied on him for work—was that every member of the working classes needed a *patrón,* who provided employment and credit, as well as protection for his workers in court should that be necessary. The patrón served as a kind of insurance policy. The only flaw in this system was that there were not enough positions for all the laborers who needed to attach themselves to a master. As a result, many men of the popular classes found it necessary to move from time to time and look for work. The difficulty of travel would then prevent their returning home regularly. Socializing with residents in the new location, along with the impossibility of living alone, might lead to new couple relationships. The true vagabond would not need to marry, of course, but the footloose and fancy-free life did not appeal to the bigamists; they wanted to settle down and have a home. The fact that they married a second time seems to indicate their desire to abide by, rather than to violate, the social rules. Sometimes the authorities had a hand in the decision to marry, since the local priest and government functionaries were likely appear at any time of day or night in their unceasing efforts to end cohabitation. Once the authorities were in the picture, marrying headed off unpleasant legal consequences, until bigamy was discovered, of course.

CONCLUSION

Like everything else in colonial Latin America, the family looked different at different levels of the social structure. The church had considerable success in enforcing Christian marriage as the portal to family life for those at the two levels where the church exercised most power: among elites and the indigenous people. Among the casta population and the community of enslaved workers, family formation was less orderly. The existence of a racially mixed population was always inconvenient for the Spanish crown and never officially acknowledged. As a result, people at this level had considerably more latitude in choosing a partner, as well as in the matter of whether or not to formalize their relationship. Family formation among the enslaved population was of less interest to the church, partly because insisting on formal marriages in this case would have brought the church into conflict with some of its most important donors. It is important to note, however, that the frequency of slave marriages by a priest was often surprisingly high, as the evidence from a frontier area of Brazil shows. This evidence indicates a commitment on the part of owners to regularizing the laboring population and an attempt by the workers themselves to seek shelter in the bosom of the church-approved family.

Families were viewed as the basic building block of society. An orderly hierarchical society depended on maintaining established social levels, and this system in turn depended on guiding the process of selecting a partner. Elite parents and the church exerted their influence over young people at the highest social level as a way of protecting and perpetuating elite patriarchal families and their property. In general, Indians married other Indians, and this was certainly encouraged, partly to facilitate the collection of tribute from that population. While things were a lot less orderly at the level of middle groups, the record shows a clear preference for Christian marriage and legitimization of the offspring among those aspiring to climb the social ladder; the documentation also shows their imitation of elite practices like the dowry. Enslaved Africans, and those free people who chose enslaved partners, had very little control over their family life, married or not. While slave owners seem to have made some effort to keep couples together, that may have been more for the sake of order among the working people on the estate than for humane reasons. Despite legal protection for marriage among the enslaved, the adjudication of a will or the whim of an owner often separated even formally married couples.

Their children were normally considered future laborers, rather than members of nuclear families, and distributed according to the best interests of their owners.

The reader may note here that the focus in this chapter on marriage as a contract between families and the basic building block of colonial society has told us little about the nature of love or affection in that society. For example, an examination of the institution of marriage provides only a partial view of colonial sexual practices and their meaning to participants. Historical documents show that people frequently employed their sexuality outside the institution of marriage, in spite of the position of the Roman Catholic Church that sex was sinful except when its purpose was procreation within marriage. The next chapter addresses this extramarital dimension of sexuality and affective life at greater length, including both heterosexual and homosexual relationships and the sex lives of priests sworn to celibacy.

NOTES

In addition to the works cited separately as sources of direct quotations and the authors' own archival research, the following sources have been drawn on for specific examples in this chapter: Mark A. Burkholder and Lyman L. Johnson, *Colonial Latin America*; Cheryl E. Martin and Mark Wasserman, *Latin America and Its People*; Alida C. Metcalf, *Family and Frontier in Colonial Brazil*; Steve J. Stern, *The Secret History of Gender*; Nancy van Deusen, "'Wife of My Soul and Heart, and All My Solace': Annulment Suit Between Diego Andrés de Arenas and Ysabel Allay Suyo (Huánuco, Peru, 1618)," in *Colonial Lives,* ed. Richard Boyer and Gregory Spurling. For full citations and other useful readings, see the annotated bibliography.

1. Asunción Lavrin, ed., *Sexuality and Marriage in Colonial Latin America* (Lincoln: University of Nebraska Press, 1989), p. 1.

2. Ramón A. Gutiérrez, *When Jesus Came, the Corn Mothers Went Away: Marriage, Sexuality, and Power in New Mexico, 1500–1846* (Stanford, Calif.: Stanford University Press, 1991), p. xviii.

3. Richard Boyer, "Women, *La Mala Vida,* and the Politics of Marriage," in *Sexuality and Marriage,* ed. Lavrin, p. 252.

4. Gutiérrez, *When Jesus Came,* p. xix.

5. Susan Socolow, "Acceptable Partners: Marriage Choice in Colonial Argentina, 1778–1810," in *Sexuality and Marriage,* ed. Lavrin, p. 228.

6. Archivo Histórico Arquidiocesano (Guatemala City), T3–114, Santa Catarina Pinula, January 1831, Joseph Maria Orantes in the case of García-Torres.

2

LOVE, SEX,
AND RELATIONSHIPS

INTRODUCTION

Love and sexual attraction are among the areas most inaccessible
to the student of history. The emotional life of our subjects is often
hidden from view. It does not emerge explicitly in statistics, trials,
wills, or other public documents historians normally use to create
a picture of life in the past. It seems clear, however, that people are
sometimes drawn to mates who might not be suitable or socially
convenient for a variety of reasons: the prospective mate might be
promised, or already legally joined, to someone else; might be from
a different social group; might not reciprocate the feelings; might
be of the same gender; or might be a religious worker bound by a
vow of chastity. In short, attraction to another is part of life and a
part that does not respect social rules. In the previous chapter, it
became clear that marriage in colonial Latin America was a contract
between families, managed by the authorities of the religious state.
While there were exceptions to the rule, generally marriage had
little to do with love or attraction.

This chapter addresses sexuality, affection, and attraction outside
marriage, including both heterosexual and homosexual relationships and the romantic lives of priests who were sworn to celibacy. Historians working in periods before the advent of widely

available and highly effective birth control methods have the advantage of following the birth of children outside marriage as one measure of premarital and extramarital relations. Children born out of wedlock become the embodiment of extramarital sex and a measure of its frequency among heterosexuals. Another indication of affective life is the fact that enslaved Africans and their descendants, whether or not they were formally married, sometimes took enormous risks to find their mates or to visit them on a nearby plantation, a fact that provides a clue to the deep attachment some people felt for one another. Homosexual relationships are more difficult to find in the past, and statistics on children born out of wedlock are irrelevant, obviously. In recent years, considerable time and creativity have been devoted to unearthing evidence of homosexual relationships, so far primarily between men. What is clear is that the church as an institution fought an uphill battle in its attempt to control sexuality and contain it in the approved channel of reproduction within marriage while seeking to eliminate same-sex relations altogether. Meanwhile, individual priests were almost as likely as their flocks, some would say more likely, to be overcome by their passions and violate their celibacy, sometimes taking advantage of their position of power over their parishioners to make demands for sexual favors.

While colonial elites seem to have gone to great lengths to achieve at least the appearance of abiding by the church's social and sexual rules, evidence abounds of the church's failure to control sexuality effectively among the common people during the period. This chapter will explore some of the differences in the romantic and sexual relationships of people of different social classes.

SEX AND SIN

There is considerable evidence that the indigenous peoples of the Western Hemisphere prior to the arrival of the Europeans held views on matters of sex, sin, and their relationship to each other that differed, in some cases radically, from those of the 15th- and 16th-century Roman Catholic Church. Some histories of the pre-Columbian period claim there was no concept equal to the church's notion of sin and that some indigenous societies included sexuality in public ceremonies and prohibited not sex itself, but sexual excess. With the arrival of the Iberians, however, came the misogynist linking of sexuality with women and the devil, who together had achieved the banishment of man from paradise. The ideal posed by the church for women became the Virgin Mary, an impossible model, as some historians have pointed out, since Mary was both a virgin and a mother.

In addition to bringing to the Americas a concept of sex linked to sin, the church also brought a deep aversion to sex acts between men, something that apparently had not been forbidden in at least some pre-Columbian societies. Even before the Inquisition arrived in the colonies, the church had succeeded in making sodomy illegal. Some historians of sexuality have observed that the church forbade homosexuality primarily because of the threat posed to patriarchy and the gender system by a man playing the sexual role of a woman. Their thesis draws strength from the fact that the partner playing the active role in a sexual act between men was not subjected to much criticism in trials before the Inquisition.

Some non-Christian American religions have retained a view of sexuality that diverges widely from that of the church; Afro-Brazilian Candomblé does not hold nonreproductive sex to be sinful by definition, nor does it forbid sexual acts between members of the same gender. In the colonial period, however, the church was the unchallenged creator and arbiter of moral standards; there were no other institutions capable of balancing or challenging that power.

PREMARITAL SEX

Despite the power of the church over their lives, it may be that the common people of the colonial period clung to some of the mores and practices that had characterized the pre-Columbian era, and indeed many of the common people of colonial Latin America do seem to have believed that sex between two unmarried people was not sinful. In addition, it seems that given the hardships of peasant life and the key role played by the wife in the peasant household, among rural people a woman's virginity occupied a position low on the list of assets to consider in the choice of a wife. Virginity in one's intended might be a nice feature, but documentation from the period shows that it was not considered a necessity by young men seeking a mate. So while elites attempted to abide by fairly rigid social rules concerning premarital sex, the records of the lives of the common people demonstrate a more freewheeling approach that granted considerable latitude to unattached women whether widows or young unmarried women.

In-Laws and Blood Relationships

The frequency of sex before marriage emerges not only in baptismal records, where a baptized child is identified either as an *hijo legítimo* (legitimate child) or an *hijo natural*, but also in marriage applications that include dispensations of impediments to marriage. According to canon law, the legal code of the Roman Catholic Church, there were several "impediments" to marriage, including a relationship by blood (e.g., being cousins), as well as various relationships considered incestuous. These incestuous relationships were based not only on blood relationships, like the modern secular definition of incest, but also on in-law relationships and those created by certain commitments. In the late colonial period, canon law required those who fell into categories defined as incestuous to apply for dispensation of the impediment that resulted. If, for instance, a man wished to marry his brother's widow—not uncommon in a situation where life expectancy was short and the dangers of rural life were many—the couple had to apply for a waiver of the impediment posed by their relationship, a link known as *afinidad lícita* (legal relationship). Otherwise the relationship between this former brother-in-law and sister-in-law would prevent their marriage.

Most applications for church waivers of impediments to marriage dealt with blood relationships, especially in small villages that might have been founded by two or three couples whose offspring would all be related within a few generations. In addition, though, dispensations were often sought for *afinidad ilícita* (illicit relationship), and it is from these documents that we get an indication of the frequency of premarital and extramarital sex. When the couple met with their priest to state their intent to marry, the interview might reveal an illicit relationship that required dispensation from the archdiocese. Records of applications for this waiver reveal a high incidence of premarital sex, although this did not deter couples from marrying. Young men of the popular classes seem to have attached little significance to the past sex lives of their chosen mates; other considerations weighed more heavily in the choice of a partner.

One suitor explained to a dismayed priest his reasons for choosing to marry a relative who, even before they began their premarital relationship, had not been a virgin: he was alone in the world, his lands were intermingled with those of his intended's father, widespread knowledge of the sexual relationship he had with this young woman would prevent him from finding another partner, and he wished to clear his conscience and avoid a conflict with the girl's father. His intended explained that she had begun her sexual relationship with her suitor because of "human weakness," out of youthful ignorance and the fact that he was working for her father and living in the same house with her, and now she wanted to marry him to escape her father's poverty and the control of her stepmother. She admitted that this was not her first sexual relationship.

Other applications for dispensation of impediments to marriage give similar reasons for wanting to marry someone with whom there was an impediment of blood or incestuous relations. One young man sought to marry because he was an orphan whose guardian had recently died leaving him with no place to go. A girl admitted she was already sexually involved with her suitor and wished to marry because she was homeless after being put out of the house of her stepfather. When one suitor sought the dispensation of his intended's illicit relationship with his brother and two of his cousins, the priest wondered why he would want to marry such a girl, but the young man refused to be budged in spite of the past experience of his bride-to-be. One engaged girl had sexual relations with a man other than her fiancé, but she assured the priest that it was not based on any commitment between them but was strictly a casual event; her suitor was unfazed. In another case, a young woman was pregnant by her mother's suitor, but about to marry someone else very soon; both mother and daughter were married to their suitors shortly thereafter.

Virginity, Honor, and Practical Considerations

In some cases, marriage was delayed due to the poverty of the suitor. Under these circumstances, the couple would frequently begin a sexual relationship. When the young woman became pregnant, they sometimes attempted to "cover her honor" by speeding up the marriage.

Certainly, there were exceptions to the low value attached to virginity by those of the popular classes. One rural woman ran away from her village, leaving her suitor of many years, because she feared for her life if he found out about her previous relationship with his brother, although the brother was long dead. In another instance, an application to waive an impediment shows a father's fears that if his daughter did not quickly marry the only suitor who had appeared, she would lose her virginity and increase the difficulty of finding a partner. In addition, one study of judicial records of sexual assault in the late colonial period shows that women's accusations of rape were rarely taken seriously, and that victims had almost no hope of obtaining a favorable verdict if they had prior sexual experience. So the historical record seems to be contradictory regarding the importance of women's virginity during the period. Indeed, the difference may lie in the nature of the documents themselves (i.e., criminal assault cases versus applications for marriage).

In any case, evidence of concerns related to the choice of a marital partner from a rural area of eastern Guatemala at the end of the colonial period shows that the Euro-Catholic value system with its equation of women, sex, and sin had not yet extended its control over the population in the matter of selection of a mate. The documentation also shows that the sexual double standard had little influence on the real expectations that men and women had of each other. While there were certainly some exceptions to this rule of the slight importance of a woman's personal sexual history, the weight is definitely on the side of practical rather than ideological considerations. Not that chastity and fidelity in a woman were not desirable, but material considerations took precedence.

The Upper Classes and Premarital Sex

The examples above give some idea of the frequency of premarital sex and its social significance among the common people. Among elites, rules were considerably more strict, and women could pay a high price for premarital sex. Since a formal commitment to marry was almost as binding as marriage itself, couples often began their sexual relationship during the engagement period. Pregnancy often complicated matters. While marrying before, or in some cases even after, the birth of the child would rescue the family name, the woman was totally dependent on her family to keep her out of sight until the baby was born and then help decide what to do with it. If the engagement went forward to formal marriage, the child, categorized as an *hijo natural* (child of unmarried parents), although born before the marriage, was easily legitimized, and there was no shame attached to the pregnancy and birth.

Sometimes an engaged couple needed to wait for official permission from the Spanish or Portuguese crown or for the resolution of some family matter before marrying. Unfortunately for a woman who became pregnant before the marriage was performed, plans to marry sometimes fell through. If the suitor changed his mind, or if his employment took him away from his intended and his return was delayed, or worse still, if he were killed, his pregnant fiancé found herself in an unenviable position. Elite families went to great lengths to conceal the pregnancy of an unmarried daughter or sister, since this occurrence threatened to make another marriage an impossibility for her and cast a stain on the honor of the whole family, thus diminishing the marriage prospects for all family members. At times, the newborn might be brought into the household under the fiction that it was an orphan and even be granted legitimacy at some point, but the honor of the child's unwed mother was lost if word spread that she had parented a child.

In one case in 17th-century Mexico, an important Spanish functionary from Mexico City was on his way to rejoin his invalid wife at a small town in the countryside when he became involved in an illicit relationship with a young woman of the family where he found lodging in Puebla. The functionary, named Francisco, stayed a few months, and eventually the woman's relatives began to pressure him to marry her, even going so far as to misinform him that his wife had died. When Francisco attempted an escape, he found himself facing the woman's angry brothers, armed and ready to kill him if he did not marry her. The woman's family brought a magistrate to the house in the middle of the night to take Francisco off to jail, and the marriage was quickly arranged. After marrying his lover, a woman quite below his status as he saw it, Francisco was free to leave town, which he hastened to do. He was never to see his new wife again, but this was irrelevant to the men of her family since they had rescued their honor by forcing Francisco to do his duty. We do not know how the young woman may have felt, now joined to a husband she would never see again and therefore prevented from marrying someone with whom she might have been able to make a good life.

Premarital Sex and Fatherhood

For every child born outside marriage, there were two parents, but of the two, the father paid the lesser price by far. Having a child out of wedlock was not, in and of itself, a blot on his honor. Indeed, while the unwed mother attempted to hide her status as a parent, the newborn's father might celebrate the birth of a child, in spite of its illegitimacy. This may be attributed in part to the legal apparatus, based on the *Siete Partidas*, the medieval Spanish law code that exempted men from the obligation of recognizing a child born outside marriage. Laws that left women and children unprotected in this way were based on the assumption that an unmarried woman who engaged in a sexual relationship was not an honorable person, so there was no way the father could be sure the child was actually his.

When a man lost honor, it was usually because of his reputation in his professional life and his business dealings. A man's honor depended on his honesty and reliability, on being faithful to his word. Breaking a contract could mean a loss of honor for a man, and since a promise of marriage was a form of contract, breaking it could tarnish his reputation. Sometimes an engagement lasted a long time, and several children might be produced before a man broke off the relationship, possibly to return to Spain or to accept an assignment in a different area of the viceroyalty. In this situation, the problem would not be his treatment of the woman involved, but rather the fact that he had given his word to marry and then gone back on it. This difference between the social status of unmarried parents also suggests that men were less fettered by community pressures since they tended to move around more than women, especially a woman with children who needed the support of her family and a stable life for her children.

Although a man might not recognize and legitimate his child, he was responsible for what was known as *crianza*, raising and providing for his children. If he failed to carry out this responsibility, he might lose honor. His main problem, though, if he did not recognize his child, would be confronting his child's loss of honor, the unlikelihood that his male child would be eligible for a professional or military career and that his female child might contract a favorable marriage.

EXTRAMARITAL SEX

Widows

In some cases, virginity was not an issue because the bride-to-be was a widow. In these cases, the documents show that attraction and what was characterized as human weakness, combined with availability or considerations of survival, led to sexual relationships outside marriage. In one case, a man sought a waiver in order to marry his brother's widow who was about 10 years older than he and had seven children; the couple had already begun a sexual relationship. Testimony shows that the deceased husband, after realizing that he was ill and probably dying, had invited his brother into the house to help his wife manage her property. It seems the dying husband in this case supplied his own replacement, and his brother and widow were agreeable to this arrangement. In another case, a young indigenous man with no financial resources of his own applied for a waiver to marry his employer, a *mestiza* 13 years older than he. He stated that he expected to be fired if he did not marry her. For her part, his employer stated that she wished to marry the young man, with whom she had been carrying on a relationship for a year, because if they did not marry she would be forced to fire him, find a replacement, and run the same risk with the new employee. What emerges in these cases is that rural common people paid little attention to the rigid rules of sexual behavior the church attempted to impose on their lives. The snippets of rural life we see in these applications for waivers of impediments to marriage indicate high levels of both premarital and extramarital sexual activity during the colonial period, in spite of the best efforts of the priests to restrict it.

Slavery

Although the chapter on marriage and the family shows that some slaveholders encouraged marriage between their workers, other owners found it unnecessary and inconvenient to allow their workers to marry, possibly because marriage could be interpreted as an obstacle in separating couples from each other and children from their parents at the time of sale or inheritance. In addition, a plantation owner's unrestricted access to his female slaves could be made more difficult, possibly even more dangerous, if the women were married. Not surprisingly, slaveholders were fond of ascribing loose morals to their workers and liked to blame enslaved women, married or not, for enticing their masters. While the true nature of such master-slave sexual relationships is often difficult to gauge and undoubtedly varied widely depending on specific circumstances, the power of the slaveholder was always an important factor in shaping them.

Meanwhile, there is evidence of strong affective life within the community of enslaved workers itself. An English manager of a sugar mill in early 19th-century Brazil noted that men sometimes risked severe punishment to sneak off to another estate to visit the object of their affections after a hard day's work. He wrote of their "determination that the feelings of the heart shall not be controlled."[1] Records from a Jesuit plantation show that although the workforce was supposed to be locked up at night, it was fairly easy to slip away; the administrator attempted to correct this by applying the whip to young men who had been caught taking off at night. While recent research into the lives of enslaved workers has shown that marriages were more common than historians previously believed, married or not, the workers preferred to live in couples if the male–female ratio on the plantation made that possible. Female-headed households were abnormal, rather than the norm, and less than 10 percent of the slaves lived alone.

Adultery

In addition to showing the frequency of premarital sex, the applications to marry mentioned earlier also reveal many people engaged in sexual relationships with partners who were already married to someone else. According to the usual definition of adultery, a married *woman* had to be involved. Monogamy was neither practiced by nor expected of men, in spite of the best efforts of the church. Although religious workers struggled mightily to encourage, even enforce, monogamy among all their parishioners, they had little hold over men of the popular classes. What is somewhat more surprising is the evidence of married women choosing sexual partners outside their marriage, and often not for any apparent economic reason. While in some cases a woman may have engaged in an adulterous relationship almost as a form of insurance in the event of the death of her husband, at other times women seem not to have had any hidden motive, but simply to have acted on an attraction. Even more surprising, the evidence does not show that adultery necessarily led to separation of the couple or couples involved. We do not, of course, know how conjugal relations suffered as a result of the adultery of a partner, but often adultery did not terminate marriage. Women's essential role in the production and reproduction of peasant life seems to have given them a little power over their own lives by reducing somewhat their husbands' control over their activities. Put another way, a wife was a necessity in the peasant household, and in rural villages finding a partner was not easy. A sexual transgression might not warrant the termination of an otherwise workable home life.

A long and interesting court case from a town on the highway between Guatemala City and San Salvador in the 1780s displays many features common to adulterous relationships. The aggrieved husband, Juan Francisco Pineda, brought a case against his wife's lover, Manuel Mendizábal, who worked for Pineda from time to time. Pineda was a successful farmer and owner of a mule train; the 25-year-old Mendizábal, who identified himself as a musician, did various odd jobs including working as a mule driver for Pineda. The relationship between Mendizábal and Pineda's wife, Petrona Rustrián, apparently continued for some years, leading to various arrests for Mendizábal and just as many jailbreaks. Several times the authorities succeeded in catching Manuel and Petrona practically in the act, once finding Manuel hiding in the bed of Petrona's young son, *under* the child. He had forgotten to move his clothes, however, which were found neatly folded at the head of Petrona's bed. Once locked up, Mendizábal would usually write to Petrona, expressing his love for her and asking for her help in contacting people who might facilitate his release. In one of these letters, addressed "Dear jewel of my heart and all my love," Manuel told Petrona, "Although enduring my misfortune in this dismal prison, I remain your *negro* (your man, husband) and faithful to my little cutie, my soul cherishes you, don't forget me. . . ." He went on to ask her to collect a debt from someone who owed him money so he could eat better in jail. Manuel finished the note, "your devoted slave who yearns to see you more than to write you. You well know his name." It is interesting to observe that this drifter seems to have been able to write the note himself, but Petrona could not read it and so asked a male neighbor to read it for her, paying him with a measure of maize. The neighbor, loyal to his gender, told Pineda who seized the note as evidence, notwithstanding Manuel's attempt at anonymity.[2]

Various features of this case make it typical of adultery cases. First, Pineda was related to the mayor, giving him a realistic hope of winning the case. He ranked high in the rural socioeconomic hierarchy, while Manuel was a floater who relied in part on his appeal to women for his livelihood—he was once arrested in the house of a local widow. Also typical is the fact that after the case got to court Petrona chose to sell out her lover and stay with her husband, certainly the more practical option. Indeed, Petrona told the court that her husband had pardoned her in the past for her relationship with Manuel and seemed to be willing to do so again as long as she repudiated the relationship with Manuel. What her husband seemed most upset about was that she had given Manuel a blanket and some clothing and that she regularly washed his clothes down at the river and sent his meals to wherever he was working. Here the husband showed more concern for the misuse of his hard-earned assets than for the chastity of his wife. And in the end, the adulterous relationship did not end Petrona's marriage. While Catholic marriage was supposed to be both lifelong and monogamous, it seems the lifelong element may have weighed more heavily than monogamy. Since the married couple was the basic building block of a stable, moral society, the sin of adultery could be forgiven, while separation, more threatening to the social system, could not be tolerated.

At times, adultery led to hidden blood relationships that could not be untangled, and dispensation of an impediment was sought just on the chance that one existed. This situation occurred in a case in which parents of both the bride-to-be and her suitor were suspected of having been fathered by men other than their mothers' husbands, which would have meant that the couple was related by blood. Since the rate of births outside marriage in many rural areas hovered around 30 percent, many children did not know the identity of their fathers. When they reached the age of marriage, they were sometimes surprised to learn of a blood relationship with their intended partner. If they themselves were unaware of a possible relationship, the community gossips could be depended upon to supply the information to the priest with alacrity upon hearing the announcement of the intended marriage.

At times, two married people would exchange a promise of marriage if both should become unattached. A couple engaged in an adulterous relationship might thereby provoke the impediment of *crimen*, meaning that they had promised to marry while one or both parties were still married to other people. Applications for dispensation of this impediment show a fear of the immiseration that was the likely result of being left without a partner, but planning to marry one's sexual partner, even if the current partner was at death's door, was a violation of canon law.

THE CLERGY

Canon law governing sexual behavior was not infrequently transgressed by the individuals most directly responsible for upholding it. Many priests were involved in heterosexual relationships, despite their vows of celibacy. In some cases, these relationships were coercive, as it was relatively easy for priests who were so inclined to exploit the power they enjoyed over female parishioners, especially inside the confessional. In many other cases, and most often in rural parishes, a priest lived more or less openly in a presumably consensual relationship with a local woman and was understood by all concerned to be the father of her children. The attitudes of parishioners toward such relationships depended remarkably little on disapproval of priests having sex. Instead, those attitudes tended to derive from assessments of a priest's overall performance of his duties.

In 1805, the native governor of the village of Huitzuco, in Guerrero, Mexico, protested against an official investigation of an illicit relationship involving Huitzuco's parish priest and a local woman. The governor praised the priest, Manuel Urizar, for his "steadfast, most honorable conduct [and] great many acts of charity," adding "we have never seen a priest with such zeal for his parishioners."[3] Urizar's active sex life, in other words, did not appear to offend villagers at all, or at least not the village head. As long as the priest performed his duties faithfully, going well beyond them in this case in the apparent interest of easing financial burdens on his flock, his contravention of church law in the matter of celibacy was a largely irrelevant trifle.

It mattered, however, whom priests singled out for their attentions. Parishioners were most likely to be upset by the sexual peccadilloes of a priest who pursued married women or young women who were presumed to be virgins, even if the attraction was mutual. Meanwhile, for church authorities the most reprehensible sexual misconduct by priests involved using the power of the confessional to extract sexual favors from female parishioners, whoever they were. Even in such cases, though, convicted priests usually escaped with relatively light punishment at the hands of their superiors. In late-colonial Mexico, even the worst repeat offenders usually retained the right to be given a new parish after serving a temporary period of exile or a similar sentence. And the very power that priests exercised over parishioners during confession, the abuse of which was of such grave concern to the higher-ups, undoubtedly ensured that many instances of illicit behavior were never reported in the first place.

The cases that do show up in the historical record indicate that some priests pressed their luck quite blatantly. In 1795, the parish priest of Xochicoatlan, a few hours north of Mexico City, persuaded the parents of at least five young women that the girls needed to come and live with him in his residence so he could oversee a careful regimen of spiritual exercises. One of the girls later reported that the priest had successfully forced his sexual attentions on her almost as soon as her mother had said good-bye. The aggrieved mother declared to church officials that "no confessor, no matter how saintly, can have women penitents in his house."[4]

The saintliness of a pair of Franciscan friars serving in the Mexican province of Jalisco, the brothers Gregorio and Joseph Yriarte, was presumably the object of some significant doubt among their parishioners. Gregorio was accused of having solicited sexual favors from at least 19 women, mostly in the confessional, before being hauled before an ecclesiastical court in 1758. Joseph, meanwhile, was said to have pursued every young woman who came to him for confession, in some cases inviting them to his quarters and in others exposing himself to them.

SAME-SEX RELATIONSHIPS

Some expressions of sexual desire were not to be tolerated at all, whether exhibited by priests or any other member of colonial society. The most unacceptable, at least on paper, involved men engaging in sodomy. Defined by the church as the *pecado nefando*, or "abominable sin," it was sufficient grounds for execution by strangulation, to be followed by the burning of the corpse at the stake. In 1595, this grisly fate befell a certain Juan González, a young shopkeeper's assistant, after he was arrested along with several other alleged participants in homosexual activities in the Andean silver-mining city of Potosí. The same year in Brazil, this punishment was decreed by the Inquisition for André de Freitas Lessa, a shoemaker from Olinda who confessed to having had no fewer than 31 male sexual partners "in his home, close to the Church of Conceição or at the top of Rua Nova, he being the one who always assaulted and begged them."[5] In both of these cases, following the dictates of both church and crown, allegedly sinful men of modest social status found themselves charged with a capital crime for participating in an unapproved expression of a basic human desire.

Significantly, the same harsh punishment was never suggested at all for the man Juan González identified up to the moment of his execution as his sexual partner on several occasions: Dr. Gaspar González de Sosa, a high ranking and well-respected local church official. Although Dr. González attempted suicide while briefly imprisoned during the 1595 investigation in Potosí, after resolutely denying all the allegations made against him he was eventually acquitted and resumed his clerical post. Within a few years, he was living openly in a far more intimate and long-term relationship with another young man, whom he reportedly showered with lavish gifts, honors, and public displays of affection. When the weight of the law was finally brought to bear against this couple, letters the two had written to each other were described by one witness as expressing "such delicate and tender things as when a man writes to a woman, calling each other my soul, my life, and other complimentary things."[6]

Despite this evidence of his passion for another man, Dr. González again escaped with relatively few negative consequences, although his longtime partner was tortured and sentenced to six years' unpaid labor at the galleys, serving as a rower in the Spanish fleet. Church authorities only reluctantly pursued charges against their esteemed colleague after failing for some time to persuade him to change, at least in public, what they viewed as scandalous behavior. Even then, an ecclesiastical tribunal cast doubt on the veracity of the testimony made against this "highly qualified preacher," declaring that "the majority of the witnesses who condemned him were vile and low people."[7] He was, nevertheless, eventually placed in seclusion and finally ordered removed to another diocese in 1614. But it appears he never suffered any of the draconian physical punishment administered to his former partners. As in cases of heterosexual misconduct on the part of priests, and perhaps even more remarkably given legal and social intolerance for homosexual activity, Dr. González benefited from the church's clear desire to protect its own.

The reader will not be surprised by now to learn that social status was an important determinant of an individual's fate, even in circumstances involving activities seen as intrinsically worthy of death under the prevailing religious and social norms. Another case from the early 17th century, this time unfolding just north of Lake Titicaca in the southern Peruvian Andes, underscores colonial society's intolerance of same-sex relations while also confirming the notion that accusations of homosexual behavior did not lead inevitably to death or even disgrace. In this instance, the testimony of an enslaved man, "Antón from the land of Congo," resulted in a 1611 investigation of another high-ranking member of the colonial elite: Damián de Morales, the appointed Spanish legal advocate for local indigenous peoples. According to Antón, Morales had propositioned him while visiting a rural estate owned by Antón's master, a close friend of Morales. On reporting the incident to another Spanish visitor on the estate, Antón was immediately asked "why he hadn't killed Damián de Morales, and [he] answered that he hadn't done that because [Morales] was a friend of his master."[8] The social implications of this conversation as recorded in Antón's testimony are clear, and rather remarkable. They suggest that in Spanish eyes an enslaved man would have been fully justified in killing a male member of the colonial elite who made sexual advances toward him. Such an attitude was far different from those commonly held regarding the prerogatives of enslaved women confronted with unwanted sexual attentions from slave owners or other elite men.

At the same time, it is important to note that Damián de Morales suffered even fewer adverse consequences as a result of his alleged behavior than Dr. Gaspar González de Sosa. Although a good deal of hearsay evidence, admissible in colonial courts, was collected against him, in addition to Anton's eyewitness testimony, he was soon released from jail and subsequently rose even higher in the colonial bureaucracy. It is possible that the authorities threw out the case against Morales as a fabrication launched by an enemy, as one scholar has suggested in the absence of a final decision in the records. What is clear is that his social status assured him a level of protection that would surely not have been accorded Antón from the land of Congo had the roles in the alleged attempt at seduction been reversed.

A narrow legal focus on the illicit sex act itself may also have saved Morales. Acceptable proof that sodomy had actually taken place, often obtained through confessions elicited by means of interrogation and torture, was another vital ingredient in securing a conviction on charges of engaging in the *pecado nefando*. News of Morales's attentions to a slave was sufficiently provocative to have become the subject of a popular verse making the gossip rounds, which ran

Captive I am, I will not say of whom
Tell it to Morales that I am his.[9]

Nevertheless, neither Antón nor anyone else claimed that sodomy had in fact occurred. Even when culpability for the act itself was under consideration, distinctions were generally drawn between participants who took the active versus the passive role, with the latter deemed particularly lacking in masculine honor as defined by Spaniards and therefore most threatening to the established order. Juan González, for instance, confessed to taking the passive role in his relations with Dr. Gaspar González de Sosa, which made him a *puto*, or male whore, in the parlance of the times. This confession perhaps ensured his payment of the ultimate penalty for engaging in sexual practices that lay outside the accepted norm of hetero-sexual reproductive sex.

Assessing the frequency of such unlawful practices in colonial society as a whole is as difficult as determining the extent of par-ticipation in forbidden religious rituals, discussed later in the book. Neither was well documented, for obvious reasons. Their social meaning is even more hotly debated, particularly with regard to their manifestation among indigenous peoples both before and after the European arrival. Some scholars argue that native groups had few qualms about same-sex relations among men, based in large part on the tendency of Iberian invaders to list sodomy promi-nently among the vices said to afflict societies they labeled heathen. Social acceptance in many parts of the pre-Columbian Americas of the *berdache*, or "cross-dressing man," is cited as additional evi-dence of this enlightened attitude. But others see instead a hyper-masculinized warrior ethos that shared the Iberian contempt for the "passive," who was deliberately and publicly "feminized" and thus relegated to a decidedly inferior status in the gender hierarchy. One thing is clear: sexuality and power are never far removed from each other, as the evidence discussed throughout this chapter in-dicates, and prevailing patterns of social hierarchy had a profound impact on all sexual relationships in both precolonial and colonial Latin American society.

It might well be asked at this point: Given all this attention to same-sex relations between men, what was the frequency of, or the reception accorded, same-sex relations between women? Ironically, we know even less about these subjects because such relations were not systematically targeted for punishment by the colonial authori-ties. We can suppose that convents provided an important refuge for women's expression of same-sex desire, strongly suggested in *I, the Worst of All*, an Argentine film on the life of the famous Mexi-can poet and scholar Sor Juana Inés de la Cruz, who may or may not have been a lesbian. But in the end, there is very little evidence to go on.

A last important point to consider is that many of our modern notions about sexual identity do not seem to have been shared by people in colonial Latin America. For example, the "sin" of sod-omy involved very specific sex acts, not sexual orientation. And it was the notion of male passivity in those acts which was seen to threaten the supposedly natural order of things most directly in a highly patriarchal society. In a seeming contradiction, this focus on specific and exclusively male acts may have allowed for the display of a wide range of same-sex physical affection, not only but perhaps especially among women, without the concomitant idea that such displays were a reflection of a fundamental essence at odds with social norms. Undoubtedly, the lower social status of women also carried with it the sense that whatever they did amongst themselves was of little consequence, anyway, with the acts being as insignificant as the individuals who engaged in them in the absence of men.

CONCLUSION

The scraps of evidence that can be gathered concerning sexuality and its expression during the colonial period suggest an interesting irony. It is both an area of life over which the authorities attempted to exert strict control and at the same time an area in which many people refused to be controlled, insisting on practicing a very personal form of resistance and rebellion. Sexuality is a tantalizing arena of historical study because it was clearly a powerful part of daily life in the past, and yet it seems to hover just out of reach much of the time. What is inescapable in the documented incidents of proscribed sexual acts is that people of the colonial era challenged the social rules that conflicted with their passionate desires. Some who transgressed paid a high price, especially those whose low social status exposed them to the harsher punishments. But surely many people found fun and satisfaction in their sex lives, and the outnumbered authorities were at a distinct disadvantage in their efforts to manage this aspect of social life.

Of course, heterosexual relations, whether inside or outside the confines approved by the authorities, also served the function of reproducing the population. Each resulting generation of children then had to be raised as much as possible in accordance with prevailing customs or imposed norms. First and foremost, young people were trained to replace their parents and grandparents, either as the workers who sustained colonial society or, in smaller numbers, as its rulers. The next chapter examines the nature and experience of childhood, including the types of education, both informal and formal, that children in the colonies received.

NOTES

In addition to the works cited separately as sources of direct quotations and the authors' own archival research, the following sources have been drawn on for specific examples in this chapter: Sylvia Chant with Nikki Craske, "Gender and Sexuality," in Chant with Craske, *Gender in Latin America*; Ramón Gutiérrez, *When Jesus Came the Corn Mothers Went Away*; Catherine Komisaruk, "Rape Narratives, Rape Silences: Sexual Violence and Judicial Testimony in Colonial Guatemala," in *Biography*; Susan Migden Socolow, *The Women of Colonial Latin America*. For full citations and other useful readings, see the annotated bibliography.

1. Stuart B. Schwartz, *Sugar Plantations in the Formation of Brazilian Society: Bahia, 1550–1835* (Cambridge: Cambridge University Press, 1985), p. 381.

2. Archivo General de Centro América (Guatemala City), A1, legajo 5441, expediente 46613, 1788–1791. Causa criminal pr. concubinato que sigue Juan Franco. Pineda contra Manuel Mendisabal.

3. Quoted in William B. Taylor, *Magistrates of the Sacred: Priests and Parishioners in Eighteenth-Century Mexico* (Stanford, Calif.: Stanford University Press, 1996), pp. 185–86.

4. Quoted in Taylor, *Magistrates*, p. 188.

5. Quoted in Luiz Mott, "Crypto-Sodomites in Colonial Brazil," trans. Salima Popat, in *Infamous Desire: Male Homosexuality in Colonial Latin America*, ed. Pete Sigal (Chicago: University of Chicago Press, 2003), p. 187.

6. Quoted in Geoffrey Spurling, "Honor, Sexuality, and the Colonial Church," in *The Faces of Honor: Sex, Shame and Violence in Colonial Latin America*, ed. Lyman L. Johnson and Sonya Lipsett-Rivera (Albuquerque: University of New Mexico Press, 1998), p. 55.

7. Quoted in Spurling, "Honor," p. 58.

8. Quoted in Geoffrey Spurling, "Under Investigation for the Abominable Sin: Damián de Morales Stands Accused of Attempting to Seduce Antón de Tierra de Congo (Charcas, 1611)," in *Colonial Lives: Documents on Latin American History, 1550–1850*, ed. Richard Boyer and Geoffrey Spurling (New York: Oxford University Press, 2000), pp. 118–19.

9. Quoted in Spurling, "Under Investigation," p. 123.

3

CHILDHOOD
AND EDUCATION

As we have seen in the realms of family life and sexuality, the inhabitants of colonial Latin America lived very different lives depending on their rank in colonial society. Thus the lives of children and youth, the focus of this chapter, were shaped in fundamental ways by social status. Among the upper classes, children were seen as the future guardians of the property of the patriarchal family. They were educated and protected accordingly, and much of what we know of their lives emerges in legal documents arising out of disputes regarding an inheritance. Other legal provisions related either to the division and stewardship of family property or to the tutorial function provided for in the last will and testament of the head of household. Meanwhile, girls and boys of the lower social ranks, who made up the vast majority of young people, were expected to become laborers, and as such they were tracked into work from the age of seven or eight. The modern-day concept of adolescence did not exist in colonial Latin America; for most people, the end of childhood and the beginning of adulthood came early. Although European tradition established the age of adulthood at 21, people functioned as adults long before they reached that age.

CHILDHOOD IN CONCEPT AND PRACTICE

Childhood among Indigenous Peoples

During the colonial era, indigenous peoples clung to their old patterns of child rearing and training of young people for adult life, and in some ways, their understanding of children differed radically from that of Europeans. The people of the Andes thought of age in terms of capabilities rather than strict chronology. In early censuses, many indigenous people did not know how old they were. In place of chronological age, people were measured by their increasing capacity to contribute to the community. The two key markers in these pre-Columbian societies were weaning, which occurred between ages two and five, and puberty. Both these milestones

A drawing by Guaman Poma de Ayala of a five-year-old girl carrying a jug of *chicha* (homebrewed alcohol). Prior to the arrival of the Spanish, the peoples of the Andes incorporated their children into the household tasks from an early age. (The Art Archive / John Meek)

indicated a shift in the individual's capacity for contributing to the larger society. At times, children were given to the government as a form of tribute, and sometimes sacrificed to the gods. One historian assessed the indigenous view of childhood thus: "It would appear that children were perceived . . . as natural resources produced by the community and therefore expected to benefit that community."[1]

In the pre-Columbian period, both boys and girls worked from about the age of five, with both sexes helping around the house; caring for younger children; and collecting water, wood, and other household necessities. In addition, the girls began to learn the weaving and cooking skills they would need as adults. From ages 9 to 12, boys became collectors of wood, makers of rope, spinners of wool, hunters, and animal caretakers, while girls continued their cooking and weaving and in addition collected plants used to dye fabric and herbs for cooking and healing. From ages 12 to 18 boys hunted and herded animals, while girls did housework, spun and wove, worked in the fields, cared for animals, and made the fermented corn drink *chicha*. Another task of pre-Columbian society that was performed by young people between the ages of 16 and 20 was harvesting the government's crop of coca leaf. When they reached 18, girls were considered adults and ready to marry, while boys continued working for their communities as messengers and errand boys for the nobility. Pre-Columbian peoples expected children to participate actively in their societies, performing useful functions at every phase of their lives.

Childhood among Europeans

The European concept of childhood differed from that of the indigenous peoples. Whereas most of the indigenous peoples of the pre-Columbian Western Hemisphere seem to have seen children as simply smaller adults, holding them responsible for their actions and expecting them to contribute to the survival of their families and communities, the European legal and social system understood children as prerational beings who needed to be educated and civilized before they could be accepted into the community of reasoning adults. While European custom made 21 the formal age of adulthood, a defendant under the age of 25 was legally entitled to a court-appointed lawyer to defend him in court, and to a legal guardian to oversee his financial interests. However, this pertained chiefly to children of upper-class families; working-class young people carried out adult roles earlier, often going into a vocation at the age of 15 or 16. Boys as young as eight were placed in apprenticeships, and girls of the same age might be "adopted" or simply farmed out as servants to wealthier families. Among people of all socioeconomic levels, the years between 20 and 25 were considered the young-adult years, and after that a person was a full-fledged adult until old age.

Childhood in Colonial Practice

The practical impact of theoretical differences between the views of Europeans and indigenous people is debatable, however. The Spanish and Portuguese were not completely successful in introducing their views into the homes of the peoples they had conquered. Because colonial societies consisted of the peoples of three continents living side by side, children's experience could look very different depending on whether their parents were Spanish or Portuguese; from West, Central, or East Africa; or from one of various indigenous societies. Certainly, African parents working as coerced laborers had less control over their offspring, due to the owner's legal right to make many key decisions pertaining to his workers, but just as certainly these parents brought with them to the Americas a notion of what should be expected of and provided to a child. So while the Spanish and Portuguese may have set up the dominant structures in the colonial period, parents continued to raise their children according to their long-term beliefs and practices.

Children and Household Relationships

Children lived in a variety of households, quite often outside of nuclear families. Children in many colonial homes were subject to various authorities such as wet nurses and nannies, aunts and uncles, as well as mothers and fathers, so they were raised by a group of adults, not just their parents. In rural areas among poorer people, married children generally lived with or close to the husband's parents, so grandparents or aunts and uncles were important authorities in children's lives, as well as channels to the world's resources (i.e., a wife/husband, a job, and a plot of land in the community where the newly married young man could build a little house and plant his cornfield).

Another feature of children's homes was that they nearly always contained women, while they might not have had any men. Spanish census records show that almost all children grew up in houses with female adults, although these women might not have been their mothers, but many of those households listed no male adults. Hardly any houses showed men and children living together without adult women in the home.

One interesting feature of the large patriarchal household was that the children of the patriarch normally grew up with other children who were not of the same race and class. For example, the child of the slave owner's family grew up in close relationship to enslaved children, later becoming the owner of his former playmates. A variety of complicated relationships developed between people in these situations, including the special relationship that often bound the master's child to the enslaved woman who had breast-fed him or her and who might continue to care for the child during its early years.

The households of the wealthier members of the community included many servants and dependents who at times functioned as servants. Indigenous children often worked in the homes of Spaniards as domestics, beginning as young as age eight. Labor contractors who supplied these child servants often referred to them as "orphans," although both parents might be living, probably a reference to the fact that their parents, although alive, were dead in the sense that they could not afford to care for the child.

Foundlings and babies left at the door of the church grew up in convents or orphanages where they might be tracked into a career as servant in the institution. The authorities of these institutions took responsibility for planning the lives of their charges, sometimes forcing these young people into marriage or church work against their will, as demonstrated by the many suits for escape from marriage or the church. At times, however, a lasting bond that imitated the biological parent-child relationship was formed between an orphan and one of the adults at an institution.

Work and Play

Most children's lives consisted of work and play, with work predominating for the majority, that is, those born into families on the lower rungs of the social ladder. Child rearing was not considered a job in and of itself, so children's daily activities had to fit around the lives of adults who had full-time responsibilities. Play was not supervised by adults, which may have been fun for a lot of children but held certain inherent dangers. Court records are full of cases brought by parents on behalf of children who had been harmed at play. One case concerned a five-year-old girl who had been abducted by a man on a horse while she was bathing alone in a stream. Another case involved three playmates: an enslaved girl of eight who was playing with the son of her owner and a slave boy and was raped by them. One mother of a young girl who had been raped while playing with two teenage boys testified that the struggle for survival among adults of the working classes meant these parents "were reduced to seeing their tiny sons and daughters living in the streets for the better part of the day."[2]

Work was sometimes unsupervised as well. Children, especially those of the serving class, ran errands for adults, so they were likely to be in the streets without an adult. Surely they took advantage of the lack of oversight to extend their time on an errand in order to include visiting a friend who lived or worked nearby, watching a passing procession, or playing a quick game of marbles. Some works of art from late 17th-century Cuzco show children taking a moment out from their workday to harass passersby with peashooters.

One form of work that was closely supervised was apprenticeship. Colonial authorities in some areas followed the practice familiar in Spain of rounding up young vagrants or poor, homeless youth and orphans and placing them in apprenticeships. By the end of the 18th century in Lima, police were instructed to take the children of beggars away from their parents if they were over five and place them as apprentices with a local artisan. Forced apprenticeship was not reserved for any particular racial group. Male children and young men of African descent, nonelite whites, and Indians all went off to work as apprentices. While elite young men got an education, these young men got vocational training. Most apprentices entered their contracts around the age of 15, although they might be as young as 8 or as old as 25. They were not paid a wage but received training and housing. The artisan or boss took over the role of the parent, meeting the young person's needs for housing, food, and clothing in exchange for the apprentice's work in his shop. If the apprentice ran away, he would be sought, probably captured, and returned to his master. Children from higher social groups, whether the Spanish and Portuguese overlords or the indigenous noble families, were educated longer, not put to work early like their social inferiors.

Youth and the Law

Some young people became entangled with the law, leaving a substantial body of court cases containing many details of young people's lives. Children younger than 10½ were not legally considered criminally responsible for their actions; those aged 10½ to 17 could be charged with a criminal offense but received sentences lighter than those meted out to adults. Once over 17, people were treated in court like adults, but they still had the right to legal counsel assigned by the court. Quite a number of crimes seem to have been committed by young people. In Lima, nearly one-third of all those arrested for criminal acts from the early 18th to the early 19th century were under age 25, with male *castas* by far the most likely to face charges. Among females, the castas were the group most likely to be arrested, and female castas represented about one-third the number of male castas arrested. The second largest group of arrestees was white (*español*) males, whose numbers reached about two-thirds of the number of casta males arrested. Male and female castas together amount to slightly more than 50 percent of all youths arrested in Lima during this 100-year period. In addition to those who faced charges, many other young people appeared in court as witnesses or victims.

Boys and young men who were arrested sometimes waited a month or more in a dark, dank cell for their turn to face the court and offer their defense. Alternatively, suspected offenders might be forced into apprenticeships without being formally charged, much less convicted, of any crime. The main goal of the justice system with regard to young people of the lower social groups was not to punish them, but to track them into employment. Parents sometimes turned their children in to the authorities to be locked up for disobedience, after which they were usually apprenticed or assigned to a workshop.

The sentences applied corresponded to the delinquent's position in the class/caste hierarchy. It was common for the court to show leniency in the case of white youths, sometimes finding apprenticeships for the convicted, while applying harsher sentences to racially mixed youths who might not even have been convicted, for instance sending them into permanent exile from their communities. This pattern of sentencing reflected the social position of the accused and strengthened the colonial social structure. In the case of enslaved minors, the law viewed the slaveholder rather than the judicial system as the proper judge of appropriate punishment, since legally this young person was the property of his owner.

Like every other colonial institution, the courts applied the law differentially in ways that reinforced social hierarchies. Culpability and sentencing of a white male looked very different from the court's treatment of a casta female, for instance, always with the goals of protecting property and producing a productive male labor force and modest, obedient girls who would become good Christian mothers raising docile, diligent workers.

FORMAL EDUCATION

As with the other aspects of childhood experience discussed above, access to formal education in the European tradition varied widely by social status. Most residents of colonial Latin America were illiterate, unable even to sign their own names on legal documents. Those possessing the basic elements of literacy, let alone any form of higher education, were disproportionately Iberian in origin and reasonably prosperous in their economic circumstances. Individuals pursuing a career in the church, the professions, or the colonial bureaucracy were the most likely to have an advanced formal education. In Spanish America, a university degree could be obtained as of the 1570s in Santo Domingo, Mexico City, and Lima, home to the three oldest universities in the Americas, and in several other cities such as Santiago de Guatemala by the end of the 17th century. During the 16th century, zealous members of missionizing Catholic religious orders, described more fully in the chapter on religion and popular culture, even sought briefly to make European-style higher education a rite of passage under Spanish rule for the sons of the indigenous nobility, particularly in Mexico. The Portuguese, on the other hand, established no universities at all in Brazil during the entire colonial era. Instead, residents of Brazil who desired a university education were forced to travel to Portugal to study at the University of Coimbra.

Practical Education

While a small if influential number of colonial Latin Americans acquired a university education that was roughly equivalent to the one offered in the institutions of the Iberian Peninsula, the vast majority of colonial Latin Americans had a few years of primary schooling at best, or none at all. An apprenticeship in a trade, which carried with it the possibility of a life that was socially and economically better than the average to be expected among the poor masses, represented the most important learning opportunity for the vast majority of boys in colonial society. Although apprenticeship provided no guarantee of economic prosperity, and as noted earlier was often used as a form of discipline for wayward youths, many parents of modest circumstances signed contracts engaging their sons for a number of years to master artisans in the hope that the skills acquired would allow them to move into the ranks of skilled tradespeople, and thus into the guilds that protected the rights and privileges of artisans. By the 17th century, the descendants of native peoples and Africans were increasingly entering skilled trades that were technically reserved for Iberians, as shortages of the latter and the disdain many of them felt for a life of manual labor in the Americas opened up spaces for castas and other non-Iberians to escape the status and experience of the unskilled laborer. Apprenticeship, therefore, was the most important potential source for poor children of the social mobility that would later come to be associated with access to a good public education.

Indigenous Peoples and Formal Schooling

Despite the greater practical significance in most cases of the education provided by an apprenticeship or training in household tasks, formal schooling was not entirely absent from the lives of the common people in colonial Latin America. While high levels of illiteracy reveal that it was not a very prominent feature of daily life for most people during the colonial era, both church and crown—at least in Spanish America—sought to promote Christianization as well as Hispanicization by means of a few years of primary-level schooling for indigenous children in colonial society. By the end of the 16th century, indigenous children in New Spain were expected to attend parish schools from ages 7 to 11, where they were to be taught the rudiments of the Spanish language, writing, and the tenets of the Catholic faith. A mid-17th-century recommendation by the bishop of Puebla for the establishment of sex-segregated schools, with male teachers for boys and female teachers for girls, indicates that the cleric took as a given the existence of some form of universal, basic education for all children. In 1716, the viceroy in Mexico City decreed as official policy the operation of separate schools for boys and girls, and he also mandated that *maestros* (teachers) be knowledgeable in Spanish, a clause obviously targeted at schools with indigenous pupils. The notion that girls should be educated as well as boys emerges yet again in a 1762 order by a Mexican archbishop that only women of good character should be teaching female students.

Despite these indications of official concern for the establishment of a basic level of mass formal education for both girls and boys, the evidence suggests that implementation was sporadic at best. For one thing, many members of the native population resisted an educational policy that threatened to undermine their children's fidelity to the language and customary practices of parents and grandparents, not to mention the detrimental impact of mandatory school attendance on the availability of hands to support families that were in most cases desperately poor. The indigenous residents of rural villages rarely campaigned for the establishment of schools in their communities; such institutions were instead usually founded on orders from clerical or royal officials. At the same time, most of the Spanish population was less than enthusiastic about ensuring that indigenous children had any sort of formal education at all, while parish priests were primarily concerned with inculcating the basics of Catholic doctrine as opposed to knowledge of the Spanish language or rudimentary literacy, which in theory were to accompany religious indoctrination.

The Mexican viceroy's 1716 decree ordering teachers to have knowledge of Spanish illustrates clearly the gap between education policy and practice. In those rural communities where the mandated parish schools actually operated, if often only intermittently, there were many indigenous teachers who gave instruction in their native tongue rather than Spanish. Although the authorities actively encouraged the employment of such teachers on the presumption that they would be more acceptable to local residents than Spanish outsiders, the intent behind the policy was to have trusted individuals facilitate the adoption of Spanish norms, not undermine them. Thus, the use by native teachers of their mother tongues in the classroom can be interpreted as one aspect of a larger pattern of cultural resistance on the part of the indigenous population.

Nevertheless, the employment of teachers who did not provide education in the Spanish language also resulted from the low status accorded to the post of schoolmaster as well as the fact that most indigenous teachers, themselves poorly educated, were underqualified for their occupation as defined by official policy. In many communities, the village teacher was chosen by and owed allegiance to the local priest, who was often the most powerful local representative of colonial authority and far more likely than the teacher to be Spanish in origin and economically secure in family background. The status differential can be seen in pay distinctions between the two positions. In the mid-18th century, the annual salary of the average rural teacher in Mexico was roughly one-tenth the amount considered to be the minimum on which a rural priest could survive.

In the late-colonial era, reform-minded administrators intensified efforts to translate policies regarding the establishment of some form of universal primary education into daily practice. According to the archbishop of Mexico, in 1754 alone some 228 parish schools were established for Indian pupils in the territory under his jurisdiction. During the succeeding decades, parish priests were increasingly likely to list the establishment and support of such schools among their notable career accomplishments. Royal officials, meanwhile, sought to make teachers more independent of church control and presumably more effective at imparting non-religious academic content to their charges by ordering that teachers be appointed by district governors instead of priests.

If anything, though, the indigenous population's resistance to formal schooling increased as late-colonial efforts to impose it on a more systematic and "enlightened" basis gathered steam. The residents of native villages complained especially about the funding burden they were forced to bear to support local schools and often delayed teachers' salaries or refused outright to pay them. At bottom, formal schooling continued to be seen in many indigenous communities as a means by which alien cultural norms were to be imposed on them as well as an inconvenient distraction from vital family labor. In 1791, the royal official in charge of the Mexican region of Guadalajara complained that "during the growing season, the Indians take their children out of school for the entire rainy season until the crop is harvested."[3] And numerous officials observed that villagers who obtained any significant degree of formal schooling continued to be mistrusted more than admired by their neighbors.

Elite Schooling

Most young people of Spanish origins, both boys and girls, received at least a few years of education, usually in an institution run by a religious order or under the guidance of a private tutor. Children from wealthier families had more opportunities to advance, including some individuals of non-European or mixed-race background, although the alleged stain of African ancestry in particular was a social and, at the highest levels of education, legal impediment to such mobility. Between the years 1651 and 1658, about a hundred girls were educated in reading and writing as well as singing and playing music in the elite convent of Santa Clara in Cuzco, Peru. Among them was the daughter of a local *kuraka*, a member of the indigenous Andean nobility. Some, although not all, of these students eventually professed as nuns. A few girls of indeterminate origins, likely either illegitimate or of modest parentage, also acquired at least some aspects of this convent education after being abandoned at the entrance to the convent as infants. But these girls were often being trained at the same time as servants and therefore held an inferior status to those whose parents paid tuition. One Santa Clara nun dictated a clause in her will favoring an orphan named Josefa Labaxonera whom she had "raised from infancy to sing in the choir." Josefa was also, however, a provider to her benefactress of "personal services" along with several other girls the nun was responsible for supervising.[4]

Boys intended for the priesthood or otherwise expected to possess advanced formal education entered a *colegio*, which we would consider to be a secondary school, as early as age 7, although not usually before age 11. A requirement for entrance into such institutions was the ability to read and write, generally acquired in early childhood through private instruction or under the guidance of a priest. Colegios were almost always run by religious orders, with those operated by the Jesuits seen to provide the most rigorous education available to the sons of the colonial elite prior to the expulsion of that intellectually oriented order from both Spanish and Portuguese America in the mid-18th century. Toward the end of the colonial era, the course of studies in a typical colegio included Latin grammar and pronunciation, the literature and philosophy of the classical Greek and Roman world, mathematics and physics, and, of course, Christian theology. In places like Mexico, proficiency in one or more native languages was also expected of candidates for a career in the church, if not necessarily achieved owing to poor instruction.

Young men entering the priesthood often spent at least six months engaged in an additional course of preparatory studies before embarking on their career. In the seminary at Tepotzotlan during the late 18th century, the day began with a half hour of silent prayer in the chapel at 5:30, followed by mass and breakfast, three hours of private study, and a morning class in moral theology. Following the noon meal, during which a biblical lesson was read aloud, students retired for several more hours of private study before a late afternoon class in church history, an hour and a half of private reflection in the chapel, an evening lecture on the obligations of the priesthood, and a late meal accompanied by the reading of another biblical lesson. One last round of private meditation preceded bedtime at 9:30.

The bachelor's degree, in theory a requirement for the priesthood as well as a prerequisite for other professional degrees, was granted at about the age the average student in the present day is finishing secondary studies. In other words, the four years of coursework necessary to acquire a bachelor's degree in colonial Spanish America roughly coincided with the period during which most modern North American youth are in high school. The colegios granting the degree, nevertheless, are best thought of as the colonial social equivalent of North American undergraduate colleges, while entrance with a bachelor's degree into more advanced studies in a colonial university at the age of 17 or 18 was akin to moving on to graduate school in the present day. Only a small proportion of would-be clerics went beyond the bachelor's degree to obtain the licentiate degree offered in universities, and even fewer a doctoral degree.

Circumstances were a bit different in fields such as medicine, where a four-year professional program in a university followed the completion of a bachelor's degree. Nevertheless, individuals finishing the eight years of higher education needed for a medical degree emerged as practicing physicians at about 21 years of age. Once again, the more advanced licentiate degree, not required to practice, was pursued by only a few students, while a doctoral degree in medicine, according to one scholar, was little different from an honorary degree in the modern university, involving no actual course work.

Some 150,000 degrees were conferred by Spanish American universities during the colonial era, an indication on the one hand of the importance accorded to higher education by colonial authorities and on the other of the elite nature of that education. On average, just over 500 degrees were awarded annually in Spanish America during the three centuries between the establishment of the region's first university in Santo Domingo in the 1530s and the end of the colonial era in the 1820s, when 20 universities were in operation. The majority of those degrees were awarded in the 18th and early 19th centuries as the number of universities, and university students, increased. But even then, the percentage of the population holding such a degree was infinitesimal and included almost no one from the poor and mostly non-European majority.

CONCLUSION

The majority of children in colonial Latin America grew up in circumstances in which the acquisition of truly functional reading and writing skills was neither directly relevant to daily survival nor a realistic expectation given limited access to formal education. The prospect of a university-level education was simply outside the realm of imagination save for an elite few. In societies that were largely rural, most children followed their parents into the fields at a relatively young age, looked after animals, or learned to carry out household duties, practical tasks that they would continue to execute in their adult lives. The majority of urban children, notably boys, could aspire at most to an apprenticeship that if it was not too abusive and actually engaged the apprentice in learning valuable skills, promised a decent economic future with a bit of status in the community as well as occupational security. Girls, especially those from the non-European majority, might find employment at a young age as domestic workers, exposed as a result to all the possibilities for sexual or other abuse that were an occupational hazard in employers' houses. Enslaved children enjoyed the least secure positions of all, even if in their earliest years they might be the much loved playmates of boys and girls who would eventually own them.

But if childhood often involved hard work or exploitative circumstances, most children lived in some sort of household context in which they enjoyed close relationships with several other household members, disproportionately women. Relatives often lived close by and cared for children if parents were not present, although girls or boys who found themselves serving in an employer's household generally had to look for kindness among unrelated fellow members of the household staff or, if fortunate, from one of the household patriarch's family. Of course, the experiences of the sons and daughters of an elite family were quite distinct from those of the children of the poor and mostly non-European majority that surrounded them, both as servants at home and as social inferiors in the wider colonial society. Both economic condition and race profoundly shaped the experience of childhood, while boys and girls generally followed very different, culturally prescribed paths from a young age, whatever their origins or economic status.

Some circumstances were common to all colonial Latin Americans, however. Such things as geography, climate, or disease vectors, which historians sometimes label the material conditions of existence, were not in most cases respecters of social and economic status, even if the wealthy had more resources than the poor with which to shield themselves from adverse environmental circumstances. The next chapter examines aspects of material culture in colonial Latin American society, focusing on the ways in which people responded to their environment in mundane but crucial areas of daily life such as the construction of dwellings, the making and wearing of clothing, and the production and consumption of food. As we shall see, the responses varied, sometimes by choice and other times out of necessity. The lives of all inhabitants of colonial society, nevertheless, were profoundly shaped by the constraints imposed by the natural world that surrounded them.

NOTES

In addition to the works cited separately as sources of direct quotations and the authors' own archival research, the following sources have been drawn on for specific examples in this chapter: Mark A. Burkholder and Lyman L. Johnson, *Colonial Latin America*; John Tate Lanning, *The Royal Protomedicato*. For full citations and other useful readings, see the annotated bibliography.

1. Carolyn Dean, "Sketches of Childhood: Children in Colonial Andean Art and Society," in *Minor Omissions, Children in Latin American History and Society*, ed. Tobias Hecht (Madison: University of Wisconsin Press, 2002), p. 44.

2. Quoted in Bianca Premo, *Children of the Father King: Youth, Authority, and Legal Minority in Colonial Lima* (Chapel Hill: University of North Carolina Press, 2005), p. 124.

3. Quoted in William B. Taylor, *Magistrates of the Sacred: Priests and Parishioners in Eighteenth-Century Mexico* (Stanford, Calif.: Stanford University Press, 1996), p. 339.

4. Quoted in Kathryn Burns, *Colonial Habits: Convents and the Spiritual Economy of Cuzco, Peru* (Durham, N.C.: Duke University Press, 1999), pp. 115–16.

4

MATERIAL CULTURE

INTRODUCTION

Since daily life is one of the more difficult features of the past to grasp, historians use various kinds of records in addition to written materials to do so. One way to understand how people of the colonial period lived is to look at their material culture, the structures in which they lived, what they wore and ate, and how they transported themselves and their goods from one place to another. Physical health can be explored not only by reading descriptions of diseases included in colonial documents, but also, within the limits imposed by cultural constraints on the disturbance of the dead, through forensic examination of human remains. Attention to cooking utensils that have survived—some, of course, still in use today and performing the same functions—provides insight into a key feature of daily life, the preparation and consumption of food. We can draw conclusions about social status by looking at the houses of people of different social levels or by examining both contemporary art and wills to discover what different people wore. This chapter examines several key aspects of the physical world that shaped and constrained the experience of colonial daily life: housing, clothing, food, transportation, communication, and health and sanitation.

HOUSING

Rural Housing

More than 90 percent of Latin Americans in the colonial period lived in rural areas in small houses scattered around in the countryside or grouped together in hamlets. Most of these dwellings were rectangular one-room structures of one story with no windows, a dirt floor, and virtually no furniture. What little furniture there was, a few three-legged stools, possibly a low wooden bed, were rough handmade pieces. The walls were of low-cost materials native to the area; in many places, that meant adobe, sun-dried blocks made of mud and straw. In more humid or hotter areas, the construction might be of rough-hewn boards or bamboo. These structures followed the ancient patterns of pre-Columbian housing constructed by the inhabitants and could be built in a few days or, at most, weeks. Whatever the material used to build the walls, all these houses were roofed with some kind of thatch made from a local material, often palm fronds. Normally, those at the higher end of the village social structure lived in the same kind of house that those lower in the hierarchy occupied. Wealth in a rural community was more likely to be expressed through the acquisition of land, animals, and laborers than through the style and appointments of one's house. Another possible difference was the size and complexity of the home altar; nearly all homes had some area devoted to a few religious objects, with people higher up on the social ladder devoting more space and resources to this feature.

There was no running water coming to these houses, so women or children went to a nearby river, spring, or lake to carry water to the house. Clothing was washed in the same stream or lake and spread on the ground or the bushes to dry. The cooking might be done inside the small house, filling the whole room with smoke, or there might be another one-room structure, which meant less smoke in the main living area, but in the chilly highlands, it also meant the loss of the cooking fire as a source of heat. The fire was laid directly on the floor or on a raised platform; a clay pot to heat food or water, or, for tortillas, the flat stone griddle known in Mesoamerica as the *comal*, would be balanced directly on the burning sticks. Most people slept either on the floor on a woven mat known as a *petate* or in a hammock; those with slightly more resources might have a bed of a few boards knocked together with only a petate for a mattress.

Housing was similar in Mesoamerica and the Andes, although the rude dwellings of the common people in the latter region were

Homes constructed of adobe and thatch in modern Ecuador, a style of housing that has been in use in some areas of Latin America for hundreds of years. (The Art Archive / Gianni Dagli Orti)

usually circular instead of rectangular. Since wood was scarce in the *altiplano,* as the Andean highlands were known, the dung of llamas and other domestic animals was used to feed the home fires. As families added members or improved their economic status, they built additional one-room structures to accommodate tools or store food, or possibly for a newly married son and his wife.

Enslaved laborers on the plantations of Brazil lived in small one-room huts no different from those of the rural working people of Spanish America, or in large structures divided into rooms with one family occupying each room. In Brazil, it was common for working families, whether made up of slaves or freemen, to be allotted a garden plot to grow at least some of their own food. Indeed, this arrangement was not only a regular but often an essential feature of plantation life owing to the notorious failure of many sugar planters to provide adequate nourishment to their slaves. A 1701 decree by

King Pedro II of Portugal reflects this fact. In it he ordered his officials in Brazil to force local slave-owners "either to give their slaves the required sustenance, or a free day in the [work] week so that they can themselves cultivate the ground."[1] At times, these small-scale cultivators might sell their surplus to the *casa grande* (main house) in exchange for a little money they could save toward the purchase of their freedom or spend on a small luxury.

Circumstances were similar on large sugar plantations in Spanish America. One such property, located just south of what is now Guatemala City and home to some 200 enslaved residents in 1630, was described by an English observer as "a little Town by it selfe for the many cottages and thatched houses of *Blackmore* slaves which belong unto it."[2] As in Brazil, the houses of the working people of Spanish America, both slave and free, often included a garden plot as well.

Urban Housing

People who left rural areas to move to a nearby town or city sometimes lived where they worked, in the homes of the wealthy. These domestic workers had a small space in the home of their employer, an arrangement that afforded protection from the precariousness of independent life, if not from members of the family they served. In exchange for this security, they had to be available for work as needed, meaning at any hour of the day or night. For those who did not find a place with a wealthier family the housing prospects were grim. Many recent arrivals found, or helped themselves to, some kind of material with which to construct a makeshift shelter, designed to serve as a temporary home, although frequently what was conceived as temporary became permanent or lasted at least until the next earthquake or mudslide destroyed it. These little dwellings clustered together, completely devoid of any formal plan, in a ravine or other area marginal to the city proper, gradually forming whole neighborhoods of slums that housed much of the working population of the city.

Priests lived in housing supplied by the church, although if they came from wealthy families, they might live in lavishly appointed homes in town or sometimes on a hacienda they had bought with family money; the servants of priests were usually Indians or *casta* members of the working classes. Secular urban professionals like lawyers, doctors, merchants, tradesmen, or shopkeepers and officers in the military lived in homes that were more or less well appointed, depending on their income.

The wealthy generally lived in town. In Brazil, plantation owners and their families might live in the countryside on their sugar plantation, or *engenho*, although they would usually have a home in the nearest city as well, and family members moved back and forth. The homes of government functionaries, most of them sent to the colonies directly from Europe as agents of the crown, and of the wealthiest colonists in both Spanish America and Brazil displayed art objects and treasures imported from the mother country. Things produced in the colonies could not compete in beauty or value with the luxury goods, possibly originating in China or India, brought over from Europe.

Architecture and Social Relationships

In the countryside, even the homes of the wealthiest owners of large estates were often like large fortresses of many rooms with almost no furniture. For the most part, the building materials were the same as those used in more humble dwellings with the exception of the roof, which would often be of tile rather than thatch. Some adornments might be added, including walls of stucco with wooden beams and interior wood paneling. Rooms, usually without windows, were arranged around a central patio, a style based on the houses of the ancient Romans that were built around an open-air space known as the atrium. Fancy houses in town might be constructed in a figure eight around two patios, a front one with a formal garden and possibly a fountain, and a functional back patio with an open water storage tank for washing the laundry and watering the horses, and with a kitchen and food storage area off to one side.

Architectural styles were also affected by the quite practical consideration of earthquakes. As a result, houses of the wealthy, especially in the Andes, were sometimes constructed for flexibility with beams linked by heavy leather bindings in place of nails. In areas of frequent tremors, wide sturdy archways might be included to provide protection for the family members.

Compared with the housing of today's industrialized world, the houses of people in colonial Latin America provided precious little comfort. Most large houses were drafty and dark; most small houses were cramped and cheerless. Furniture, what there was of it, was built for function rather than comfort. This generalized lack of comfort at home reflects an important aspect of life in the colonial period, however, which is that people spent a lot more time outside in public spaces. A great deal of work was done outside, either in the fields or in the streets and open-air markets. Going to the local spring or well for water, or going to wash the laundry at a local stream or public wash house became an opportunity to chat with others, exchange news and gossip, and spend parts of the day outside the house. This was more true for the working people than for their social "betters," however. Women from elite families were expected to stay at home unless they were heading out to church, usually in a group of other women from the household. If the family could afford a carriage, the women would make use of it to avoid the streets, which were sometimes filthy and, depending on whether it was the dry or rainy season, were likely to be a dustbowl or a sea of mud.

Another interesting feature of housing in the colonial period is that it was more crowded than the houses many people are used to in today's world. The homes of the wealthy included the patriarchal family and might also house maiden aunts, a widowed mother, or a ne'er-do-well brother; a quantity of domestic servants, free or enslaved, commensurate with the family's wealth; possibly one or more illegitimate children of a family member; and the occasional visitor. The families of poorer people may have lacked this wide variety, but their homes were smaller and often did contain an extra member or two, possibly a farmworker, a "girl" to help with the housework, a widowed mother, or an unwed sister or aunt. To some extent, family members were driven out into public space because there were so many people in the house.

CLOTHING

In colonial Latin America, clothing truly did "make the man," as the saying goes. There was no greater marker of social class than clothing. A humble home is left behind when one goes out into the public arena, but a person's dress conveys his rank in society. The more European the style of one's clothing, the more respect he commanded. Even wealthy people had fewer clothes than modern industrial production provides many people of today's world, but the clothing they did have was designed to communicate their social standing. People dressed in the most elegant style they could afford in their attempt to assure their position in high society. Clothing represented a necessary investment in social standing.

Elite Clothing Styles

Elites or people aspiring to elite status adopted European clothing, meaning, for men, leather shoes or boots, silk hosiery, silk or linen underwear, knee breeches or other pants imitating the latest European fashion, a jacket and shirt with sleeves, an overcoat, and a hat of felted wool. Women of high society possessed different clothes for different activities, outfits for riding and going to church, as well as everyday dresses, party clothes, and various capes, shawls, and lace head coverings. They favored silk underwear and nightgowns; many petticoats; long-sleeved, ankle-length dresses, possibly of Asian silk trimmed with lace; and footwear of fine leather.

Clothing Styles among the Common People

The common people dressed in practical clothing of home manufacture, constructed of local materials, especially cotton or at times wool from the sheep brought by the Spanish in the 16th century. The working men of New Spain generally wore durable cotton fashioned into loose-fitting pants and shirt. In addition, they frequently wore some kind of handwoven cloak that replaced the overcoat of their social "betters." Many people went barefoot, but they might have had a pair of sandals made of hides. On their heads, they often wore a straw hat with a wide brim for protection from sun and rain. In colder areas like the Andean highlands, men wore more wool and a hat made of some fiber. Since the clothing of working people was usually made of local materials and had to suit local weather conditions, areas based on a cattle economy tended toward leather clothing, while cotton was preferred in warmer areas, and wool in the chilly highlands.

Women wore homespun cotton or wool skirts, sometimes covering several petticoats, and over their blouse, or *huipil,* they threw a shawl of cotton or wool that doubled as a carrier for the latest baby or for goods on their way to or from market. Underwear was nonexistent for both men and women of the working classes.

Most enslaved workers, especially those employed in plantation labor, were not in a position to buy their clothes; they wore what was provided for them. While conditions varied somewhat

Independence-era image of an indigenous family dressed in simple clothing in the Bogotá region of what is now Colombia, appearing in an account by the Frenchman Gaspard-Théodore Mollien of his travels in the region in 1823. (The Art Archive / Neuchatel Public and University Library / Gianni Dagli Orti)

from one work site to another, the general rule was for owners to spend the absolute minimum to clothe the workforce. They might allot each worker a few yards of the cheapest cloth to fashion into pants or a skirt. Sometimes the workers would receive a new item of simple cotton clothing once a year or every other year. In very hot conditions like the sugar-boiling house, the workers might go naked or nearly so. Some contemporary accounts relate that the slaves went naked, but most drawings show them with pants or a skirt of handwoven cotton cloth.

Enslaved workers who earned wages, paying their owner his share and keeping a share themselves, sometimes invested that money in items of clothing or jewelry for use on festival days. Foreign observers often remarked on the strikingly elegant clothing worn by some women of color, including slaves, in Mexico City, Lima, and other urban areas. This phenomenon was widespread enough to prompt a number of apparently ineffectual royal decrees prohibiting such displays of finery by anyone outside the colonial elite. In some cases, it was status-conscious slave owners who purchased the "extravagant" clothing worn by women (or men) who served them, although considerations of status were no less important when an enslaved person acquired a fine article of clothing on her own. Public display of the article served to establish its wearer's claim to the upper rungs of the social hierarchy, in this case the slave hierarchy.

FOOD

Food and Cultural Conflict

In addition to being the fuel our bodies need to function, food is an expression of our culture and basic to our feelings of comfort and security. Both Spanish and Portuguese colonists devoted their energies to maintaining the diet they had enjoyed back home. Urban areas, especially at the mines, grew up quickly in Spanish America, and suppliers established themselves in marginal areas surrounding urban centers from which they carried fruit, vegetables, and meat into the city markets every day. In Brazil, where there had been no sedentary empires in pre-Columbian times with tribute systems funneling food to the imperial core areas, there was less urban life than in Spanish America. By the later colonial period, however, farms had been established around cities in Brazil, and laborers might work in the countryside on a large farm, growing food to bring to the owner's city home. Some plantation owners went into the business of supplying food to urban areas, establishing fruit and vegetable farms on properties surrounding cities and towns.

From the earliest days of the colonial period, food production was an arena of conflict between Iberians and indigenous peoples. The Spanish tried to force the Indians to produce wheat for bread, an essential of the Spanish diet and an item the Europeans ranked far above the humble corn tortilla, staple of the masses. For their part, the Indians struggled to find the time and the land to continue producing the diet that had served them well for millennia: a starch of potato in the Andes, maize in Mesoamerica, or manioc (cassava, yucca) in Brazil and the Caribbean. Women ground maize and manioc into corn meal or farinha (manioc flour) to make the staple of the diet, which was supplemented with beans, squash, and chiles and washed down with a fermented drink of *pulque, chicha,* or *cachaça.*

New World Foodways

The diet of the common man in Mesoamerica was based on the tortilla, prepared by women who cooked the corn for hours, ground it on a concave stone called a *metate* using another stone shaped like a rolling pin, and then kneaded the dough and formed a flat pancake to be cooked on a griddle called a *comal*. A stack of tortillas served as the basis of every meal; sometimes tortillas and salt made the whole meal. Luckier families ate *frijoles* (beans) with their tortillas along with one of many different kinds of squashes and *chiles* (hot peppers) chopped up with tomato and onion. In tropical areas of Brazil and in the Caribbean, the staple of the diet was manioc, a starchy root crop that had been cultivated in those areas for hundreds of years.

In the Andes, one of many different kinds of potatoes made up the basis of the meal. Often potatoes were freeze-dried, becoming *chuño* by a process that involves alternately freezing the potato and thawing it to express water and then freezing it again, producing a preserved food that can be stored a long time, even years. *Charqui*, jerky made of llama meat in the Andean highlands and, after the European arrival, of horse or beef, was another common preserved food. The grain *quinoa* continued to serve as an important cereal in this area as it had before the Spanish arrived. Indeed, most of the crops mentioned above resulted from pre-Columbian agricultural experimentation in the Americas and were unknown in the rest of the world prior to 1492.

Nonalcoholic drinks also accompanied, or at times took the place of, the meal. These might be a fruit drink made from handy oranges or lemons, or *atol* (hot drink, often of cornstarch) of maize, plantain, or some other starchy grain or vegetable. A chocolate drink made from cacao beans was a luxury for special occasions, often restricted in Mesoamerica to the nobility except in areas where cacao was readily available; where cacao grew naturally, chocolate drinks might be a normal part of the diet of the common people. In southern South America, the drink would be a tea of *yerba mate*, and in the Andes, the tea might be made of coca leaf. With no potable water system piping water to the houses in town, drinking water had to come from public or private wells or natural sources like rivers located outside the towns.

In the early days of Portuguese colonization, enslaved Indians were sent into the backlands to pursue the pre-Columbian food-gathering activities of hunting, gathering, and fishing. In areas near a forest, Indian and African workers might be sent to bring back armadillos, lizards, rodents, monkeys, and various birds that found their way into the well-supplied kitchen of the Brazilian plantation owner. Indians continued to engage in the activity of gathering tropical spices and fruits, bringing them to the city for sale. Honey and insects collected in the wild rounded out the diet of many Brazilians.

Another important pre-Columbian activity that continued into the colonial period was fishing. Fresh fish were caught in rivers, and the ocean continued to supply seafood such as turtles, octopus, and large ocean fish. Launches braved the ocean to bring back shark and whales, which supplied oil in addition to meat. Most fish was salted to preserve it, then carried to market. Since the Portuguese were fond of salt codfish, they continued to import salted Newfoundland cod for themselves, feeding salted beef and fish to their workers.

Old World Foodways

The newcomers from the Iberian Peninsula and Africa introduced other products and culinary styles to the Americas. Old World grains and legumes like rice, oats, and lentils all appeared after the European arrival. Indigenous peoples enthusiastically adopted chickens, and those who could find the resources raised a few pigs and occasionally feasted on pork. The sheep brought by the Spaniards not only served as an important source of warm wool clothing and blankets but also added lamb to the American diet. In some areas, goats became the key provider of leather, meat, and milk, which was sometimes made into cheese. Often the goats were herded through the city and milked on demand when a customer appeared.

Larger domesticated animals from the Old World, like cattle, mules, and horses represented a larger capital investment and were normally the property of the estate owners, although they were tended by the estate workforce. Hundreds of head of cattle would be driven to cattle fairs for sale and then driven to slaughterhouses in the city. Demand for beef was high, and cattle raising could be a lucrative business. Cattle were sometimes driven to the cities from many leagues away, all the way from Honduras and El Salvador, for instance, to be sold in Guatemala City. Once butchered, beef not eaten fresh was preserved by salting or drying it, since there was no refrigeration. People without the resources to buy their beef sometimes found ways to help themselves to an animal, in spite of stiff penalties for cattle rustling. They would then drive it surreptitiously to a local butcher who would not inquire deeply into its origins. The exception to this picture of beef as a luxury food was the cattle-raising areas where beef was so common it could be almost the only food available and might be eaten several times a day, according to contemporary observers.

Those in Spanish America who could afford the diet they had followed in Europe imported olive oil, wine and other liquors, flavored vinegars, and candied fruit, luxuries that worked their way into the Latin American diet. Crown policies forbade the colonists from competing with Spanish producers of some goods, especially wine and olive oil, so those in New Spain who required those products had to rely on imports coming from the metropolis except during certain times when smuggling from Peru flourished. Other features of the upper-class diet were homemade cheese from cow or goat milk, and bread and fancy cakes and pastries produced in bakeries aimed at the Spanish or Portuguese consumer and supplied in many places by sugar produced on local plantations. These desserts might also be made with chocolate, derived from the cacao bean produced originally by the native peoples of Mesoamerica and grown later in the colonial era, often by slaves, in Ecuador and Venezuela as well. In Brazil and sometimes in Spanish America, baking was done by enslaved laborers, with even the managers being slaves.

Some foods introduced to the Americas in the colonial period came from West Africa where the Portuguese had become familiar with bananas and okra, for instance. The West African peoples brought their knowledge of how to use these foods with them, and such dishes as *gumbo,* a word probably rooted in an African name for okra, entered the American menu. Many enslaved laborers had no opportunity to savor these dishes, however, since the norm for the American slaveholder was to maintain the workforce with simple fare and little of it. Slaves in Brazil lived primarily on the tropical staple, manioc. This high-calorie starch was supplemented with a bit of salted meat produced on the region's vast cattle ranches as well as other starches, rice, and various kinds of bananas. Slaves on the west coast of South America lived on a corn-based diet, although they might receive some meat or fish and whatever starchy food was most accessible, potatoes from the highlands, a bit of bread, or a few plantains. In many areas of Latin America these workers had access to small plots of land on which to grow some vegetables, thereby reducing the amount of food provided to them by the slaveholder.

TRANSPORTATION

Movement of people and goods is a problem that falls into several categories. Since the primary reason for colonization was to extract wealth, the Iberian crowns lost no time in establishing a system of moving goods, especially bullion, from the New World to the Old World. Another problem to be solved was disembarkation of people and goods arriving in the Americas. Thus colonization required moving goods on their way to Europe toward the ports and distributing people and goods coming from Europe across the interior, which in some cases meant far inland. Where waterways existed, they were the ideal route, but even then, porters were necessary to load and unload the barges and riverboats, and some miles of land transport might be required to bring goods to their point of departure at riverside. Another category of transportation was the movement of goods and items necessary to sustain life, like food and water, within the colonies.

Transatlantic Shipping

In the 16th century, the Spanish inaugurated the *Carrera de Indias*, the fleet system, involving convoys of 10 or more ships scheduled to sail annually between the Caribbean and Spain. The system was designed to provide some protection for American gold and silver from Dutch and English pirates, and it did so fairly effectively, but it was unwieldy and inefficient. At the beginning of the 17th century, the average shipment of silver from Potosí arrived in Spain more than four months later. From 1600 to 1650, instead of its scheduled annual departure, the fleet sailed about every other year; a total of 29 fleets sailed from Spain to Panama during that 50-year period. The occasional and unreliable schedule of the fleets contributed to the growth of contraband trade, especially in the Caribbean. Since illegal activities are only sporadically recorded, the extent of contraband trade is impossible to estimate with any degree of accuracy, but it must have been extensive.

Land Transport

Once arrived in Panama, people and goods were carried to land on the backs of the longshoremen of the day, Indian or African slaves. Until adequate port facilities could be constructed, this was the only means of getting ashore. Africans followed their custom of carrying heavy objects on their heads, while Indians generally employed the tumpline, known in Mesoamerica as a *mecapal,* a wide leather strap placed across the forehead with long strings attached at each end that secured the load behind the porter. Some objects were carried tied to poles held up by pairs of porters. To reach inland locations, people of some importance were usually transported in sedan chairs carried by pairs of slaves; these porters might be elegantly dressed if the chair's occupant was a person of high social standing. The common people either walked or were carried in hammocks hoisted by slave porters. Hammocks were also used to transport people of low social status to the cemetery after they died.

Mining provided a strong motivation for extending roads and building ports. In the Andes, the Spanish found useful the many miles of carefully constructed road the Incas had built for imperial trade and troop movements. These roads were too narrow for use by carts, since the pre-Columbian peoples had had neither the wheel nor large draft animals, but the Spanish widened and improved these roads for carts and mule trains. Indian porters, or *tamemes*, did most of the transporting of goods and people in the early days of the colonial period; later most goods went by mule train that often included hundreds of animals.

The colonists also added roads from Lima and Cuzco to the coast to enable the transport of silver to Spain, and they built a road across the Panamanian isthmus in order to transport silver arriving at the Pacific side from Peru to the Caribbean coast for departure for Europe. In Mexico, roads were constructed from Mexico City northward to the mines at Zacatecas and later to other mining areas that lay farther north. At the beginning of the 17th century, the vehicle for transporting goods was a large cart known as a *carro* that ran on iron-rimmed wheels at least six feet in diameter. These carts were pulled by as many as a dozen mules. The muleteer, or *arriero* in Spanish, often an enslaved worker in Brazil and sometimes in Spanish America as well, played a key role in transportation since by the midcolonial period most goods that traveled any distance did so on the backs of mules. By the end of the 18th century, the mules of Central America were moving goods worth about two million pesos annually. In Costa Rica alone, one of the smaller economies of the region, tobacco growers required the services of more than 3,000 mules per year. The bigger economies of the isthmus, those of Guatemala and El Salvador, would have required significantly more mules per year to transport their products.

The growth of urban areas in the last third of the 18th century also had an impact on transportation. As the urban population grew, suppliers of food for these areas reached farther into the interior to satisfy demand, which meant transporting agricultural products over greater distances. This became another impetus for the widening of transportation networks. Nevertheless, by the end of the colonial era, transportation remained slow and laborious in many areas of Latin America, an obstacle to regional integration.

Obstacles to Transportation

The difficulties of travel by road in many parts of Central and South America, where rugged mountainous topography often alternates with soupy coastal lowlands, is illustrated in mid-18th-century descriptions of time spent in Ecuador by Jorge Juan and Antonio de Ulloa, two young naval lieutenants sent out by the Spanish government on a scientific expedition. They described one lowland road as "so deep and boggy that the [mules] at every step sunk almost up to their bellies." A very different road experienced a few days later in the process of ascending to the highlands around Quito was "[i]n many places . . . so narrow that the mules have scarce room to set their feet; and in others a continued series of precipices." Travel by sea along the coast, when a viable option for getting from one point to another, did not always constitute a more attractive alternative. It took Juan and Ulloa eight full days simply to make their way by boat from the port of Guayaquil to another spot along the Ecuadoran coast. In complaining about this method of transportation, they cited "the usual impediment of the current," just one of several environmental obstacles to rapid seaborne transportation along the Pacific coast of South America, in addition to "several unfortunate accidents."[3]

Another 18th-century traveler gives us a contemporary description of the laborious overland passage of oxcarts from Buenos Aires to Jujuy in the northwestern Argentine interior. He first explained that mule trains, the normal mode of land transportation, were not even used on this route "because much of the way is through thick woods, where many mules would get lost," aside from the "many rivers in flood that [the mules] could not cross with loads on their backs." Sure-footed teams of four oxen apiece, by contrast, could be trusted to conduct fully loaded carts across all but the deepest riverine obstacles. Nevertheless, drivers of these teams spent much of their time prodding the animals forward by means of a special goading device suspended over each team. The device had been adapted precisely to a task in which it was "essential to jab all four animals nearly simultaneously." According to the observer, most of the helpers who sustained a fleet of oxcarts and their drivers during a journey that might take two months or more were "recently arrived from Africa." In his estimation, these enslaved laborers were not to be trusted with handling valuable goods, although his description suggests they were in fact vital to this particular trade.[4]

COMMUNICATION

The many obstacles to transportation in colonial Latin America had a direct impact on the efficiency and speed of long-distance communication. Such communication, at least in the form of letter writing, was generally of vital interest only to a small minority of the population, notably merchants and royal officials in addition to those individuals, disproportionately from the colonial elite, who maintained personal contacts with relatives and friends far away. While colonial archives in both Latin America and the Iberian Peninsula are filled with correspondence written by people from these sectors of the population, most of the inhabitants of colonial Latin America communicated almost exclusively by word of mouth, forced to depend on the memory of a traveling friend or acquaintance in cases where they wished to convey a message to someone at a distance. There was little alternative for an illiterate majority whose members were mostly too poor to engage a notary or other educated individual to write letters for them, except perhaps as absolutely necessary in situations of urgency.

The sectors of the Spanish American colonial population for whom letter writing was an important tool of communication were able to depend by the 17th century on a postal service that connected most of the larger urban centers. The system was run more or less privately until the late colonial era by the *correo mayor* (postmaster general) who, like most other officeholders, was required to purchase the office from the crown and then, one way or another, recoup that fee and make a profit through his operations. Where overland transport was feasible, the mails were carried at first by runners of mostly native or African origins and later by mounted riders. In Brazil, where all major urban centers were located along the Atlantic coast prior to the mid-18th century, maritime communication was most efficient. As a result, no formal system of overland postal service was organized there until the last decades of the colonial era.

The time it took written correspondence to travel in the preindustrial Iberian empires, especially when crossing the Atlantic, had a profound impact on the nature of Iberian rule and its influence on the daily life of the residents of colonial Latin America. It was not unusual for a dispute of local interest in a remote area to take several years to make its way across the ocean, receive consideration from either the Spanish or Portuguese crown, and finally return accompanied by a royal decision. By this time the local situation might have changed dramatically; for example, one or more of the parties involved in the original case might well be dead. As discussed at more length in another chapter, the slow pace of communication placed a substantial amount of power in the hands of local officials, who frequently made judgments that did not accord with the king's wishes even when the officials were already aware of what those wishes were. Not surprisingly, these judgments often worked to the benefit of powerful creole landowners or other local notables, a much more immediate presence in the official's life, whether as important social connections or potential threats, than the distant crown. Even when the Iberian monarchs genuinely sought to ameliorate the harsh living and working conditions imposed on Indian and African workers by the colonists, time and distance worked against the king's efforts.

HEALTH AND SANITATION

From the perspective of human health, the conditions under which the majority of the population of colonial Latin America lived were decidedly less than optimal. In the first place, public health systems of the sort that we take for granted in the modern industrialized world, aimed at such basic tasks as the sanitary disposal of human waste, either did not exist or were at best rudimentary. Meanwhile, bleeding and other widely accepted practices of medical professionals were less often beneficial than directly harmful to their recipients, with the most effective and least noxious treatments often to be found among various folk remedies administered by traditional *curanderos/as* (healers), frequently women of native or African origins. In this world, even the wealthy and powerful had little protection against the spread of epidemic disease or the more mundane infections and other physical maladies that plagued the average individual in a preindustrial society. Infant mortality was high among all social sectors, women regularly died while giving birth, and most families experienced the loss of at least one member in the prime of life owing to disease or a badly treated injury.

Water and Sanitation

Assured access to clean water for drinking and sanitary purposes, often judged to be the most significant contributing factor to recent improvements in general human health, was something few individuals could count on with any certainty. The open and communal water sources on which most of the population depended included public wells and fountains, or streams and rivers, although some people owned wells or fountains privately, selling water to their neighbors. Authorities in the bigger cities were pressed hardest to organize the large-scale acquisition and distribution of water for drinking and washing. In Santiago de Guatemala, capital of Spanish Central America, a system of aqueducts was constructed for bringing water from outside the city to its various public fountains. As elsewhere, domestic servants or, at lower social levels, the women of the family gathered at these fountains to bring home water for drinking, cooking, and washing. A very few wealthy families were able to use Santiago's system to bring water directly into their own homes, however, and the city's better neighborhoods enjoyed disproportionate access to it.

Given the lack of septic systems, another major problem in urban areas involved disposing of various kinds of household waste. Once again, domestic servants, often enslaved workers, daily removed household garbage and chamber pots of night soil from the houses of the wealthy, while people lower on the social ladder were obliged to carry out their own waste or simply throw it out the door into the street. Often there was no designated area for this waste, so it simply collected in a vacant lot or on the streets where it attracted all forms of bird and animal life and contributed to the unsanitary, disease-ridden conditions of the colonial city. The issue of public sanitation was somewhat less pressing in the countryside simply because population and housing were less dense there.

Epidemic and Endemic Disease

Epidemic diseases such as smallpox, measles, and typhus periodically ravaged colonial populations. The postconquest devastation of native peoples in the wake of their initial exposure to these and other Old World diseases extended well into the 17th century, and the population as a whole suffered from regular if less deadly rounds of epidemics throughout the colonial era. One observer noted that a 1631–1632 typhus epidemic in Guatemala largely singled out Indians, adding that the disease "rotted their mouths and tongues, and made them as black as coal before they died."[5] The Bogotá region of what is now Colombia experienced major smallpox epidemics in 1558, 1588, 1621, 1651, 1667–1668, 1693, 1756, 1781–1783, and 1801–1803, with the earlier outbreaks striking disproportionately at native communities. In Ecuador, a slow process of demographic recovery among highland Indians during the 17th century was temporarily reversed between 1691 and 1695, when as many as one-half of their number died in a series of epidemics of smallpox, measles, typhus, and diphtheria. Just over a decade later, in 1708, an outbreak of what may have been influenza killed numerous residents in the regional capital, Quito, this time striking people from all social sectors with little distinction. In 1724, city councilors reported the apparent return of smallpox and lamented that "many people had died as a result of the pestilence that has been introduced."[6] The city continued to be visited on a regular basis in subsequent decades by epidemics of smallpox, measles, dysentery, and scarlet fever, sometimes in combination. The most noteworthy outbreaks occurred in 1746, 1763–1764, 1769, and, worst of all, 1785, when at least 2,400 people died during the two worst months alone of an epidemic of measles that was still killing people well into the following year.

Many of the diseases that flared up from time to time in virulent epidemic form remained endemic among surviving populations during the lulls between outbreaks. Meanwhile, a variety of other unspecified fevers, coughs, and intestinal irritations seem to have been relatively constant companions in the average household. No doubt some of these illnesses had their origins in unhealthy sanitary practices. Others flourished or not in accordance with patterns of social interaction, including those of a sexual nature. The visiting Spanish naval officers Juan and Ulloa claimed that syphilis was so common in Quito during the 1730s "that few persons are free of it, though its effects are much more violent in some than in others."[7]

Formal Medicine

For relief from their various ailments, the sick, especially those with some means, were able to turn at least in larger urban areas to a variety of licensed medical practitioners, notably physicians, surgeons, and pharmacists. All of these were approved in Spanish America by the *protomedicato,* a regulatory body charged with oversight of the healing professions. Transferred to the Americas from Spain in the 16th century, the institution was initially embodied in a single inspector known as the *protomédico* and gradually transformed into an examining board composed of three or more licensing officials in each of the major cities where it existed. A royal charter of 1646 gave this board a formal institutional structure in New Spain that was largely mirrored in Lima and several other major cities. By this time, most of these cities also had one or more hospitals founded and run by religious orders, often the Bethlemites, as did many smaller urban areas.

The formal medical infrastructure described above was quite inadequate to public need, however. In 1608, Quito's municipal council was unable to confirm the presence of a single salaried doctor in the city, and as late as 1785, there were just four licensed physicians working there among an urban population of more than 20,000 inhabitants. A few years later, the 9,000 residents of Ecuador's main port of Guayaquil were left with just one doctor to serve their needs after a second died and a third found himself imprisoned for debt. Meanwhile, one of the two hospitals operating in Quito in 1785 served exclusively as a sanctuary for 22 victims of leprosy, while the other one was little more than a poorhouse except in times of epidemics. Circumstances were far more dire in rural Riobamba, home to five times as many people as the capital held, where there was no hospital at all.

A more abundant supply of licensed medical professionals and formal medical institutions would not necessarily have improved either access to medical services or the quality of those services, however. Physicians had developed few truly effective methods for confronting illnesses, surgeons and barbers were one and the same, and pharmacists dispensed curatives that were frequently indistinguishable from those proffered by unlicensed healers and thus generally of no more (or less) utility. Indeed, the reigning pharmaceutical handbook in early 18th-century Spanish America recommended the ingestion of dried frog intestines for kidney stones, dried and powdered fox lungs for asthma, and ground up tapir toenail or human cranium—although only when obtained from a person who had died violently—for epilepsy. In any case, such expertise as the formally qualified medical professionals possessed was beyond the reach of the majority of the population, given the prohibitive fees they charged in ordinary circumstances. During Quito's 1785 epidemic, the municipal council had to order the city's four resident doctors to treat patients who could not afford to pay, and it also promised to partially reimburse two pharmacists who had succumbed to pressure to dispense free medicines to victims of the outbreak.

A growing impulse among royal authorities to reform and improve public administration toward the end of the colonial era did produce some efforts to introduce a more scientific approach to medical practices. Autopsies were mandated for some of the victims of Quito's 1763 epidemic, for example, although the doctors who performed them reported no findings of value. In 1790, officials faced with a smallpox outbreak among the independent native peoples of southern Chile ordered the local Spanish population to prepare for inoculation, a procedure introduced into the Western world earlier in the 18th century and still state-of-the-art treatment prior to Edward Jenner's development of a vaccine a few years later. Royal officials also sought increasingly to crack down on unlicensed medical practitioners and their nonsanctioned cures. But even toward the end of the colonial era, there continued to be little evidence that the methods employed by these individuals posed any greater danger to the general public than those of their licensed counterparts.

Informal Medicine

Efforts to eliminate unlicensed medical practitioners were almost entirely ineffective during most of the colonial era, in large part because of a chronic shortage of approved providers. The University of Mexico, the most prestigious institution of its kind in colonial Spanish America, conferred on average fewer than four bachelor's degrees in medicine per year between 1607 and 1738, with laws barring the nonwhite majority from access to higher education helping to keep numbers low. Officials faced with frequent medical emergencies were therefore willing to put up with and sometimes even encourage the presence of a variety of unlicensed health workers in the areas under their jurisdiction, especially among non-Spanish populations. The king of Spain himself determined in 1652 that laws meant to restrict the practice of medicine to legally qualified professionals did not apply in native villages. Thus there was a proliferation in colonial Spanish America of the usual array of charlatans and con men who are attracted in all ages to the informal practice

of the healing arts. Literate European foreigners, notably French-
men and Italians, appear to have found this area of enterprise to
be especially appealing, constituting the sort of lucrative economic
niche profitably filled by individuals able to carry off the pretense
of possessing great and esoteric learning.

Quite distinct in the provision of unlicensed medical services to
the public were midwives, who attended most births in colonial
Latin America. Offering as they did a vital service, midwives were
tolerated out of necessity even if generally disparaged by the formal
medical establishment. A decision taken by the city of Caracas in the
17th century to accord small housing allowances to local midwives
gives us one indication of their value to society, however reluctant
such official acknowledgement may have been. At the same time,
their overall status and living conditions at the time can be sur-
mised on the basis of the city council's description of the midwife
Ana Jiménez, who despite having assisted many of the city's "principal persons" in their hour of need was "destitute" and burdened
down by the needs of her many children and blind husband.[8] A
clear sense of the status distinctions drawn among medical providers, and of their relative economic circumstances, emerges in a comparison of Caracas's allotment to its midwives of between 1/2 and
1 peso annually for their housing needs with an appropriation of
public health funds ordered by Lima's city council a few decades
earlier. In 1572, the council set the salary of a physician assigned
to care for the health of workers in local tile and brick factories at
30 pesos per year, allotting another 10 pesos annually for the services of a barber/surgeon.

In part due to economic need, many midwives doubled as *curanderas,* offering clients a mix of herbs and potions intended variously
to work magic on lovers or enemies, relieve pain, cure chronic aches
or illnesses, or heal wounds. Often of non-European or mixed origins, such women frequently drew the suspicion of the authorities,
including in some cases the Inquisition, which smelled *hechicería*
(witchcraft) in their practices. At the same time, they were regularly consulted by people from all social sectors, which probably
explains much of the hostility exhibited toward them by both medical and religious authorities. Even official representatives of the
colonial government turned to these unlicensed healers. In Mexico
City in 1618, a Spanish officer of the law named Bartolomé Ruiz
acknowledged to the Inquisition that he had been treated by the
mulata Ana de Pinto for internal discomfort. Pinto had applied a
poultice to his stomach, given him a mysterious drink, which may

have included peyote as an ingredient, and sewed a small bag containing loose hairs into his shirt. Crucially, she had also "made the sign of the cross over the chest and ears of the sick man, at the same time making crosses everywhere in the name of the Holy Trinity, God the Father, God the Son, and God the Holy Spirit" and incorporating other, indecipherable words into her healing ritual. Ruiz's rationale for submitting to Pinto's "witchcraft" is indicated clearly in his statement "that to have health there was nothing that he wouldn't take."[9]

In dispensing medical advice and cures, Pinto and other *curanderas* competed not only with physicians but also with pharmacies, which women of any ancestry were explicitly prohibited from operating under a 1593 Spanish law. Ironically, the traditional knowledge on which their unapproved cures were often based— a knowledge combining material and spiritual understandings of illness informed by various African and European precedents, as well as indigenous beliefs and practices—was sometimes judged efficacious by the same authorities who professed to despise that knowledge. Reporting the abatement of the 1790–1791 smallpox epidemic among native peoples in southern Chile, the local Spanish commander attributed the turn for the better in part to "the strange and barbarous manner in which they treat themselves."[10] Local remedies included the use of medicinal plants like *palqui*, noted by a Jesuit observer to be a treatment for high fever. Effective or not, such medical practices were no less scientific in origin than bleeding or many of the other recommendations yet to be excluded from the arsenal of the licensed physician. In some cases, they were likely to have been more so, sources of consistently demonstrable health benefits as determined by a lengthy course of experimentation.

CONCLUSION

The material realm in which colonial people operated—from the houses in which they lived to their modes of transportation and communication, from the food and drink that sustained their bodies to the physical afflictions that undermined the health of those same bodies—circumscribed the lives they lived in many and varied ways. Even the wealthy had few protections from most infectious diseases and lived in dwellings that if palatial in comparison with those of the poor majority were bereft of many of the comforts enjoyed by the average individual in today's richer nations. Long-distance connections were unimaginably slow from our perspective, with the glacial speed at which people, goods, and news traveled imposing precise temporal limitations on everything from commercial transactions to the efficiency of royal bureaucracy to relations with far-flung family members. As in all times and places, material constraints profoundly shaped human lives. The activity that may have shaped daily life in colonial Latin America more than any other, however—taking up the majority of waking hours for most individuals—was work. The next chapter examines its central place in the history being told in this book.

NOTES

In addition to the works cited separately as sources of direct quotations and the authors' own archival research, the following sources have been drawn on for specific examples in this chapter: Lowell Gudmundson, "Middle Groups," in *The Countryside in Colonial Latin America*, ed. Louisa Schell Hoberman and Susan Migden Socolow; Mary Karasch, "Suppliers, Sellers, Servants, and Slaves," in *Cities and Society in Colonial Latin America*, ed. Hoberman and Socolow; Lyle McAlister, *Spain and Portugal in the New World, 1492–1700*; Eric Van Young, "Material Life," in *The Countryside in Colonial Latin America*; Stephen Webre, "Water and Society in a Spanish American City: Santiago de Guatemala, 1555–1773," in *Hispanic American Historical Review*. For full citations and other useful readings, see the annotated bibliography.

1. Robert Edgar Conrad, ed., *Children of God's Fire: A Documentary History of Black Slavery in Brazil* (Princeton, N.J.: Princeton University Press, 1983), p. 61.

2. Thomas Gage, *The English-American his Travail by Sea and Land: or A New Survey of the West-India's* (London: R. Cotes, 1648), p. 134. Italics in original.

3. Quotations from Jorge Juan and Antonio de Ulloa, *A Voyage to South America*, intro. Irving A. Leonard, the John Adams translation, abridged (Tempe: Arizona State University, 1975), pp. 96, 97, 100.

4. Quotations from "Concolorcorvo's Description of Travel by *Carreta* in the Argentine (1773)," in *Colonial Travelers in Latin America*, ed. Irving A. Leonard (New York: Alfred A. Knopf, 1972), pp. 195, 196, 199.

5. Quoted in W. George Lovell, "Disease and Depopulation in Early Colonial Guatemala," in *"Secret Judgments of God": Old World Disease in Colonial Spanish America*, ed. Noble David Cook and W. George Lovell (Norman: University of Oklahoma Press, 1992), p. 80.

6. Quoted in Susan Austin Alchon, "Disease, Population, and Public Health in Eighteenth-Century Quito," in *"Secret Judgments of God": Old World Disease in Colonial Spanish America*, ed. Noble David Cook and W. George Lovell (Norman: University of Oklahoma Press, 1992), p. 164.

7. Quoted in Alchon, "Disease," in *"Secret Judgments,"* p. 160.

8. Quoted in John Tate Lanning, *The Royal Protomedicato: The Regulation of the Medical Professions in the Spanish Empire,* ed. John Jay TePaske (Durham, N.C.: Duke University Press, 1985), p. 43.

9. Quoted in Joan Cameron Bristol, *Christians, Blasphemers and Witches: Afro-Mexican Ritual Practice in the Seventeenth Century* (Albuquerque: University of New Mexico Press, 2007), pp. 149–50.

10. Quoted in Fernando Casanueva, "Smallpox and War in Southern Chile in the Late Eighteenth Century," in *"Secret Judgments of God": Old World Disease in Colonial Spanish America,* ed. Noble David Cook and W. George Lovell (Norman: University of Oklahoma Press, 1992), p. 209.

5

WORK AND LABOR

INTRODUCTION

The main impulse behind colonization of the Americas was the desire for wealth, shared by whites at every level from the kings and nobility to the most humble person who made the trip across the Atlantic. Before industrialization introduced forms of labor in which machines did much of the work, the accumulation of wealth depended on human energy. The key to wealth was organizing workers to perform manual labor, then appropriating the product of their labor. One of the cardinal principles of life on the Iberian Peninsula was that doing manual labor, having to work in order to live, was a sure sign of low social status; therefore, carrying their values across the Atlantic, the Iberian colonists committed themselves to the project of getting rich without doing the necessary work themselves. That meant putting in place systems of coerced labor at all sites of production. As a result, the exploitation of human labor was an essential component of colonial life from its inception. The labor systems put in place by the Spanish and Portuguese will be the focus of this chapter.

When the Spanish first set up colonies on Hispaniola in the last decade of the 15th century, they simply rounded up the native Taínos and forced them to do whatever manual labor was necessary for the establishment of the colony. The indigenous population of the island was devastated by the combination of epidemic diseases against which they had no antibodies, poor treatment, and the abrupt change from their former agricultural focus on production for their communities to a life of labor-intensive agricultural production in an extractive economy. Some estimates place the native population of Hispaniola around 1 million before the arrival of the Spanish. By the time 15 years had passed, their number had been reduced to 30,000. Alarmed at the results of the enslavement of the natives, the king approved establishing the *encomienda*, a system that had been in use during the Reconquest by Christians of the Iberian Peninsula.

ENCOMIENDA

The encomienda was a grant of workers to a person known as the *encomendero*. The word *encomienda* comes from the Spanish verb *encomendar*, meaning "to entrust," so in the literal sense, the encomienda was an entrustment of native people to a Spaniard. They worked for him and paid tribute to him. In theory, the encomendero accepted the responsibility to protect these workers and to Christianize them, thus saving their souls from eternal damnation. In the view of the Iberians, the Christian god was the greatest gift they could bring to the heathens of the New World. In practice, of course, the encomendero was more concerned with organizing the efficient payment of the tribute, which took the form of bolts of woven cloth, fowl, and agricultural products, than he was with saving the souls of the Indians. In addition, the way the encomienda system was put into practice made it not much different from outright enslavement. The tribute demands imposed on the natives held in encomienda were a major factor in the demographic collapse. Another factor was the lack of time people had for the work that had sustained them in their pre-Columbian communities, that is, finding food and medicinal herbs, weaving cloth, building shelter, and appeasing the gods that provided for the community's needs. In the first two decades of Spanish colonization of the Caribbean, the colonists came close to accomplishing the total depletion of the native population. As the native workforce died, the Spanish saw the need to supplant it with other workers and brought in a new group of laborers from across the Atlantic. Most of the population of the Caribbean today is descended from this African labor force.

Encouraged by the sermons of the Dominican priest Father Antonio Montesinos, the Spanish crown passed the Laws of Burgos in 1512 in an effort to protect the native population. The laws regulated the Indians' working and living conditions, as well as the forms of punishment that might be used. The colonists, however, paid little heed to the legal niceties, and the crown displayed greater interest in the appearance of moral correctness than in enforcing these regulations, especially since more effective exploitation of the workforce meant higher tax revenues for the crown. Another effect of Montesinos's sermons was the conversion of the encomendero Bartolomé de las Casas who came to be known as the "Defender of the Indians." After Las Casas renounced his encomienda and became a Dominican priest, he wrote extensively on the exploitation of the native people by the Spaniards, writings that figured in the construction of the "Black Legend," the narrative that accuses the Spanish of being the cruelest of all the European groups that settled the Americas. Having established the labor system of encomienda in the early Caribbean colonies, the Spanish transferred it to mainland Mesoamerica and later to the Andes when the Pizarro brothers conquered the empire of the Incas. The conquerors viewed their encomienda as the principal form of booty, a right of conquest. Hernán Cortés assigned himself a grant of more than 100,000 Indians and received the crown's stamp of approval. His followers were granted somewhat smaller, but still impressive, numbers of workers whose labor supported a sometimes lavish way of life.

The tribute provided to the encomendero varied according to location, always with the chief goal of bringing him the greatest wealth. Some of these products were profitable exports, others entered the local markets of the domestic economy. Either way, control over tribute put the encomendero in charge of the area's economy and made him both wealthy and politically powerful. Typically, tribute payments would be feed for animals, wood for fuel, corn and wheat, woven cotton cloth, chickens, eggs, coca leaves, cacao beans, and cochineal, a red dye popular in Europe. The production of some of these goods fell to the lot of the women of the community. As the Indian population declined and men were removed from the villages to join public works projects, tribute demands fell more heavily on the shoulders of the women who were left behind.

In 1542, the Spanish crown finally heard the accusations of Bartolomé de las Casas against the colonists and responded with the New Laws, an effort to limit the power of the encomenderos and protect the native population from the harshest demands of the encomienda. Another concern of the crown was the growing wealth and political power of the encomendero families who were approaching the level of the Spanish nobility. The New Laws took the encomienda out of the realm of inherited property, providing for any Indians held in encomienda to revert to the control of the crown upon the death of the encomendero. However, the colonists rebelled against the New Laws. In Peru, they even joined forces to seize and execute their viceroy. The viceroy of New Spain learned from that event and judiciously decided to ignore the New Laws rather than experience the same fate. The crown removed the restriction on inheritance, but when encomenderos died without heirs, their encomiendas reverted to the crown anyway. By 1570, three out of four encomiendas in central Mexico had already returned to the control of the crown and were being managed by the crown's agents. By the end of the 16th century, the encomienda had largely run its course in the major centers of colonial rule, although it persisted in Paraguay and other peripheral areas.

REPARTIMIENTO AND MITA

The system that replaced the encomienda was the *repartimiento*, a system that granted an allotment of Indian laborers to the colonial administration for a public works project or to a colonist for a specified task or period from a week to as long as several months. The workers were supposed to receive a small wage for this work, along with food and housing, but since there was no supervision of the colonists, the workers' wages and subsistence were frequently overlooked. By the mid- to late 16th century, the repartimiento had been instituted in Mesoamerica, the Andes, and parts of Colombia, with workers assigned to different kinds of work in the different regions. In the viceroyalty of New Spain, the repartimiento laborers worked in agriculture and the mines. In some areas, it was customary to assign workers to *obrajes*, weaving workshops in which the workers were practically enslaved. In other places, Indians were assigned to dye manufacturing, largely indigo production, where many became ill as a result of wading up to their knees in the vats of fermenting leaves.

In the mining areas, repartimiento took the form of the *mita*, a labor system adapted from a similar system of labor drafts used in Incan times, known by its Quechua name *mit'a*. There was no way to exploit the precious metal strikes without an enormous labor force. While the Potosí mine owners had relied on Indian labor from the earliest days in the 1540s, it fell to Viceroy Toledo in the 1570s to shape the mita into the system that continued throughout the colonial period. The mita system called for every adult male to go to the mines every seventh year. In the beginning, Toledo's restructured mita supplied about 13,000 native workers to the Potosí mines. As the colonial period wore on, it became common for those Indians who could afford it to avoid their mita obligation by paying for a replacement. The wealthy and powerful mining families collected this cash tribute and used part of it to pay wages to the mine workers, keeping the rest as income. Some workers, called *mitayos*, came to the mines to work and stayed on after completing their assignment to work as *mingas*, or wage workers, doing the more highly skilled tasks. Eventually, the mitayos came to be those who were too poor, or too unlucky, to avoid the draft, working alongside, or in some cases supervised by, Indian wage laborers or people of African origins, some enslaved and others free.

The Mita and Silver Mining at Potosí

Potosí, the site of the great silver strike in Upper Peru (now Bolivia) a decade after the conquest of the Incan Empire, was described by a 16th-century miner, Luis Capoche, as "sterile and unproductive, and almost uninhabitable because of its unpleasant and nasty climate."[1] The description goes on to say that the mountain is treeless, cold, snowy, and buffeted by strong winds. According to this source, no one lived there before silver was discovered because it was so inhospitable that only potatoes would grow there. While more recent accounts tone down the severity of the climate and point out that the early mine owners had an interest in exaggerating the difficulty of their task and showing how hardy they had to be, certainly the climate and geography made for a hard life for the mine workers. Others who have been to Potosí describe a mountain more than 13,000 feet high that has an annual average minimum temperature of 27 degrees Fahrenheit and average high of 52 to 56 degrees. The area receives about 25 inches of rain a year and supports, in addition to potatoes, varieties of corn, beans, vegetables, and fruits that thrive in cold climates.

In the earliest days of the mita the mitayos were collected in their villages on the appointed day, along with their families, making a group of thousands. These people were joined by the animals being sent to the mines, and all marched off to their assignment. Upon arrival, communities would likely be split up; at least no effort was made to keep people from the same communities together.

The work may have been rather bearable in the first few decades of the mid-16th century when there was a lot of silver and it was located near the surface, but as time went on, the silver became harder to reach, and the work became more arduous. Some of the original workers may have been miners in Incan times, and due to the need for skilled workers, they would have been the earliest of the skilled mine workers, who were freer than the unskilled mitayos. According to one survey by the crown, some groups of workers preferred Potosí to other options for producing tribute, and they were able to supply a better, more varied diet to their families working at Potosí than in other forms of tribute production. The survey should not be taken too literally, as it would have been in the interest of agents of the crown to show that the lives of the mitayos were not too unpleasant.

Mine workers were divided into different groups, depending on the type of service they provided. Already in the middle of the 16th century there were two basic categories of workers: the mitayos, who were working to provide tribute, and the *yanaconas*, who were domestics serving a Spanish master. In Mesoamerica, the term *naboría*, borrowed from the Caribbean Taíno, designated a group equivalent to the yanacona of the Andes. These yanacona workers were a bit more free than mitayos, since they had the privilege of leaving to seek another master. They also did not pay tribute before the 1570s when Viceroy Toledo abolished their exemption. Another category was that of *indios varas*, Indians in charge of working a certain number of *varas* (a measurement roughly equal to a yard). The vara Indians hired other indigenous people to work for them so they could exploit their assigned section most efficiently and effectively.

Mine Work

There were various types of mine work: cutting the ore out of the face of the rock, carrying the ore from inside the mine and piling it on the platform at the mine entrance, picking over it on the platform (sometimes done by women), and taking away the useless part of what had been dug up before the ore was taken to the refinery. In addition, stonework structures had to be built to hold up the roof of the tunnel because the altitude made for a lack of the large trees that provided wooden supports in mines at lower altitudes. All this work might be directed by Indian supervisors.

In the refinery, the ore was fed into the crusher, then shoveled into a sieve to cull out the silver. Women and young people also sieved ore by hand. The silver then went into the refining process where it was mixed with amalgam and other inputs, a step usually performed by a Spaniard or *mestizo*. The amalgamation process involved Indians tramping bare legged through the mixture, after which washers ran the amalgamated silver through water in a tub designed to remove the waste. Workers moved the ore from one step to another on their backs. In some cases, there was a provider of wood or charcoal for the refining process and someone to tend the ovens used in the amalgamation process.

Working Conditions

Working conditions in the mine were primitive. There were day and night shifts of 12 hours each to keep the mine working around the clock. When the work was going on a thousand or so feet below the surface, the workers carried the ore to the surface on a series of ladders, each one 50 feet long. To tie the ore onto his back, he used a square of wool blanket that he provided himself. This sack could be tied to his feet when he had to wriggle through small spaces pulling the ore behind him. Often the air quality was poor due to the dampness, and some mines were plagued by flooding. Many miners probably got silicosis, but this was not a clinically recognized disease until the end of the 19th century. Walls frequently collapsed, although this was not as much of a problem at Potosí as elsewhere due to the sturdiness of the igneous rock there. Punishments were severe, with mine workers being whipped if they were slow.

Accidents were common. One estimate puts deaths in mining accidents at several hundred annually. In addition, 50 or more Indians died every year in the hospital from accidents that occurred in mining and in the refining process, according to a contemporary observer. Other deaths were the result of illnesses related to mine work, especially breathing the dust created in the crushing of the ore. Workers often contracted pneumonia passing from the heat of the mine to the cold of the outside air. The remains of colonial workers around Arequipa show signs of tuberculosis, and some workers surely died of lead poisoning or mercury poisoning caused by breathing the mercury vapor or by absorbing mercury through the skin while treading the mixture of ore and mercury in the amalgamation process. Most mercury came from a mercury mine at Huancavelica that had its own detachment of mitayos. Mercury contaminated the water and air of the area, poisoning everything the workers breathed, touched, or ate.

In addition to working in the mine, there was plenty of other work to be done in the mining regions. In the view of some historians, the mita workers could not have worked continuously throughout their four-month shift because they would not have survived it. Some sources indicate that the Indians did other work around the mines for two out of every three weeks. When they were not working in the mines, Indians at Potosí were put to work as porters, vendors, woodchoppers, and charcoal makers.

Women and Silver Mining

Women, mostly the wives of mitayos, worked at the mines as well. Toward the end of the 16th century, women took over the *guayra* process of smelting ore using the wind-driven furnace of pre-Columbian times. Women also brought the miners' food to them one day a week and received selected pieces of ore from their husbands who came to the surface to collect their food. Some research indicates that the mine worker's practice of passing a chunk of ore to his wife was widespread and accepted by the supervisors. Women added these rich bits of ore to the tailings they had pulled out of the heaps of discarded ore. The mitayo's wife and children either worked at tasks connected with mining or performed other jobs like raising animals for food to make up the difference between what the mine worker earned and what it cost to support the family for the year. The population of women at Potosí grew until by the end of the 18th century it made up just over 50 percent of the mining center's population.

Life in the Mining District

Living conditions were not much of an improvement over working conditions. Twenty to 30 Indians might live in each house in the section of town set aside for the workers; the rooms were small, barely allowing for a bed, a fireplace, and a few jugs of homebrew made from fermented corn known as *chicha*. The gathering together of many Indians in one spot may have exacerbated the epidemics, causing the demographic collapse that one historian estimates at 50 percent between 1570 and 1620.

By the beginning of the 17th century, the work week was supposed to be six days long, leaving Sunday for rest and attendance at Mass. However, Monday was the day to gather together the week's workers, a process that took most of the day, due in part to the fact that many workers had taken the opportunity to get drunk on Sunday and had to be collected from their dwellings, thereby delaying the process of distributing workers on Monday. This task of rounding up the week's workers on Monday meant that effectively the work week was from Tuesday through Saturday afternoon. Workers were supposed to be paid on Saturday evening but often spent much of Sunday waiting for their pay.

The life of the mitayo was not much different from that of a slave in some respects. The wage was so tiny that it served more to assuage royal guilt, since after the 1540s the Spanish system officially opposed enslaving the Indians, than to provide for the worker and his family. Around the beginning of the 17th century, the wage for the mitayo was between 2.75 *reales* and 3.5 reales per day (with eight reales making one *peso*), depending on the type of work performed. Out of this wage the mine worker provided his own candles, which might cost him one-quarter of his weekly wage. (*Minga* workers, who performed the more skilled tasks, earned 4 to 4.25 reales per day, plus either some ore for the mine workers or some coca leaves for those working in the refining process). In addition, the mitayos were whipped if they failed to meet their weekly quota. And like enslaved workers, they might be sold or rented out. So while this form of "slavery" came to an end after a year of work—unless the mitayo stayed on because he had not met his quota—during that year, there was little difference between the life of a mitayo at Potosí and that of an enslaved worker in any other part of Latin America.

AFRICANS, SLAVERY, AND MINING

Many years before the discovery of silver at Potosí, the mining of gold was already well underway. By 1499, enslaved native laborers were engaged in gold mining in the north of Hispaniola, and African workers were soon being transported to the Americas to join them. Africans and their descendants worked alongside

Indians in mining, although in general the mining of gold relied more heavily on Africans, while silver mining was done primarily by indigenous workers.

The processes by which these two precious metals were extracted differed greatly. Mining silver involved going deep into the earth, with all the engineering problems that entailed, while gold mining was done by scooping out deposits of gold-streaked rock in streams and separating out the gold dust, a process that required neither construction of tunnels nor great capital investment. Both forms of mining were labor intensive, and in both, the work was divided according to gender. In silver mining, those who went down in the mine were usually men, while women played a supporting role, keeping their partners fed, clothed, and housed; women also combed through the slag heap searching for silver to retrieve. In gold mining, men excavated the banks of the rivers, and women panned the gold to separate it from the water and dirt.

Gold and silver were not the only desirable metals. By the first decade of the 16th century, underground copper mining was being done near Cap Haitien on Hispaniola by enslaved indigenous people and Africans. At first, indigenous people were rounded up and brought to the mines to work a shift of six to eight months. The inadequate shelter and food provided for the workers left many suffering from malnutrition that lessened their resistance to European epidemic disease. As the native population declined, Africans were brought to replace them. Queen Isabella even proposed that the Africans be used as mine workers, with indigenous workers being used in farming to produce food for the African mine workers. Where was the "Defender of the Africans"? No equivalent to Bartolomé de las Casas rose up to challenge the abuses inherent in the labor system of slavery, although questions were occasionally raised about the legality of the enslavement process in Africa itself. Las Casas himself explicitly advocated the substitution of African for native labor in his initial appeals to the crown for reform, only repenting of this morally curious stance later in his life.

Gold Mining in Colombia

Mining had the same effect in Colombia as on Hispaniola; the indigenous people were nearly wiped out by the combined effects of disease and extreme exploitation, and the colonists turned to

African laborers who became the critical element in the accumulation of wealth by the colonists. Gangs of hundreds of enslaved Africans and their descendants worked in colonial Nueva Granada, especially in the Chocó area on the northern Pacific coast of modern Colombia, where people of the African Diaspora predominate today. Enslaved African miners were supervised by an overseer who himself might be of African origins; the workers lived in camps at the mining site on the coast, while their owners lived in the highlands where the climate was cooler and more healthful. A quota was established for each worker, and if the laborer managed to accumulate gold above his quota, usually by working unclaimed areas on Sundays and holidays, he might use it for purchases at the store or save it toward the purchase of freedom for himself or a family member.

Africans and Silver Mining

While most silver mining was done with Indian labor, there were enslaved workers from Africa in all the mines, at times a lot of them. African workers were expensive, especially due to the cost of transporting them to the interior of New Spain and Peru, far from the slave markets of the eastern coasts of the Americas, so that may account for their smaller numbers in this type of work. In addition, some mine owners apparently believed the altitude of silver mining was too great for the Africans.

At Potosí in Upper Peru, thousands of Indian mita workers represented the bulk of the workforce, but there were also many Africans and people of African descent. Statistics from 1600 show that just under 70 percent of workers were Indian wage workers, about 18 percent were mita workers, and about 14 percent were enslaved Africans and their descendants. Some Africans in Potosí took the place of mules, pushing the mill wheel at the *Casa de la Moneda* (the mint); others performed household labor or some form of artisanry. By 1780, there were around a thousand people of African descent in Potosí in a population of 23,000.

In New Spain, there were more than 800 enslaved Africans working at the silver mines of Taxco in 1569. In Honduras, most underground mining of silver was done by enslaved Africans rather than Indians. This suggests that when the mining site was closer to the slave markets of the Atlantic, making enslaved Africans less expensive to purchase, mine owners were just as happy to exploit African workers as indigenous ones.

At the end of the 18th century in the Mexican city of Guanajuato, which replaced Potosí as the most important silver-mining area in Spanish America after 1740, nearly half of the mine workers were people of African descent, with white and indigenous workers about evenly divided to make up the remaining 60 percent. All were wage workers; none of them were slaves. In many mines—Zacatecas in New Spain is one example—wage labor eventually replaced the mita system of drafting laborers. In Zacatecas, debt held the labor force at the mine. Although ostensibly free, workers were tied to their work sites by contracts and the threat of violence at the hands of a special armed force called the *Santa Hermandad* (Holy Brotherhood), which hunted down workers who ran away.

PEONAGE

One way of ensuring a necessary workforce, not only in mining but on the farms and plantations of Spanish America, was to tie the workers to the work site through debt. Haciendas needed laborers. Indeed, the colonial period experienced a severe shortage of labor throughout much of its history. Land was often readily available, but without people to work it, land could not produce wealth for its owner. The hacendado's chief problem was finding laborers he could rely on. As long as the peasantry retained land, laborers resisted working for wages, preferring the life of subsistence farming. It may have been a hard life in some ways, but by growing their own food, building their own houses, and weaving their own clothes, peasants met their own basic needs and maintained control over their schedules of work and play.

Various methods were employed to induce workers to come and live on the hacienda, where they would generally be paid through some form of barter, given the shortage of currency at the time. Frequently, workers were offered a small hut, a garden plot to grow their own food, possibly some food ration for themselves and their families, or a loan, by which they were indebted to the landowner. In addition to these benefits, a worker gained the opportunity to form a vertical relationship with a powerful person who could serve as his *patrón*, so both parties had something to gain: the landowner got his crops tended and harvested, as well as getting domestic work done by the female members of the peasant family, while the worker gained the protection of a powerful person in dealings with the law.

In an effort to retain his laborers, the patrón defended them from labor drafts or service in the militia, vouched for them in court, and lent money to cover their family emergencies. A debt, once contracted, was generally impossible to pay off, given low wages and the likelihood that the debt would accumulate interest, fees for such privileges as buying goods at the hacienda store, and possibly a fine for some infraction. Workers tied to the plantation in this way were known as indebted peons; if they died without canceling the loan, it would likely be passed on to their children.

While this system of debt peonage was one way to ensure that there would be laborers available when they were needed, workers sometimes abandoned both the work site and the debt, so the system failed to provide an ironclad guarantee of a dependable labor force. In general, however, a worker probably could not expect a better life by breaking the law and trading in one hacienda for another or leaving agricultural work to go into the mines. Staying on the hacienda with neighbors he had known all his life, marrying the girl next door, and living the life his father had lived before him might be a relatively attractive option, given the other choices.

This system of a large landowner, a patrón, with a group of dependent laborers continued past the colonial period in some areas. While some evidence indicates that peonage and other forms of coerced labor diminished during the 1700s, vestiges of these systems lived on in the unsettled years of the 19th century, and even into the 20th century, when a patrón might deliver his peons to the polls to ensure their participation in the voting process. Once there, in the absence of poll watchers and international observers that would not come on the scene until late in the 20th century, the peons would have found it in their interest to follow the recommendations of the patrón in casting their ballots.

SLAVERY

The labor system that had perhaps the greatest impact on Latin America as a whole was plantation-based slavery, especially in sugar production. An understanding of this form of coerced labor and its significance is central to any study of work life in the colonial period. From the point of view of whites who dominated colonial society, the function and purpose of Indians and Africans was to work, so to a great extent it was work that defined not only their daily lives but the meaning of their existence. It is this fact that makes the historical evidence of enslaved workers refusing to be reduced to simple beasts of burden all the more inspiring. Their insistence on their humanity in the face of a brutal and unrelenting system of dehumanization is what makes their story remarkable.

Slavery in Europe

Iberians had considerable experience with slavery as a labor institution. While slavery in most of Europe had been replaced by other labor systems by 1300, it continued on the edges of Europe where there was contact with other peoples, and where laborers were sold in slave markets. Many of these were of eastern European or Slavic origins, with the medieval Latin word *sclavus*, or Slav, also becoming the root word for "slave" in most Western European languages. Meanwhile, Africans from south of the Sahara had been brought north across the desert as enslaved laborers for centuries, if in relatively small numbers. Beginning in 1441 when Portuguese traders got as far south as Senegambia in their exploration of the western coast of Africa, these numbers began to increase dramatically. During the remainder of the 15th century the Portuguese brought about 900 African laborers annually back to Portugal. European traders, therefore, were already supplying enslaved African workers to Europe, mainly as domestic help, long before the colonization of the Americas began. In addition, the conjunction of African labor and sugar production, with its highly labor-intensive process of harvesting and refining, began on the Iberian Peninsula. From there, the Portuguese transferred sugar production based on enslaved African workers to Madeira and other offshore Atlantic islands as they moved down the western coast of Africa.

Origins of African Slavery in Latin America

Slavery in Spanish America began with the enslaving of the native peoples of the Caribbean, especially in the search for gold on Hispaniola. As the indigenous people fell victim to epidemics and the need for more laborers grew, the colonists came to rely on workers from Africa, justifying the practice by arguing that through baptizing their workers they extended to them the Christian promise of eternal life. When Iberian colonists in the Americas sought to augment or replace the labor of the native people, they turned to the thriving markets of West Africa to buy these workers.

In the Portuguese colony of Brazil, the area that ultimately received more than one-third of all the Africans who landed in the Americas, colonists first enslaved the native peoples. Indian laborers were obtained by offering them a wage, by barter, or by *resgate* (rescue), the practice of trading for slaves with native groups who held them. The justification for resgate was that a harsher fate awaited them at the hands of their captors, that of being cooked and eaten in a cannibalistic rite. In the 16th century, the usual system of Indian labor was for the colonists to trade tools, knife blades, or other goods desired by the indigenous people in exchange for their work on a specific project. By the 17th century, working for a wage had become more common and joined slavery, *aldeia* (village) labor, and the barter system, all methods of ensuring that the *engenho* (sugar mill) would have the necessary labor.

Among enslaved Indians the male–female ratio was about three to two. When an indigenous male head of household entered slavery, his whole family went with him to the engenho, where the women often worked on the farm producing food for the workforce. In this form of agriculture, women predominated, as they had in pre-Columbian agriculture.

At first, the Portuguese bartered for labor on short-term jobs, but the Indians, feeling no need for a wage, refused to do longer-term work on the barter system. Also, barter became more expensive for the Portuguese. Some native groups tired of the trinkets Europeans sought to trade and began to demand pricier items in trade for the brazilwood they cut and dragged to the coast. The natives of Brazil were uninterested in profit since social status in their societies derived from their prowess in war and from the capture of future victims of ritual cannibalism rather than from wealth; this affected their trade partnerships with the Europeans who lived by different economic principles. The Portuguese viewed the native peoples as lazy because of their lack of interest in accumulation. Often workers simply did not show up for work. If the opportunity arose, they were likely to run away and disappear into the territory they knew so well. Even as late as the late 16th century, however, they constituted the majority of laborers in the sugar engenhos. There were Africans, but the cost of buying them was prohibitive for many sugar mill owners until later in the colonial period after they had grown wealthier.

Like the native workers in the Caribbean, those in Brazil contracted and died of diseases brought by the Europeans. The first reports of an epidemic, possibly smallpox, in Brazil came in 1559. Estimates of indigenous dead in settled areas reached 30,000; no count could be made of those who died in the wilderness. Shortly after that, a measles epidemic carried off an equal number. This first round of epidemics lasted from 1559 to 1563, disrupting the community's agricultural production and causing some Indians to enter slavery to avoid dying of hunger. So the epidemics joined restrictions imposed by the crown on Indian slavery and the ever-increasing demand for sugar in Europe to create the motivation for restructuring the workforce and increasing the reliance on African workers.

The Europeans' growing fondness for sugar as a sweetener and the rising international price in the first 20 years of the 17th century were key factors in the dramatic increase in the numbers of Africans brought to the Americas. On one engenho, 7 percent of the workforce was African in 1572; only 19 years later, that had increased to 37 percent, and by 1638, 100 percent of the workforce was African or African-descended, a dramatic change in just over 50 years.

Why Africans?

What was behind this rapid conversion from an Indian to an African labor force? According to some historians, the Africans and the Europeans were culturally closer to each other than either group was to the indigenous people, and this led the Europeans to value African workers more highly. The agricultural practices of West Africa and the use of iron had enabled the people of that area to become accustomed to agricultural work, whereas many of the Indian groups lived by gathering the fruits of the land and by trapping wild game. In addition, the Portuguese already had experience with African workers in sugar cultivation on the Atlantic islands of Madeira, the Azores, and the Canaries. The African workers also resisted European diseases better than the indigenous people because Africans and Europeans had been in contact for centuries. While African workers cost more—they sold for three to five times more than Indians with the same skills—they were more productive, and Portuguese colonists wrote that this outweighed the difference in price. Among free workers, the native people were always paid less than Africans or their descendants, and sometimes they were paid in bartered goods, food, cloth, or alcohol. While other free workers were often paid by the day, Indians might be paid at the end of the task or the end of the month. New protective legislation that increased the cost of Indian labor, the tendency of the native people to run off into the forest they knew so well, and their lower resistance to European diseases all combined by the late 16th century to make African workers preferable in many areas of Latin America.

Sugar Plantations and Slave Life in Brazil

So what was life like for an enslaved African on a Brazilian engenho? Answering that question requires taking a close look at sugar production in preindustrial Bahia, the center of the Brazilian sugar economy. Until the middle of the 17th century, sugar constituted the entire economy of the Portuguese colony and the primary motor driving the colonization of Brazil. In late July or early August, the Bahian planters began the *safra* (harvest). Preparation of machinery and building repair occupied the few weeks before the first day of the harvest. On the day it began, everything and everybody was blessed by the priest with holy water that was scattered on the machinery, animals, and workers before the initial canes were put through the press by the priest or the owner. Without this blessing, the workers refused to work; some went to special lengths to ensure that a few drops of holy water fell on them.

The work schedule during the safra called for cane grinding to begin in the late afternoon and continue through the night till late morning of the following day. Work in the fields was done during the day. The slaves worked in shifts but might be required to work double shifts, so during the harvest period, they were exhausted and might fall asleep almost anywhere. The safra in Bahia lasted from 8 to 10 months until the end of May. The Bahianos could harvest longer than the growers in the Caribbean whose climate permitted a harvest period of only 4 to 6 months. This climatic difference contributed to a highly efficient exploitation of slave labor in Bahia, as workers produced income for about three-quarters of the year.

The only breaks for the sugar workers resulted from broken equipment, including the equipment that brought water to the engenho to turn the mill wheel, shortages of wood for fuel, rain that made cutting and hauling cane impossible, and holidays. In the early 17th century, there were 37 Catholic holidays observed annually on the Jesuit engenho Sergipe, and Sunday was an additional day of rest. This probably represents one extreme of holiday observance, since Jesuit authorities tried to make sure that engenhos run by their order observed Sundays and all the Catholic holidays. Private owners often worked the labor force throughout the week, not observing the Sunday holiday. Most planters observed Sundays, but many believed that giving the workers time off encouraged lewd and licentious behavior such as drinking and dancing.

A sugar estate in the Brazilian region of Pernambuco, with the *engenho* (mill) in the foreground and the planter's *casa grande* (mansion) behind. The image appears on a map produced by the Dutch cartographer Joan Blaeu during the 1640s, when the Dutch briefly controlled the major sugar-producing areas of northeastern Brazil. (Courtesy of the John Carter Brown Library at Brown University)

Producing Sugar

The production process required work in the fields and in the mill, supplemented by various kinds of labor to keep the production process going. Once cut, the cane had a time limit of around 24 hours, or at most two days, before it soured, so cut cane had to be milled within that time frame. The requirement of keeping the mill supplied with cane, water, and wood lent urgency to the work, with the result that the needs of the machinery controlled the lives of the workers. Slaves participated in all forms of work at the engenho; not only were they field hands and domestics, but also skilled workers.

Sugar production began with fieldwork. Workers, men and women, got up at 5:00 for a morning prayer and went to the fields, some of the women with babies strapped to their backs. There they worked until 9:00 when they were given a small breakfast; the midday meal was eaten about 1:00, and the work lasted until about 6:00. Depending on the time of year, the work might consist of planting new fields of cane, weeding existing cane, or harvesting the cane.

Planting new cane involved making a trench in the wet heavy soil favorable for sugarcane, and it was hard work. A line of male and female workers with hoes dug a trench for the cane, then the whole line shifted back to make the next trench. They were supervised by the overseer with a rod to discipline slow workers. Weeding the cane was not as arduous, but there was the danger of snakebite and cuts in the skin from the sharp edges of the cane leaf.

During the harvest period, assignments were made in pairs, a man to cut and a woman to bind the cut stalks into bunches of 10 and load them onto the oxcart or boat for transport to the mill. During harvest time, even domestic workers were sometimes assigned to work in the mill in addition to their domestic work. Often the fieldwork was done as piecework so when the day's quota was done the workers might have time to work in their gardens.

After the field workers brought the cane to the engenho, a team of seven or eight workers took over. Two or three workers, usually women, put the cane stalks into the rollers to extract the juice. Two carried away the crushed cane stalks to be thrown away or for use as animal feed. One woman kept the oil lamps burning; another threw water on the machinery to keep it running smoothly and cleaned the kettles that collected the cane juice. One worker was responsible for the hoist that swung the kettle full of cane liquid over to the boiling house. The work was supervised by the sugar master or general overseer during the day, and by night, his assistant took over; by the 1700s, this subordinate was usually one of the slaves.

While the more technical jobs of sugar master and kettleman were sometimes performed by white technicians, often people of African descent performed these highly skilled tasks. Transporting the cane, whether by cart or boat, was also skilled work often done by slaves or free black workers. The Portuguese colonists found the Africans to be reliable workers, easily capable of managing the most complicated steps in the sugar production process; over time, Africans and their descendants took over most of the skilled work at the engenho.

Most new workers straight from Africa, known as *bozales*, were put to work as field hands since new workers were normally purchased to maintain or increase the level of production. People of African descent who had been born in Brazil and therefore spoke Portuguese were more likely to have the opportunity to rise into the ranks of skilled workers. Sometimes these *crioulos*, Brazilian-born slaves, were the children of the white master, one of the men in his family or of a white technician at the mill, a fact that meant the work hierarchy tended to reflect the hierarchy of color on the engenho as racially mixed people moved up the ladder.

The skilled workers made the difficult decisions on when to add the lime, ash, and water required to maintain the proper temperature in the kettle. Skimming the boiling cane juice also depended on skill and experience. When the right point had been reached, the liquid sugar was poured into pottery forms and set aside for the liquid to leak slowly out the bottom. Wet clay was smeared on top of the forms, and the water traveled through the sugar clearing it of impurities and creating three different kinds of sugar: the clearest at the top, the darkest at the bottom, and a medium grade in the middle. Women normally did many of these tasks, also participating in tamping down the sugar into the large crates that would take it away to market. Field hands might also do this work, after working in the fields all day cutting cane.

The last part of the process was supervised by the crater who managed the packing and calculated the number of boxes of sugar produced. The crater also totaled up the payment due to any independent farmers that had brought their cane to the mill for processing, as well as the tithe due to the church. All these skilled tasks might be done by smart and responsible enslaved workers. There was an ongoing debate among the engenho owners on whether it was more efficient to hire skilled wage workers or to train enslaved labor for these tasks. At times, a slave who worked in a position of skill and responsibility might be provided a small wage designed to motivate him to work harder and do his best.

The preindustrial boiling house resembled the early factory of the Industrial Revolution. In a time before it became customary for machines to set the pace of work, the sugarhouse must have seemed like an anomaly, something so unlike anything on Earth that some contemporary observers turned to biblical images of hell to find a comparison. Clocks were not used to control the speed and duration of the work until at least the middle of the 18th century. Instead, it was the job of the manager of the sugarhouse to regulate the work and to balance the speed of various parts of the process in order to keep production moving at the speed set by the mill wheel. Some mills ran three shifts, a schedule that required at least 100 workers.

The work was dangerous, and the workers were prone to accidents. Due to the length of the workday during the *safra*, those who fed the rollers were at particular risk. If they were sleepy or inattentive to their job, a hand could easily be caught in the rollers, and the arm or even the whole body could be pulled into the rollers and crushed. Water-powered mills were the most dangerous in this respect because of the delay in bringing the rollers to a halt. Since most feeders were women, it was not unusual to see women workers on the plantation who had lost one or both arms. Stokers fed the hot furnaces and faced the danger of falling into the fire; this work was sometimes used as a punishment for slaves who had run away or been disobedient. One man who had run away repeatedly finally took advantage of his assignment stoking the fires and threw himself into the furnace to end his days.

In addition to working as cane binders in the field and feeders in the grinding house, women tended the lamps in the mill, poured water on the cogs of the machinery, and worked in the finishing process, spreading clay over the pots of sugar, separating the final product into the three different grades, and packing it into boxes. About one-fourth of the women on a plantation worked as domestics in the main house. There they cared for children, prepared food, made lace, and stitched clothing for the owner's family or worked as servants to the female family members.

In addition to the main work in the canefields, the field and mill workers were assigned other tasks, depending on the time of year. In the off-season, between harvests, the slaves spent much of their time cutting wood to fire the mill during the harvest period, and they worked another four to eight hours on miscellaneous jobs around the plantation; they mended fences, constructed and maintained buildings, and ground manioc into flour.

Living Conditions on the Plantation

Life outside the workday was quite limited. For the most part, workers were restricted to the estate on which they worked; in addition, by the time they had accomplished their main task of the day, they had little time left for other activities. The assignment of a quota gave workers an incentive to finish their daily assignment in order to have time to work on their garden plots, a feature of the system designed to reduce dallying. Slaves might sell the excess product of their plots, often to the engenho itself, which bought it for below-market price.

At night, the average worker returned to a one-room hut with walls made of mud and roofs of thatch. Huts might be small separate structures or long buildings divided internally into separate spaces, each occupied by a different family. For clothing, the workers might receive a few lengths of rough handwoven fabric. On some plantations, slaves received a new outfit every other year.

One observer reported that the workers on the plantation he visited were issued a pair of cotton pants or a skirt, two shirts, and some material to sleep on. Some observers noted that slaves were naked, but most paintings of the workers of the period show them in simple cotton clothing.

Throughout the colonial period, descriptions of the workers' diets indicate that the food was insufficient in both quantity and quality to maintain a healthy workforce. Some observers noted that the food was too coarse to be digested. Some documents include instructions from the colonial authorities to the slaveholders to feed their workers adequately or give them time and space to grow food for themselves. A record from 1750 shows that slaves were given a bushel of manioc flour to last 40 days, along with salted meat or fish; this diet might be supplemented by bananas and rice. One slaveholder of the early 19th century who considered himself generous in the food he provided gave the field hands bread and rum in the morning; a breakfast of rice, bacon, and coffee; a midday meal of meat and vegetables; and supper of manioc flour with vegetables and fruit. The fact that the workers preferred to work their own plots, even when they had little free time to do so, may be one indication that the food issued by the engenho owner was insufficient and of little nutritional value.

Labor Discipline on the Plantation

One of the assumptions of the Brazilian slaveholder was that physical coercion was necessary to keep the slaves working. In the absence of any institution charged with overseeing the slaveholder's choice of coercive methods, he was free to apply extreme forms of physical punishment and even death with virtual impunity. The authorities assumed that an owner would not lightly cause the loss of his investment, but while this concern may at times have stayed the owner's hand, it was balanced by the desire to set an example that would keep the fear of punishment alive. Many plantation owners and administrators viewed terrorizing the workers as the only way a small number of white owners could control a much larger number of black enslaved workers. Even plantations run by religious orders relied on fear to keep the workers working. One 18th-century writer offered the opinion that the Portuguese peasant treated his oxen better than the Brazilian slaveholder treated his workers.

When one slave who sued for freedom due to her master's abuse won her freedom in court, Bahia's governor refused to enforce the decision, claiming the case set a dangerous precedent for other abused workers. There is considerable evidence of the dehumanization that was an essential characteristic of slavery. Frequent references are made to castration as a form of punishment of black men whether enslaved or free; this punishment does not seem to have been applied to workers of other races for their transgressions. In a case from 1737, a slaveholder who had one of his enslaved workers "hung . . . by his testicles" until dead escaped punishment because he was from a wealthy and important family. He also killed two enslaved workers of a different owner and a freedman because they had injured one of his oxen.[2]

Punishment could backfire however. A disgruntled worker might cause problems by taking out his vengeance on the product. Workers' sabotage, not to mention frequent instances of running away, discussed in a later chapter, delayed the production process or ruined the sugar. For this reason, most plantations adopted an approach that mixed punishments with rewards. Incentives sometimes turned out to be a stronger motivator than the whip. These incentives usually took the form of distributing *garapa*, a form of alcohol made from sugar, or assigning piecework that allowed the diligent worker to finish his task while there was still time to pursue his own activities. Some workers, especially the more highly skilled, might receive a small wage, or a worker might be given a tip for running an errand. The opportunity to sell the excess product from a garden plot also served as an incentive. The possibility of rising on the occupational ladder was an incentive, the threat of demotion another. The strongest incentive may have been the possibility of buying one's freedom, along with hope of manumission. One Jesuit observed a direct connection between a slave's hope of gaining freedom and how well he worked.

Plantation Owners

Any study of labor in the colonial period must devote some attention to the work of those who did not do manual labor, but rather other kinds of work. In much of Latin America, the most important people in society were the owners of large estates. In order to understand the planter class and its work, the plantation must be seen as a business run by a group of owners, the planter family. There was no such thing as a personal decision that did not affect the business. All decisions were business decisions, and every family decision was organized around the imperative of keeping the business alive, marching into the future. As one historian has written, "Property and family were intimately entwined in the planters' minds."[3]

It may be impossible to get an accurate idea of the daily life of the planters in the colonial period, but certain conclusions suggest themselves. In the Iberian Peninsula, the nobility was made up of landholders who ruled over many dependents, so this social structure served as the model on which the American colonists fashioned themselves. The Brazilian planters have been called "men of new wealth seeking traditional forms of social legitimacy."[4] Frequently, they lived in town where they could enjoy the comfort and social life of their equals. In Brazil, the wealthiest planters lived mostly in the city of Salvador, while their engenhos were located farther in the interior of Bahia where they could be reached in a couple of hours by boat.

The lives of the planter families were ruled by public opinion. They built an honorable reputation through their faithfulness in meeting government, church, and military obligations. A good engenho owner ran his business honestly, controlled his workers, paid his bills, equitably divided his gains with those who provided cane to his mill, and paid his skilled workers a fair wage in a timely fashion. While he did not do manual labor, his work was his life and vice versa. The way he conducted his family affairs reflected on his reputation as a businessman, and the respect he commanded in business raised or lowered his family on the social ladder.

The planter families were fashioned on the patriarchal model widely accepted by the colonists and their descendants. The contract in this model—whether followed or not—was that the father/master managed the family in the best interests of all its members, and they repaid him with gestures of respect and obedience. Dependents, children, and slaves regularly sought and received the blessing of the head of the family. He was also responsible for disciplining family members and for defending the family honor, in part by conducting his own affairs in an honorable way. This was the context within which female seclusion was enforced. Chaste women were a sign of a well-ordered home, and this order was imposed from the top: "The honor of the house was tied to the honor of the women."[5]

As we saw in the chapter on marriage and the family, however, the patriarchal model was violated in various ways. In spite of society's rules, regulations, and expectations, at times the head of the engenho family was a woman, usually a widow who had inherited that position. In Brazil in 1817, women owned 10 percent of farms supplying cane to one engenho, and 15 percent of all engenhos had women owners.

Others among the planter class were of Jewish origins, in spite of the prohibition against New Christians in the colonies and the best efforts of the Inquisition to locate them and send them back to Europe. Often they had been merchants, a group not held in high esteem in 15th- and 16th-century Spain and Portugal, who had found their way to the Americas in spite of the restrictions against New Christians. Once in the Americas, they employed the capital gained in commerce to buy land and sometimes accumulated an amount sufficient to set up a mill of their own. Toward the end of the 16th century, a synagogue was discovered on one engenho. A brief period of rule by the more tolerant Dutch over much of northeastern Brazil (1630–1654) revealed a more widespread Jewish presence, as fear of the Inquisition was temporarily suspended. But a vicious campaign against Portuguese merchants suspected of secretly practicing Judaism in Peru during the 1630s ensured that many of their counterparts in Dutch-controlled areas of Brazil departed when Portuguese Catholics regained control over the area, bringing the Inquisition with them.

Cane Farmers

Just below the planter class were the *lavradores,* or farmers. Because of the importance of sugarcane in the Brazilian economy, the cane farmers ranked highest among the lavradores, followed closely by tobacco farmers. In Brazil, the cane farmers played a crucial role in sugar production since engenho owners relied not only on the sugar produced on their own estates, but also on cane supplied to the mill by the lavradores. Income from sugarcane was normally divided equally between the lavrador who had supplied the cane and the engenho owner, but because a good supply of cane was the key to a profitable season, some lavradores were well positioned to bargain with the mill owner for extra benefits. These benefits might include the loan of slave labor or the best position on the grinding schedule. Often cane-growing lands were rented to lavradores by the engenho owners with the lavrador paying his rent by turning over one-quarter to one-third of his half of the crop to the owner. In this case, the lavrador would end up with an income that was only one-sixth to one-quarter of all the cane he produced.

Engenho owners normally preferred renting their land to selling it outright and thereby reducing the size of the estate. The mill owners also tried to avoid granting long-term rental contracts, since lavradores on long-term contracts tended to behave as if they owned the land. If the contract was not renewed, they might refuse to leave the land, preventing new renters from taking possession of it. Without title to the land they farmed, however, the lavrador families had no long-term stability apart from maintaining good relations with the engenho owners. In the 17th century, the terms of the lease usually ranged from 6 to 18 years, tending to increase as the century wore on. Some leases were as long as 50 years, or even perpetual (*emphyteusis*), with stipulations, for example, that the cane be supplied only to the owner of the engenho that leased the land, or that another engenho could not be put there.

Even when their cane was under contract, lavradores often sold their cane to other mills, running the risk that the landowner might invoke the law against them and even call out his private armed force to seize their cane or remove them from the property. Different leasing arrangements defined the social structure within the lavrador group; there were people of considerable wealth and power, generally holding their lands without restriction, followed by those who owned their land with restrictions, and finally by sharecroppers and tenant farmers. The last group had at best a precarious hold on the land they worked.

Many of the lavradores owned slaves but also participated in manual labor on their farms. In the early 18th century in the area around Bahia, lavradores owned oxen and carts to move the cane to the mill and to provide wood for the milling process, and a small workforce of between 1 and 40 slaves, with 10 being the average. At times, the mill owners lent field hands to the lavradores who were under contract with the engenho to ensure a steady supply of cane for the engenho.

The social origins of the lavradores who occupied the upper levels of that social category were the same as those of the engenho owners. In early colonial Brazil, nearly all lavradores were white. At the turn from the 17th to the 18th century, there was only 1 *pardo* (person of color) in 400 Bahian growers. By the end of the 18th century, however, almost one-sixth of the lavradores were people of color. Some lavradores were women, mostly widows; some were priests, merchants—sometimes New Christians—and militia officers, government functionaries, and judges with aspirations to owning an engenho. Some of the lavradores were religious orders, and in some cases, these orders went on to establish an engenho and enter the milling business.

The owner of the engenho wielded power over the lavradores since he might refuse to mill a particular batch of cane before it went sour, thereby ruining the lavrador, or he could short change the lavrador when returning to him his portion of the sugar or payment for it. The engenho owners and their families viewed the lavrador families as dependents with obligations to the mill owners' families. The bigger and more successful owners tended to be more dictatorial, often treating their sharecroppers and tenants like servants. For their part, the lavradores could also cause problems for the mill owners by not supplying wood and cane on schedule.

The most important lavradores aspired to become engenho owners. They shared the political, social, and economic interests of the mill owners to a great extent. They also relied on the same inputs: slave labor, oxen, and carts. Since the lavradores used their status as a stepping stone to mill ownership, they viewed their interests as similar to those of the planters rather than to those of the groups below them in the social hierarchy. The lavradores did not promote social change or challenge the sugar economy hierarchy. As the colonial period continued, the mill owners tended to solidify their power, while the lavradores tended to grow weaker. The larger planters, defended by the armed men on their payroll, found numerous ways to cheat the lavradores, who had little recourse but to accept the deal offered by their more powerful neighbors.

Wage Labor in the Economy of Slavery

Occupations

One function of wage labor in plantation society was to foster the hope among the enslaved that they might climb the ladder of upward mobility and join the wage workers. Various kinds of skilled workers were hired at the mill. The jobs of sugar master, kettleman, and boatman or cartman were often filled by wage laborers whose pay might be supplemented with food or housing. Other tasks usually carried out by wage workers were carpentry, blacksmithing, coppersmithing, and masonry; some contemporary observers noted that wages were paid on an annual basis or every two years, with the workers being housed, clothed, and fed in the meantime and a record kept in order to deduct these costs from the salary to be paid. Within plantation society, these workers occupied the level of artisans or craftsmen; sugar could not be made without their skill, which gave them some negotiating power and social status. Blacksmiths and coppersmiths, whose skills made them among the best-paid workers, might even set up their own workshops on the engenho and run them with their own equipment and their own slaves.

The professionals constituted another group of wage workers, either in the countryside or in nearby urban areas. The mill owner retained a lawyer and agents in the city to defend and advance his interests. The owners also employed professional workers on their estates; there was usually a chaplain, as well as semiprofessionals like nurses, midwives, doctors, and herbalists.

Overseers, those who supervised work in the fields and the mill, earned about as much as the skilled mill workers, and they were essential to the functioning of the engenho. They might be black, racially mixed, or white, free or enslaved. In early Brazil, they were often Portuguese immigrants, but as time went on, they were more likely to be people of part-African descent. Overseers held a low position on the social ladder, as demonstrated by their marital prospects; often they married enslaved women.

The lowest form of wage labor was that done for a specific task or period. Finding and returning a runaway slave, clearing land, day labor in the fields, taking down a tree, messenger service, all these tasks would be done by rural subsistence farmers and their family members for a small wage. This economic relationship reflects the patronage system in which local peasants were dependent on the nearby estate owner for wages to supplement the family economy.

Wage Labor and Racial Status

Like everything else in colonial Latin America, the wage structure was racialized. The usual expectation in Brazil was that whites would be paid most, blacks second, and Indians third for the same work, although workers sometimes leveraged more, depending on their proficiency and the demand for their skill. The colonists tried to set up a rigid hierarchy with whites in management positions, blacks in the fields, and Indians doing occasional tasks, but as Africans and people of African descent learned the skilled tasks of the mill, they upset this neat system. It was to the owners' advantage for enslaved laborers to perform skilled labor, since they could be paid nothing or granted a small privilege for their labor. Brazilian-born slaves, *crioulos*, came to be disproportionately represented in artisan and skilled positions in the engenho, as well as in the house as servants. Indeed, the 1788 census in Bahia shows that the dominant class had been quite successful in maintaining a division of labor into three levels: mill owners and administrators were white, field hands were black, and the skilled positions in between were held by racially mixed people of African descent.

Other Variables in the Status of Wage Labor

Various factors affected the wage and social structure of wage workers. Gaining a skill improved a worker's bargaining position as the rise in status and wage of the *mulato* Alvaro demonstrates: he appears on the engenho records in 1625 as "Alvaro mulatto kettleman," reflecting the usual identification of workers by a first name, a racial designation, and their occupation. At that time, he earned 24 *milréis*. Nineteen years later, he had gained a last name, and his salary had nearly doubled; in 1644 he appears as Alvaro Fernandes at a salary of 42 milréis.[6] The records of another engenho list a black carpenter among the highest-paid workers on the estate.

Another factor that affected the wage structure was the market price of sugar. When the price fell, wages also fell. In an effort to economize in difficult times, mill owners opened up skilled positions to people of color who lacked bargaining power and therefore worked for less. Literacy was another factor. Some positions at the mill, especially administrators, general overseers, and craters required reading, writing, and some arithmetic. Since enslaved laborers were not given the opportunity for education, they were normally excluded from these positions, but in all skilled labor not requiring literacy, Africans and their descendants became dominant as the colonial period matured.

Sometimes freed slaves worked as wage laborers on the engenho, but they were in constant danger of being seized as property in punishment for an action deemed disrespectful or simply to pay a mill owner's debt. In one case from late in the 17th century, the freedman Domingo Lopes da Silva from Angola worked for a year as a specialist in the boiling house, but when he sought payment of his wages, he found himself branded and in chains. In these cases, the whim of the wealthy and politically powerful mill owner carried the day; there was little recourse for the injured party.

Temporary or intermittent wage labor was normally done by indigenous people. Indians filled unskilled or semiskilled positions that included supplying wood, catching and returning runaways, and working in transportation. They might be paid in goods rather than cash, at the end of either the month or the task. Their wage was often a small fraction of that of others doing the same work. Often they were not listed in the records by name, but by the designation *indio*. To make matters worse, while wages increased slowly over the course of the 17th and 18th centuries, prices went up faster so that real wages for Indians fell as the colonial period continued.

Working on the Ranch

Cattle ranching, which occupied vast tracts of grasslands in the interior of Brazil, the Río de la Plata region, and Venezuela, was the specialty of the cowboy, known in parts of Spanish America as a *vaquero* after the Spanish *vaca* (cow), a *llanero* (plainsman) in Venezuela, and a *gaucho* in the Southern Cone. Wild cattle roamed all of these regions, as well as parts of Mexico and Central America, within a few decades of the European arrival in the Americas. Along with imported sheep and horses, great herds of these cattle quickly produced widespread environmental devastation, adversely affecting native agricultural activities in many areas.

At the same time, growing demand for beef, hides, and tallow (for candle wax) made cattle ranching an important economic activity. Small numbers of skilled horsemen, mostly people of color who varied in their ethnic makeup depending on the racial mixture of the area, hunted and herded these cattle under the direction of a Spanish or Portuguese landowner who might have laid claim to tens of thousands of acres. To give an idea of the scale, in 1772 the largest ranch in the Brazilian captaincy of Piauí was twice the size of the modern country of Lebanon, yet the entire captaincy, with 582 ranches, was home to only 26,000 people. The employees of such estates might include a mix of wage laborers, debt peons, and even slaves. All enjoyed a rough sort of personal freedom based on the nature of the enterprise, which frequently took them far away from the immediate oversight of their supervisors.

Some idea of that independent life can be seen in the records of investigations into illegal cattle slaughter on the Pacific coast ranches of Guatemala in the early 17th century. Royal officials set out to track down gangs of ranch workers, identified as a mix of black slaves, free *mulatos*, and Indians, who were accused of killing cattle owned by landowners other than their own employers. One investigator found an abandoned hideout used by a group of rustlers, perhaps with the support of their boss, to prepare hides and tallow for sale without royal approval to buyers in the nearest large town. The investigator had less luck apprehending a *mulato* ranch foreman who was said to be the gang's leader. That trail ran cold in the man's home village, where the official encountered nothing but a few personal belongings left behind in haste and stony silence from his neighbors.

Women: A Special Class of Workers

While it is apparent from some of the descriptions above that women worked in many of the same occupations as men, women's work was shaped by the gender system. The work site for most women, whether urban or rural, was the household. Indeed, the household was so important as a locus of work that it often produced most of what its members needed to be self-sufficient. Pottery and hides, bread and tortillas, honey, candles, soap, liquor, and clothing were all made at home. Cleaning and maintaining of clothes was done in the household, as was haircutting. Women produced all these goods and services. Most of the work women did in the colonial period sprang from women's customary work in the household and was simply expanded from the private to the public sphere. This meant that work for most women was related to food preparation, sexual services, or caring for clothing, children, the sick, and the elderly.

Social standards prevented women of elite households from working publicly, although in most elite homes, the domestic help was supervised by the women of the patriarch's family. At times, however, a wealthy businessman's widow or daughter inherited a position of economic power upon his death. It was by this route that some women came to be the owners and managers of sugarcane plantations in Brazil or great haciendas in Spanish America. Some of the farms that supplied food to mining areas were run by women, and in late colonial Bahia, 10 percent of the cane farmers supplying local sugar mills were women.

While women of the elites supervised the servants' work, at lower social levels the housewife usually worked alongside the domestic help. A middle-class woman might also run a boarding house or manage rental property. Some became girls' governesses or seamstresses, the latter earning less than their male counterparts, the tailors. Other women from the middle groups became booksellers or tobacconists. The wives of tradesmen like printers, weavers, or bakers sometimes inherited their husband's business upon his death, and by the end of the 18th century, some guilds were admitting women. In 1788, women silk spinners even formed a guild of their own.

Certainly, there were some women of the elites and middle groups who worked, generally inside the house, but most women who worked during the colonial period were of the working classes. Many were employed as domestics in the homes of their social "betters," sometimes earning nothing more than room and board, although after learning a domestic skill, they might leave and establish themselves as self-employed laundresses, cooks, seamstresses, or nurses. Of these, the best paid were the child-care workers and wet nurses. As women migrated to urban areas seeking domestic work, urban populations became heavily female. In the early colonial period, poor white women sometimes worked as domestics, but by the beginning of the 17th century, domestic jobs were filled by Indians and Africans. Market vendors were usually women of color who sold food, flowers, and woven goods; most meat vendors in Guatemala City were black women and *mulatas*.

One occupation that was exclusively women's work was that of midwife, and it was a short step from midwife to *curandera* and herbalist. For this reason, the local midwife was often the main rural health care provider, knowledgeable about pain management, the health-giving properties of different plants, and even birth control methods. By the end of the colonial period, however, male doctors had begun delivering the children of elite families, and many of these "professionals" employed bloodletting rather than the midwife's herbal concoctions that may have been both safer and more effective.

There was a fine line in colonial Latin America between street vendors or market women and sex workers. Since according to the dominant values women who worked outside the house were corrupted by contact with men of all social levels, their work made them fair game. By definition, they were morally inferior to housewives who worked in the seclusion of their homes, completely dependent on the goodwill and protection of their fathers, husbands, or brothers. Since men viewed these market women as having loose morals, the women's honor was in jeopardy at all times. Of course, there were also women officially engaged in prostitution; they at least managed to collect a fee for their services, and their work paid better than many other types of work open to women. Prostitution was especially lucrative in areas with high concentrations of unaccompanied men, like peddlers or sailors. Not surprisingly, records show high levels of venereal disease among women of the lower social groups in urban areas.

In the early colonial period, women worked as weavers in *obrajes* where they were locked in and lived tied to the loom in a system very like slavery. Later, in the 18th century when the colonial government set up factories where tobacco was rolled into cigarettes, women flocked to the factories to enter this trade. At the end of the colonial period, Mexico City was home to 9,000 cigarette workers who left their young children in the factory child-care center. At times, women managed to work their way up the factory hierarchy to low- and mid-level management positions. Women sometimes paid a high price for the independence they found in factory work though, contracting tuberculosis and other diseases as a result of malnutrition and poor living and working conditions.

Although men generally earned more for their labor than women, in both urban and rural areas women's work was essential to sustaining life and creating wealth in the colonial period. In the countryside, finding a partner was a prerequisite to the establishment of the peasant farm, and subsistence farming was impossible without the mothers, wives, and daughters of the family. In addition to producing the pots, candles, soap, and clothing mentioned above, women participated in the planting and harvesting of crops and cared for the farm's small animals, chickens, pigs, and goats, as well as the sheep that produced the wool for weaving some of the family's clothing.

The especially onerous work of preparing the staple of indigenous life in Mexico and Central America, the corn tortilla, took many hours by itself. The process involved simmering the kernels of maize with lime and then laboriously grinding them on a stone implement called a *metate* to produce dough. Flattening this dough into small disks, which were then heated briefly on a *comal*, or griddle, created the finished product, the basis of every meal. Preparation of manioc, the staple of the lowland South American and Caribbean diet, and potatoes, the central Andean crop, had always been women's work as well. After the conquest, native women sustained these methods of food preparation in the highlands of Spanish America, even in the homes of people of European origins where wheat bread was preferred. Despite European prejudices against native cuisine and its main ingredients, these remained vital, owing in significant measure to the backbreaking daily labor

A woman and girl in 1908 El Salvador grind corn to make tortillas using the pre-Columbian tools of the *metate* (grinding stone) and *mano* (an elongated stone like a rolling pin). These tools are still used in parts of Latin America more than 500 years after the arrival of the Europeans. (The Art Archive / Keystone View Co / NGS Image Collection)

of millions of indigenous women. In the colonial period, women's work truly was, in the words of the old adage, never done.

CONCLUSION

Whether working in encomienda, the mita, as an indebted peon, in the sugar economy, in cattle ranching, or in the home, most people in colonial Latin America worked long and hard. Prior to the Industrial Revolution that changed the nature of all work and coincided with the late colonial period in Latin America, work was labor intensive. The great majority of people, whether weavers, domestics, enslaved or indebted agricultural workers, cowboys, peasant farmers, or silver, gold or diamond mine workers, were engaged most of the day in heavy manual labor. It was this labor that produced the enormous wealth extracted from the American colonies by the crowns of Spain and Portugal, and it was this labor that supported the lavish lifestyles of the few colonists who were able to realize the colonial dream of power and riches.

Work also defined one's position in the social structure. The owners of mines and large estates were the ones who could provide employment for working people, as well as the ones who relied on the labor of these workers to support a comfortable life. In the absence of government restraints, this system tended to give the patrón unlimited power over the lives of his workers. At times, he might punish them severely, while at other times he assumed a fatherly role, giving protection and advice to the families that depended on him. He played the role of banker, lending money to his workers, and of advocate for a worker facing a legal problem.

However, the working people of the colonial period were not without powers of their own. If workers depended on the patrón to provide work opportunities, the patrón needed them just as much, for without workers there could be no production. The labor shortage that prevailed in most areas of Latin America throughout the colonial period gave workers a bit of leverage as they negotiated the obstacles of their situation. Some ran away to live in outlaw communities in the woods or to seek a better opportunity, some managed to earn or buy their freedom, and some developed personal relationships with those above them in the work hierarchy that paid off in better working conditions. In short, working people pursued their own interests within the parameters of the labor systems that organized their lives as they sought to improve their lot and the prospects for their children.

In this struggle for power over their lives, they found an ally at times and an opponent at other times in the form of the Roman Catholic Church, that all-important colonial authority. The church played an ambivalent role in enforcing the labor systems, as it did in other areas of colonial life. On one hand, the church hierarchy acted as an arm of colonial government, enforcing royal decrees and aligning itself with colonial elites in the colonization project. In this role, the church generally supported the interests of the Iberian colonists and defended their impunity in disciplining their workers. In addition, since church workers depended on the colonial elite for their livelihood and for promotion to higher levels of the church hierarchy, they were understandably reluctant to alienate powerful miners and hacendados and normally maintained a respectful distance from the intimate details of running an estate.

On the other hand, the church took seriously its ministry to the souls of all the faithful. Catholic holy days, of which there might be more than 30 in a year, served as a brake on the patrón's tendency to keep the productive process going seven days a week. In addition, quite a number of priests employed their sermons to remind estate owners that concern for their eternal soul demanded gentler treatment for their workers. Whether this had any effect remains a subject for conjecture, but the church made an effort to remind authorities and elites of their Christian obligation to love their fellow man, and some parish priests took seriously their role of providing spiritual, and at times temporal, comfort to their flock. The next chapter will examine the role of the Catholic Church in shaping daily life and the place of various religious practices, both Christian and others, in people's efforts to find ways within and around their work lives to pursue their own interests and enjoy themselves. In spite of the demands placed upon working people in the colonial period, there was, after all, more to life than work.

NOTES

In addition to the works cited separately as sources of direct quotations and the authors' own archival research, the following sources have been drawn on for specific examples in this chapter: Arnold J. Bauer, *Goods, Power, History*; Kris Lane, "Africans and Natives in the Mines of Spanish America," in *Beyond Black and Red*, ed. Matthew Restall; James Lockhart and Stuart B. Schwartz, *Early Latin America*; Susan Migden Socolow, *The Women of Colonial Latin America*; William B. Taylor, *Drinking, Homicide, and Rebellion in Colonial Mexican Villages*. For full citations and other useful readings, see the annotated bibliography.

1. Quoted in Peter Bakewell, *Miners of the Red Mountain: Indian Labor in Potosí, 1545–1650* (Albuquerque: University of New Mexico Press, 1984), pp. 3–4.

2. Stuart B. Schwartz, *Sugar Plantations in the Formation of Brazilian Society: Bahia 1550–1835* (Cambridge: Cambridge University Press, 1985), p. 134.

3. Schwartz, *Sugar Plantations*, p. 291.

4. Schwartz, *Sugar Plantations*, p. 265.

5. Schwartz, *Sugar Plantations*, p. 290.

6. Schwartz, *Sugar Plantations*, pp. 322–23.

6

RELIGION AND POPULAR CULTURE

INTRODUCTION

Christianity Comes to the Americas

As the previous chapter makes clear, the desire for wealth drove Iberian expansion in the New World and, in the process, shaped the various labor systems that played such an important role in shaping the daily lives of the people of colonial Latin America. But the primary justification given for the establishment of Iberian rule in the New World was not economic. It was, instead, religious: the spread of the "one true faith" to formerly unknown peoples who had evidently never been exposed to it, and the consequent salvation of souls "hitherto lost," as Columbus put it in his first letter to Isabella and Ferdinand. The introduction and development of exclusively Christian forms of religious practice throughout the newly conquered lands soon emerged as a priority, with the church's influence gradually extended into daily life at all levels of colonial Latin American society. That influence was profound, and not merely in the spiritual realm. At the same time, the church never dominated the arena of popular culture, of which religious practices were an integral part, quite as fully as either religious or royal authorities might have preferred.

The early decades of Iberian expansion in the Americas coincided with a Western European religious crisis brought on by the sudden eruption of heretical Protestantism after 1517. The eventual response to this religious rebellion was the Roman Catholic Counter-Reformation, a process formalized during the Council of Trent (1545–1563) and intended to establish more effective and systematic regulation of the religious practices of ordinary people in the interests of rooting out heterodoxy. In propagating and defending its version of the faith, the Roman Catholic Church enjoyed the full support of royal government in territories under Iberian control. The church, in fact, was in an important sense an arm of the monarchy. From the late 15th century forward, both the Spanish and Portuguese crowns exercised ultimate authority over clerical appointments and other aspects of church administration in lands under their jurisdiction by means of a concession from the Vatican known in Spanish as the *patronato real* and in Portuguese as the *padroado real*. Another 15th-century innovation, the Holy Office of the Inquisition, was transferred across the Atlantic to New Spain and Peru in the 1570s, further contributing to the consolidation of a militant Catholicism throughout the overseas possessions.

Role of the Clergy

Two types of clergy performed the groundwork for the introduction and consolidation of the new faith: *regular* and *secular*. The first Catholic missionaries in the Americas came mostly from the regular clergy, members of monastic orders who lived according to the specific *regla*, or "rule," formulated by the founder of the order to which they belonged. At least some of these early missionaries appear to have been motivated by a near-ecstatic evangelical fervor, whose manifestations included intensive efforts to learn and communicate in native languages as well as a less admirable tendency to destroy material evidence of non-Christian religious practices and other aspects of precolonial societies. Franciscans and Dominicans were especially prominent among the missionaries working in early colonial Spanish America, while the Jesuit order, founded in 1534 during the initial wave of Counter-Reformation zeal, soon took precedence in Brazil.

The members of these and other orders often exhibited an independence that did not endear them to the church hierarchy, in part because they were not directly subject to the authority of the bishops and archbishops who were eventually named to posts in the

Americas and in part because of disagreements over policy and methods. As a result, following the Council of Trent, church authorities strove to enhance the presence and power of the secular clergy instead. The latter, made up mostly of ordinary parish priests, operated under direct episcopal authority and ultimately, in the Iberian world, the authority of the royal patron who made episcopal appointments. As of the late 16th century, the task assigned to this branch of the clergy in the Americas was the routinization of the church's, and by extension the crown's, authority in societies whose every member was by this time presumed to be subject to it.

The regular clergy did not easily cede its control over native parishioners, however, nor did its members submit willingly to episcopal dictates. As a result, parallel and sometimes feuding clerical administrations developed in many places. Nevertheless, in a larger sense, crown-supported Catholicism now dominated all areas under Iberian control. Whether a given layperson fell under the spiritual jurisdiction of the regular or the secular clergy, his or her life was firmly expected to be book-ended by the Catholic sacraments of baptism and the last rites, with the years in between marked insistently at regular intervals by the church's interventions in daily affairs, as at confession or Mass. The clergy also governed and closely scrutinized key life changes, notably marriage, which was for many people the most profound shift in formal social status they would undergo during their entire lives. And if marriage was far from a universal experience, unlike birth or death, the only major institutionalized alternative to it for both men and women was the taking of religious vows. These vows, incidentally, performed as vital a reproductive function in the eyes of the church as marital ones. After all, they alone created the new generations of celibate priests, friars, and nuns who would perpetuate the institution's central role in shaping colonial society.

Expansion of Church Wealth

In the process of organizing and managing an all-encompassing belief system, the church quickly grew to become the largest single holder of wealth in colonial Latin America. This development owed something to the generosity of its better-off members, but far more to a royal fiscal system under which it was allotted a share of native tribute payments as well as the proceeds of a mandatory tithe collected for the most part from Spaniards and other nonnatives. Moreover, both individual clerics and entire religious orders actively engaged in agricultural production and other wealth-generating activities. The Jesuits, for instance, developed a network of plantations and other rural enterprises that by the 18th century collectively employed thousands of native workers as well as the largest pool of enslaved laborers of African ancestry in Latin America. And they were not alone. Take the example of just one relatively marginal area of the Spanish American Empire: Guatemala. During the 1670s, the Mercedarian and Augustinian orders each owned a sugar plantation worked by dozens of slaves in the region just south of present-day Guatemala City. Yet these sugar-producing enterprises actually ranked among the smallest operated locally by religious orders. A nearby Jesuit plantation held more than a hundred enslaved residents, as did three of four Dominican-owned plantations scattered farther afield around the Guatemalan countryside.

A key consequence of the church's acquisition of great wealth was that it came to operate in effect as the primary lender in colonial society in the absence of a modern banking system. Carefully skirting its own proscriptions on the practice of usury, it circulated its liquid assets by means of creative financial instruments like the *censo al quitar,* which functioned like a modern property mortgage while avoiding the language of debt and interest. Representatives of the institution would "purchase" an annual income from a local notable, with that income conveniently equaling five percent of a lump sum transferred by the church to the "seller," who then guaranteed the income (we would say interest payment) with land or other pieces of property. The vast resources of the church, both financial and spiritual, also made it the most important patron of the fine arts in colonial society. In fact, a good portion of the wealth it collected was tied up more or less permanently in the fabulous baroque structures that came to dominate urban landscapes throughout Latin America, whose construction and ornamentation occupied all manner of artisans, painters, and sculptors, including many of racially mixed or non-European origins. Village churches, if modest by comparison with their urban counterparts, often represented an even greater investment of local resources on a per capita basis.

Church Power and Its Limits

Wealthy and powerful as it was, the church was not quite as omnipotent as is sometimes thought. Even its control over religious practices varied widely according to time, place, and social group, despite the desire of its representatives to extend their reach into as many corners of daily life as possible. At the height of its power, the mighty Inquisition lacked all jurisdiction over the native population of the Americas and often concerned itself less with uncovering witchcraft or other suspect ritual practices among the nonindigenous lower classes than with exposing *Judaizers*, or Jews masquerading as Christians, among the small colonial elite. Those unlucky enough to be targeted by the Inquisition suffered greatly, as when it terrorized small communities of Portuguese merchants who were in many cases "New Christian" descendants of *conversos:* individuals who had converted, at least publicly, from Judaism to Catholicism to avoid persecution and, ultimately, expulsion from the Iberian Peninsula. The allegedly guilty parties were identified by means of a lengthy, bureaucratic procedure that involved intensive interrogation and, where necessary, torture. They were then humiliated publicly in an *auto-da-fé*, a highly ritualized, penitential ceremony that culminated in the *relaxation*, or transferal, of the worst sinners to royal authorities for burning at the stake. Eleven convicted participants in a "Great Jewish Conspiracy" suffered the latter fate in Lima in 1639 at the end of a 4-year investigation that may have had as much to do with punishing affluent Portuguese outsiders for their wealth as correcting heresy. A similar campaign in Mexico City 10 years later resulted in 13 more executions.

Such spectacular events were in fact relatively rare in colonial Latin America. Death sentences for heresy or witchcraft were far more common in Europe. In any case, both the power and the weaknesses of the church are best revealed in its day-to-day efforts to sustain a monopoly on religious as well as broader cultural practices through such means as the Mass, confession, and the sponsorship of lay organizations and religious *fiestas*. The impact of these efforts was profound, although the church never entirely eliminated competition either from non-Christian religious traditions or from some of the more secular aspects of Iberian culture and in some cases found it easiest to accommodate them. A new challenge to the church's influence emerged during the later 18th century, when royal authorities seeking to curb clerical independence enacted a series of reforms aimed at strengthening the central authority of the crown through the application of Enlightenment principles of rational, secular governance. In the meantime, though, the institution and its representatives loomed large over daily life throughout a region that remains even now, at least nominally, the world's most staunchly Catholic one.

RELIGIOUS LIFE

Nuns, Priests, and Racial Hierarchy

In 1679, Juana Esperanza de San Alberto, born some eight decades earlier into a family of West Africa's Bran people, died in a convent of Discalced (barefoot) Carmelite nuns in Puebla, near Mexico City. Brought to New Spain aboard a slave ship as a child, and transferred soon after to the convent by her original owner, Juana had served the Carmelite nuns for some 68 years by the time of her death. According to one historian, during this lengthy period of service Juana had acquired such a reputation for saintly humility that news of her demise brought crowds of local residents to the convent's door to beg for whatever modest objects had been hers to use during her long life. The deceased's popularity was broad enough, moreover, to impel the city's leading officials to spare no expense in preparing for and staging a lavish public ceremony to commemorate her passing. Nor was Juana's fame a merely local phenomenon. Several years earlier, no less an eminence than the Marquesa de Mancera, wife of New Spain's viceroy at the time, had visited the convent looking to meet the virtuous black woman whose embodiment of Christian virtue had won such wide acclaim.

This somewhat unexpected story of an African-born popular saint in Mexico provides an entry point for elaborating on the church's place in colonial Latin American society. First, we should note that despite her great fame as an exemplary Christian, Juana Esperanza de San Alberto herself was evidently not granted permission to profess as a nun until she fell mortally ill. The church, in other words, like the larger society within which it operated, reflected Iberian efforts to maintain a racial hierarchy in the New World. In the old Inca capital of Cuzco, Peru, not even the wealthy *mestiza* descendants of Spanish conquerors or the daughters of the native Andean nobility escaped treatment as second-class residents in local convents. Indeed, a distinction was developed between higher-status nuns of the black veil and lower-status nuns of the white veil in part to exclude women of supposedly inferior ancestry from full participation in the life of those institutions.

Naturally, the slaves, native commoners, and poor free people of mixed ancestry who constituted the majority of the colonial population were even less welcome in the life of the religious professions, unless, like Juana, they entered that life in the service of more acceptable persons. In the late 18th century, nearly 300 years after the Spanish arrival, Indians made up no more than 5 percent of parish priests in central Mexico, and fewer still were of known mixed ancestry. This situation persisted in the face of an explicit 1771 recommendation by a council of Mexican bishops that one-third of seminary students in the region be drawn from either the native or *mestizo* populations, which together represented the vast majority of Mexico's inhabitants. Given that the bishops themselves continued regularly to characterize members of these groups as inferior even after making the recommendation to expand their numbers in the priesthood, it is no surprise that long-standing barriers to their participation were slow to fall.

The people who came to dominate the religious professions in colonial Latin America were members of the creole minority, supplemented by a steady if proportionally decreasing stream of clerics coming from the Iberian Peninsula or other parts of Europe. Thus the church was represented officially to a largely non-European membership in the Americas by priests, friars, and nuns who were mostly European in ancestry, if not birth. Even among creoles it was the wealthier and better-educated urban families who were most able to send their sons or daughters into the religious life, and certainly into its higher ranks. These individuals were often sustained comfortably in their chosen vocation with the support of family resources that might be used, for example, to establish an endowed chaplaincy to be filled by a son who had been designated for the priesthood. More striking were the lavish "dowries," often including servants and slaves, which accompanied young creole women entering prestigious convents like Cuzco's Santa Clara as "brides of Christ." These offerings of wealth secured a daughter's place among the convent elite at the very moment she was taking a solemn vow of poverty, not to mention access on favorable terms to the institution's credit services. To be sure, there were humble parish priests scraping together a paltry living under trying circumstances in remote and isolated rural communities, including some who won the affection of their parishioners by regularly foregoing the customary fees levied on everything from baptisms to masses for the dead. Even when protecting his charges from outside impositions, however, the church's local representative was almost always both better off and more European in origin than the vast majority of his flock.

A woman of Juana Esperanza de San Alberto's humble origins, already restricted by her gender, could in most cases hope for nothing better than incorporation into convent life as a *donada,* a lay sister who spent much of her time performing the manual labor that sustained the day-to-day existence of her superiors. Alternatively, she might enter a *beaterio,* an institution housing a community of laywomen (*beatas*) who were only permitted to take informal religious vows. Even if she won accolades for demonstrating one of the qualities most highly valued in the religious life, like the 17th-century mystic Ursula de Jesús, a Lima-based donada of African origins, she was not usually eligible for the sort of earthly reward to which higher-born individuals might aspire. After all, the humility demonstrated by Juana Esperanza de San Alberto earned the praise of her social superiors precisely because it set a good example for those people from her own background who were less willing than she was to accept what the authorities viewed as their proper place in society. If anything, lives like Juana's were celebrated as *exceptions* to the moral weakness alleged to be natural in people of non-European, particularly African, ancestry. Moreover, credit for these exceptional lives was not to be found in an examination of the character of the individuals who lived them. When José Gómez de la Parra, a Puebla cleric, published a history of the convent in which Juana had lived her life in 1703, he celebrated her remarkable virtue only to attribute it entirely to the beneficent Christian influence exercised on her by the nuns she had served nearly her entire life.

Religious Deviance and Punishment

For us, there are other conclusions to be drawn from Juana's story, and not only its usefulness as an illustration of the hierarchical nature of Catholicism as practiced in colonial Latin America. Buried in the account of her life and death are hints of the existence of popular forms of religious practice that may not have adhered very closely to the narrow orthodoxies of the Counter-Reformation Catholic Church. The report of a scramble at the convent door for her effects on news of her demise suggests a desire on the part of local people to acquire objects they viewed as sacred, either as souvenirs or to conduct unapproved rituals. The latter sort of activity, especially if it deviated enough from Christian practices to be labeled witchcraft, was associated most closely with women of either African or native origins. Given that native women were exempt from the Inquisition's jurisdiction, the tribunal particularly targeted black and *mulata* women for corrective measures, which might include whipping and imprisonment. But they were hardly the only ones to engage in forms of spirituality that were officially frowned upon. Even members of the Spanish elite consulted their Indian servants and African slaves for assistance with incantations or potions when they wished, for example, to obtain a favorable outcome in the realm of love.

Vexing as such practices were to the religious authorities, the persistence of what the church characterized as idolatrous activities in Indian communities was perhaps even more frustrating. While off-limits to the Inquisition owing to the church's conception of native peoples as naive and childlike, such behavior had been targeted for elimination by crusading priests and friars since the earliest years of the colonial era. An extended if never wholly successful campaign focused on ending indigenous Andean peoples' veneration of *huacas:* stones or other natural objects held to be sacred. Between 1640 and 1750, a series of investigations of idolatry were carried out in the archdiocese of Lima, resulting in "processions of shame," public floggings, and similar punishments for the alleged sorcerers and witches whom investigators claimed to have identified in native communities. Church authorities also attempted to neutralize the power that Andeans associated with the natural world by smashing sacred stones, erecting crosses in places that were considered to be especially holy, and otherwise endeavoring to erase the presence of non-Christian symbolism from the landscape. Popular religious enthusiasm, in other words, was always seen as a grave threat to the church when directed to unapproved ends. Clerics, therefore, were given the crucial task of channeling such enthusiasm into organizations and activities under the church's direct control.

Confraternities and Clerical Control over Lay Religious Practices

The church's efforts both to foster and to restrain the religious enthusiasms of its lay members in Spanish America are well illustrated in the history of the *cofradía,* or confraternity, a lay religious brotherhood known in Brazil as an *irmandad.* This institution developed quickly into the most popular authorized vehicle by which ordinary parishioners could participate in religious life after its introduction to Latin America in the late 16th century. Comprised in many cases of both men and women, cofradías were generally devoted to the veneration of a particular saint, governed by elected officers, and supervised closely, at least in theory, by both clerical and royal authorities. Each cofradía raised money from its members for a variety of purposes, among them helping to pay for the day-to-day expenses of celebrating the Mass, making ornamental or structural improvements to parish churches, and celebrating an annual festival in honor of its patron saint. The communal resources of the organization were often put to more secular uses as well. For example, in many cases they constituted a sort of mutual aid fund for members in distress.

Largely in the interest of producing more revenue to help pay their expenses, cofradías often ended up acquiring a good deal of property over time. By the mid-18th century, many of those operating in native villages in the diocese of Guadalajara, Mexico, owned between 150 and 500 head of livestock, along with some land on which to graze the animals. Such resources made these organizations and their treasuries an attractive target for parish priests and others in a supervisory position who were on the lookout for convenient sources of extra funds. In 1675, for example, members of a native cofradía in the village of Quezaltepeque, in present-day El Salvador, complained bitterly to the bishop of Guatemala that their priest was working with local nonnative residents to usurp control over the cofradía's lands and livestock. The bishop sided with the native cofradía in this case, although such victories were often temporary. Enterprising members of the clergy employed a wide variety of strategies in their efforts to derive benefits from the development of these lay associations. Some priests were accused of encouraging their proliferation simply to multiply the fees that could be collected from each cofradía operating within the boundaries of the parishes they served.

Nonetheless, many parishioners appear to have been intensely devoted to their cofradías. Since priests were often less zealous in overseeing the religious than the financial affairs of these associations, members frequently enjoyed a good deal of autonomy in their ritual practices. By most accounts, native peoples, as well as Africans and their descendants, were especially enthusiastic participants in the life of the cofradía. Many scholars emphasize the likelihood that the organization provided these groups with an ideal cover for the practice of non-Christian rituals. Church and royal authorities certainly feared this possibility and ordered close supervision of both native and black cofradías. The actual evidence for specific deviations from Catholic doctrine was often thin or ambiguous, however, given that departures from orthodoxy were unlikely to be widely advertised.

Whatever the motivation, participation by the non-European majority of the population in the organization and maintenance of cofradías was widespread. There were several hundred cofradías in existence in the largely native Valley of Mexico alone by the end of the 17th century. A little farther south, some indigenous villages in Guatemala had a dozen or more each by this time, to the great consternation of Spanish officials. A century later, in 1789, the 419 churches under the jurisdiction of the Archdiocese of Guatemala had a total of 1,982 such associations, an average of roughly 5 per church.

African and Native Confraternities

As might be expected in societies organized on the basis of racial distinctions, cofradías devoted to a particular patron were often split along ethnic or racial lines into two or more chapters. Thomas Gage, a renegade English Dominican friar who served as a parish priest in Guatemala during the 1630s, reported that the cofradía of Our Lady of the Rosary in the village of Mixco, located on the outskirts of the modern capital, had three separate branches "belonging unto the *Indians*, the *Spaniards*, and the *Black-mores*."[1] In larger urban centers like Lima or Salvador da Bahia, the existence of numerous lay brotherhoods—15 alone for people of African ancestry in Lima in 1619—allowed for the emergence of more narrowly defined memberships. During the early 17th century, when Portuguese merchants contracted by the Spanish crown sharply boosted the numbers of enslaved Africans transported to both Brazil and Spanish America, new arrivals contributed to the emergence of brotherhoods that were directly identified with particular African regions or "nations" (ethnicities), such as Angola or Mina. The emergence of these national brotherhoods may have owed a good deal to priests' efforts to counter the influence of councils the slaves organized among themselves to oversee the affairs of each nation among them, including the selection of a king and queen. Catholic brotherhoods' adaptation of such practices reveals that processes of cultural transmission, however powerful the church's influence may have been, flowed in more than one direction.

Although segregation among cofradías was not always as rigidly maintained as the above examples suggest, official backing for racial and ethnic distinctions had both symbolic and practical effects. For example, certain patrons came to be tightly associated with specific groups, a development that helped to shore up Iberian policies of social hierarchy. In Brazil, the prestigious Third Order of St. Francis sought to exclude all nonwhites from its ranks. Meanwhile, brotherhoods with memberships of African ancestry tended to be dedicated to Our Lady of the Rosary, like similar organizations founded earlier for Africans and their descendants in Portugal itself following the Portuguese initiation of Atlantic slave trading during the 1440s.

The precise meaning of Our Lady of the Rosary to Africans during this early era of the Atlantic slave trade is not very clear. The transfer to Africans of the cult of the prayer beads is explained at least in part by the simple fact that the Portuguese themselves were experiencing a surge in enthusiasm for the Rosary and its association with the mother of Christ during the 15th century and sought to impose that enthusiasm on the peoples they were then enslaving. Three centuries later, recent arrivals to Brazil from the Mina Coast, roughly speaking the southwestern portion of modern Nigeria, are said to have associated the Roman Catholic Church's Virgin of the Rosary with the Yoruba divinity Yemanjá. Such blending of Christianity with non-Christian African or native religious traditions, commonly known as *syncretism*, was a regular feature of religious practice throughout colonial Latin America.

Our Lady of the Rosary was also important in Spanish America as a patron for cofradías with memberships of African ancestry, although other patrons eventually gained many adherents as well. Notable among the other favorites were the Ethiopian Saint Iphigenia, Saint Nicholas of Tolentino, and Saint Benedict of Palermo (ca. 1524–1589), himself reputed to have been the Italian-born child of enslaved Africans. Benedict's cult appeared as early as 1602 in the Canary Islands, and just five years later in Venezuela. While it took another two centuries for the Vatican to canonize Benedict formally, his cult had soon spread among Africans and their descendants in the Andes, Mexico, and even Central America, where at least five cofradías dedicated to him were established in the territories of modern Guatemala and El Salvador between 1645 and 1679.

The clergy, of course, exercised a good deal of influence in the choice of patrons, and often for reasons other than those which motivated parishioners. For the church's representatives, careful selection of an individual saint or other object of devotion for a cofradía could produce substantial benefits beyond purely spiritual ones. In 18th-century central Mexico, the primary cofradía in native villages was frequently dedicated to the Holy Sacrament (i.e., the Eucharist) rather than to any individual saint with whom a particular community identified. The explanation for this naming practice appears to lie at least in part in the obligation of cofradías of this advocation to underwrite the expenses of celebrating Mass, whose most vital ritual was the transformation of bread and wine by means of the sacrament for which the cofradía was named. Given the variety of innovative methods by which clerical incomes were extracted from poor, rural communities, it is not hard to imagine that priests made the establishment of this cofradía a priority in each village they served as a means of reducing the likelihood they themselves might have to assume any of the costs of celebrating Mass.

Confraternities and Popular Culture

Whatever the reasons for their founding, cofradías tended to have a central place in the cultural life of the communities in which they functioned. As already noted, on at least some occasions they provided a vehicle for unauthorized practices, which might include the secret worship of idols behind altars or the clandestine performance of outlawed dances. Among the more public, Catholic-oriented forms of popular ritual undertaken by their members were elaborate processions mounted for religious festivals. These events, versions of which may still be seen in many places in Latin America today, often involved lavish expenditures on such things as the construction of floats on which to conduct images of a patron saint or other sacred items through the streets. Nowhere were these processions more elaborate than in the fabulous boomtowns of 18th-century Minas Gerais, Brazil. There, the initial flush of a gold- and diamond-mining industry produced riches in such abundance that brotherhoods made up of free people of African ancestry, and even slaves, were able to contribute to the staging of sumptuous public displays of religious devotion in communities like Vila Rica de Ouro Preto. An observer of a 1733 procession launched in celebration of the Eucharist in nearby Mariana reported that members of the local black irmandad of the Rosary made their way through the town robed in white silk and carrying images of their patron and other favored saints bedecked in rich cloths and adorned with gold and diamonds.

Such processions might be as striking for the behavior of the brotherhood members who took part in them as for the display of the resources they had succeeded in acquiring and converting into items which signified their religious devotion. Public self-flagellation as a form of penance for sins may be one of the more alien and remarkable of these behaviors for many present-day readers. Somber processions by crowds of penitents flogging themselves were a common response to epidemics or natural disasters, like the earthquakes that struck frequently along the geologically active zone that stretches from northern Mexico to the southern tip of Chile. In explaining this practice as it occurred among black cofradías in 17th-century Mexico, one historian has observed that "Baroque Catholicism valued humility and emphasized infliction of suffering on the self."[2] To the extent that these values, embodied in a popular saint like Juana Esperanza de San Alberto, were accepted by the marginalized majority, they lent support to the prevailing, hierarchical social order. Ironically, the agents of that order often viewed such activities on the part of nonwhite brotherhoods with a good deal of suspicion, unsure either of their true meaning or their propriety.

Late-Colonial Curbs on Confraternity Activities

By the late-colonial era, royal authorities intent on applying principles associated with Enlightenment thinking to the reorganization of society began suppressing the sort of irrational excess that expensive fiestas and rituals of self-flagellation were thought to represent. In part this was to be accomplished by reducing the large number of obligatory holy days on the calendar. By one estimate, there had been 95 of these, including Sundays, during the 16th century, even though employers often ignored them, as indicated in the discussion of working conditions on Brazilian sugar plantations in an earlier chapter. The church, nonetheless, had always fiercely defended the sanctity of these holidays against efforts to increase the number of legitimate working days, whether out of genuine concern for parishioners' souls or the health of its own revenue base, given that priests collected fees for their role in fiestas.

But late-colonial reformers, seeking above all to enhance economic productivity, set out both to rein in clerical independence and to eliminate the ills associated with fiesta days. On top of the obligatory elements of Catholic ritual, fiestas usually involved some combination of heavy alcohol consumption, dancing to exhaustion, gambling, and fireworks. Much to the chagrin of officials, such celebrations were extremely popular, at least in part because they provided a welcome break from daily routine. Efforts to interfere with them could spark serious protest. Between 1774 and 1782, the native residents of the village of Zapotlan El Grande, Guadalajara, rioted four times in response to their priest's largely unsuccessful attempts to eliminate, or at least tone down, various allegedly excessive aspects of celebrations for Holy Week and other religious holidays. Among the cited excesses was the construction by drunken work parties of lavish and allegedly wasteful flowered arches for fiesta days, a custom with roots in the ceremonial life of the Mexica and other Nahua peoples of precolonial central Mexico. Even worse was the *mojiganga*, a masked and evidently non-Christian ritual in which men dressed as bulls threatened, injured, and sometimes, or so the priest said, killed each other.

At the same time, some of the behaviors that now offended the authorities were also seen less favorably by previously marginalized groups whose members were striving for greater social respectability. Self-flagellation, for example, appears to have been deemphasized in Mexico's black cofradías during the 18th century, as free and often mixed-race, or *mulato*, descendants of enslaved African migrants worked to shed the marginal social status experienced by their ancestors, a task made easier by the marked decline locally in slavery's economic importance. This accommodation to Spanish colonial social norms evidently extended to gender relations as well. Whereas cofradías with memberships of African ancestry had been receptive to female leadership during the 17th century, an attitude possibly derived from African antecedents, such was no longer the case in the 18th century. This shift is especially striking in light of indications that women of African ancestry, along with their native counterparts, had long been more active participants in the day-to-day affairs of cofradías than Spanish women. Just south of Mexico, in early 17th-century Santiago de Guatemala, a number of free black women had left wills bequeathing a portion of their meager estates to cofradías in which they claimed membership and, in at least one case, a leadership role.

The supposedly enlightened attack on the ills associated with cofradías was in many ways an attack on the larger, religion-infused popular culture of which these organizations were an integral part. Indeed, dividing that culture neatly into religious and secular categories makes little sense for much of the colonial era, especially since the division itself is largely a legacy of Enlightenment-era thought. A lavish spectacle in celebration of a saint's day, attended by heavy bouts of drinking, was a leading source of entertainment for people from all levels of society in colonial Latin America, whether in a small village or a major urban center. The religious and nonreligious aspects of such an event are difficult to distinguish, as neither theatrical performance nor the use of alcohol were entirely devoid of religious significance. In fact, church officials tried hard to restrict the theater to employment as a form of Christian education while attempting at the same time to stamp out native peoples' precolonial understandings of alcohol's spiritual attributes. The actions of these officials presaged those carried out later by 18th-century reformers of popular culture who saw themselves as representative of Enlightenment-era progress.

DRINKING, PLAYS, AND OTHER ASPECTS OF POPULAR CULTURE

Alcohol and Its Many Uses

Drunkenness may appear to most present-day readers as a condition that ought to fall squarely into a discussion of secular popular culture. Yet for many native peoples of the pre-1492 Americas, the use of alcoholic beverages, not to mention substances like peyote in Mexico or the coca leaf in the Andes, had clear religious overtones. Of course, wine was a fundamental element in the central religious ritual of Iberian Catholics, the Mass, but not for its virtues as an intoxicant. By contrast, ritual drunkenness as a means of communing with the spirit world was evidently a feature of fertility ceremonies and other important events on the religious calendar of many precolonial societies in the Americas. Among the Mexica and other Nahua peoples of central Mexico, participation in these rites was often restricted by law to the nobility, with severe penalties mandated for unauthorized consumption of intoxicating beverages by anyone, whether noble or commoner. Nevertheless, in many areas, community-wide ritual drinking did take place, although again with the emphasis on inebriation as a collective, ceremonial act. The beverage at the center of these celebrations was *pulque*, a cloudy, weakly fermented liquid derived from the *maguey* cactus and the major source of intoxication in Mexico before the Spanish arrival. Whether consumed or sprinkled on a fire as an offering to the gods, it seems to have held near-sacred status in precolonial societies, as did the Andean corn beer to which Spaniards gave the Taíno name *chicha*.

The consumption of alcohol by natives, especially commoners, appears to have increased dramatically under colonial rule. Nevertheless, patterns of collective drinking continued in many ways to reflect an understanding of its social role that was at odds with that held by Iberians. For the latter, wine was an essential complement to food at mealtimes in addition to being indispensable for the celebration of the Catholic Mass, not to mention being in every way a superior product to pulque or chicha, just as supposedly civilized wheat bread and olive oil were in comparison with the despised Mesoamerican diet of corn, beans, and squash or the potato-based Andean cuisine. Beyond these status considerations, drinking to the point of losing control over one's senses was considered in any circumstance to be a sign of weakness or excess, and therefore uncivilized by definition. "God created wine for the enjoyment of mankind, not for drunkenness," thundered one friar living in 17th-century Mexico City, expressing a sentiment common enough to make "drunkard" a highly offensive insult among his fellow Spaniards there.[3] Even other Europeans were alleged to lack proper self-control in their drinking habits, let alone the local native peoples whose patterns of alcohol use were viewed as nothing short of barbaric by their alien rulers.

Any consideration of inebriation as a fundamental aspect of spiritual life was entirely unacceptable, not to say incomprehensible, to a Catholic priest watching raucous native celebrations of a saint's day. For many such priests, the collective drunkenness of native parishioners only served as further proof of their irredeemably sinful natures. The misinterpretation of festive drinking by ethnocentric Europeans does not, however, disguise the fact that a good deal of alcohol consumption occurred among native peoples for reasons apparently unrelated to any formal ritual practice and more probably reflecting the ills of conquest. One disapproving cleric reported in the late 17th century that in the native villages surrounding the Valley of Mexico's sanctuary of Churubusco, "hundreds of men are continually drunk."[4] The social ills produced by the increase in nonfestive alcohol use were often profound, even if Spanish analysis of those ills reflected the typical attitudes of ruling elites toward the ruled.

Producing and Consuming Alcohol

The factors contributing most heavily to behavior that Spaniards characterized as barbaric included the establishment, with royal support, of an official network of roadside taverns. In addition to the native pulque, these establishments served wine and distilled liquors like brandy, all of them previously unknown to Mexico's native peoples. Revenue-starved royal officials also eagerly encouraged the expansion of alcohol production, finding it a reliable source of taxation with which to fund public works projects. Nor was there a shortage of willing producers among the Spanish population; some of the wealthiest families in Mexico held substantial investments in the production of pulque, a drink they generally professed to despise as Indian and therefore barbaric. As of the 1650s, this beverage was available for consumption in some 212 *pulquerías* in the capital alone.

By the late colonial era, many Mexican villages had a dozen or more drinking establishments. In general, only one or two were true taverns with the rest consisting of little more than private doorways from which a small-scale entrepreneur, in most cases a woman and frequently a widow, dispensed pulque to passersby from a jug in return for cash or payment in kind. At the same time, the collective, ceremonial aspects of pulque consumption had not been entirely forgotten by native peoples, especially in rural areas. Precolonial prohibitions on solitary drinking or the participation of women and children in ritual drunkenness on festival days continued to inform community norms regarding the proper social uses of alcohol, if not necessarily actual behavior.

In Mexico City, by contrast, the alleged excesses of urban commoners so alarmed Enlightenment-era bureaucrats that they introduced a series of regulations aimed at eliminating pulquerías altogether. These establishments, encouraged in earlier times, now came to be viewed by the authorities primarily as potential incubators of rebellion rather than reliable generators of revenue. Only 35 were left in existence by 1793, at least officially. The violence often associated with such establishments was always of most concern to the colonial elite when it occurred in an important urban center, whether Mexico City or faraway Buenos Aires, an up-and-coming port city in the late 18th century where common people gathered in neighborhood shops known as *pulperías* to drink cheap brandy and socialize. Violence aside, from the perspective of the urban poor there were few other places in which to find respite from a daily struggle for survival that regularly brought them grief at the hands of the same social superiors who were so intent on restricting their pleasures for their own good.

Power and the Theater

Aside from alcohol consumption, other diversions from the mundane aspects of colonial life did exist, notably the theater in its various manifestations. The power of theatrical performance, whether understood in a narrow, formal sense or broadly enough to encompass cofradía processions and similar popular activities, was such that control over it was considered vital by both religious and royal authorities. Indeed, colonial theater originated at least partially in the presentation of religious plays by 16th-century clerics as a fundamental element in their efforts to Christianize the native peoples of the Americas. Like painting, sculpture, and music in churches, such plays were employed as a means of educating the targets of conversion in key details of the new faith that they were expected to accept.

Native Peoples and Colonial Theater

The inhabitants of what we refer to as the Aztec and Inca empires already had their own traditions of grand public spectacles when Spaniards arrived. These traditions may have made them especially receptive to the new Christian theater, although probably as much for its value as entertainment as for the intended religious instruction. Eventually, saint's day festivals and other Catholic celebrations tended to feature native actors presenting their own versions of theatrical work. A performance still put on in places like Guatemala, with its large Maya population, is a stylized rendition of the conquest titled *moros y cristianos* and set ostensibly in the pre-1492 Iberian Peninsula with its conflict between Moors and Christians. Another theatrical practice has persisted in Peru, a ritual conflict called *tinku*, rooted in precolonial fertility rites as well as historical conflict both within and between local native communities. Tinku generally took place during the days immediately preceding Ash Wednesday and the beginning of Lent and often involved actual violence and even death. The mix of imported and native elements in shaping such theatrical practices is not easy to judge; indeed, their meaning is rarely entirely obvious to observers or even, perhaps, many of the participants. And if Catholicism clearly influenced their development, the impact was not necessarily the one intended by the church.

Processions and Playhouses

The introduction of Christian-themed plays by friars in early colonial Spanish America was followed quite quickly by the emergence of a more secular European variant of theatrical performance, despite strong reservations on the part of many clerics and the imposition of strict censorship by the Inquisition after 1574. This development owed a good deal to the desire of Spanish immigrants to reproduce the rich theatrical tradition of their homeland, just entering what would come to be known as its golden age. Public plays were a popular feature of the grand civic festivals mounted on the arrival of a new viceroy, for example, when the urban masses thronged the streets to enjoy grand processions and a series of popular entertainments. Prominent among the latter was the *mascarada*, a lively parade through the streets by masked performers representing well-known personages from the realms of myth or history, as well as characters from popular literary works. In 1621, one such event in Mexico City featured the leading figures from *Don Quixote*, Miguel de Cervantes's great 1605 novel. Thus were crowds made up largely, no doubt, of illiterate individuals introduced to Sancho Panza and other characters from a book published not long before on the other side of the ocean, only to make the story their own in ways we can only guess at.

Mascaradas focusing on local themes often presented didactic interpretations of Mexican history and culture. According to the observations of one of Mexico's leading 17th-century scholars, Carlos de Sigüenza y Góngora, a 1680 mascarada in the town of Querétaro unfolded in four distinct sections that added up to a version of the Spanish conquest as Mexico's salvation. First came "a disorganized band of wild Chichimeca Indians who swarmed about the thoroughfares garbed in the very minimum that decency allows," which was followed by an evidently more disciplined, and properly attired, creole militia unit. The third section involved a procession of actors representing precolonial Aztec and other native monarchs, who prepared the way for the arrival of a figure meant to be Charles V, Holy Roman emperor and king of Spain when Cortés conquered Tenochtitlán. Last came a float carrying an image of the Virgin of Guadalupe, whose reported appearance to a native man named Juan Diego in 1531 had recently begun to be celebrated widely by Mexican creoles after the story's publication in the 1640s. The accompaniment of the float by "a lovely child garbed in the native raiment of the Indians" and kneeling at the foot of the Virgin's throne capped off a performance that was clearly intended to emphasize the triumph of both the church and the Spanish crown over indigenous Mexico.[5]

A more exclusive variety of theatrical performance was the formal play presented in an enclosed space designed for that purpose.

Members of the colonial elite had been accustomed to taking in such entertainment in the privacy of the viceregal palace or a similar venue since the early colonial era. By the late 16th century, playhouses known as *corrales*, privately owned and usually very basic in their amenities, were offering such performances to the wider public in Mexico City as well. The survival of these private playhouses was always precarious, however, as the crown had granted a formal monopoly on this type of performance to an officially licensed theater that began operating in the city's Royal Indian Hospital during the 1560s. A similar, officially sanctioned theater opened in Lima in 1601, in the Royal Hospital of San Andrés.

Audience Expectations and Public Morality

Audience expectations of the theater appear to have varied greatly by social condition, especially in public circumstances where people from more than one level of society were thrown together. In the late 18th century, elite patrons of Mexico City's New Coliseum, opened in 1753 as the last in a series of buildings constructed to house the performances allowed under the Royal Indian Hospital's license, complained frequently about the boisterous behavior exhibited by audience members from the city's poor, mostly *casta* majority. The latter, congregated in the cheap seats, talked and ate during performances, called out to the actors, and loudly applauded a variety of between-acts dances and other short entertainments that were often criticized instead by the authorities and the "better" sort of patron as lewd or otherwise morally suspect. After the play was finished, the actors, poorly paid for the most part, often accompanied the lower-class audience members to a nearby alley where the festivities were renewed through the presentation of crowd-pleasing puppet shows. These gatherings provided a little more income for members of the performing classes and an even less restrained ambience for audiences uninterested in the supposedly more refined pleasures of the upper classes.

Like 16th-century missionaries, appalled advocates of 18th-century Enlightenment values sought to transform the theater into a form of moral education for the common people. The emphasis of that education was shifted somewhat, however, from a focus on religious doctrine to principles associated by their advocates with reason and order. To this effect, New Spain's Theater Regulations of 1786, implemented by one noted proponent of these principles, Viceroy Bernardo de Gálvez, *strengthened* existing forms of censorship, sharply restricted the apparel and behavior that actresses in particular could exhibit on the stage, and prescribed a standardized set of penalties (up to and including eight days' imprisonment!) for audience members found guilty of creating "disorder." Gálvez also had his perspective on the theater's purpose inscribed on the curtain of the New Coliseum, for the benefit of all audience members. It ran as follows:

Drama is my name
and my duty is to correct mankind
in the exercise of my profession
friend of virtue, enemy of vice.[6]

As in the crackdown on the social ills associated with religious festivals and pulquerías, the marginalized segments of society bore the brunt of theater reforms intended to improve them. Women, for example, had been gradually increasing their participation in the theatrical world during the 17th and early 18th centuries, despite church disapproval, to the extent that several were able to assume posts as directors in New Spain. But the last of them, María Ordóñez, was eventually locked up for years in a series of *casas de recogimiento*, institutions in which women were sequestered for various reasons including "moral lapses." When Ordóñez finally won release in 1794, it was only with the warning that the slightest misstep in conduct would result in her immediate reincarceration.

DEATH, DYING, AND CULTURAL CONFLICT

The contest between colonial authorities, whether religious or secular, and colonial subjects to define the nature and parameters of daily cultural practice culminated in the rituals associated with the end of life. For its part, the church had a key stake in the issue, given its fundamental concern with determining the manner in which all significant life passages were observed. As with two other important transitions, birth and marriage, a Roman Catholic priest was to administer a sacrament—in this case extreme unction, also known as the last rites—to all individuals experiencing the transition. The ceremony involved anointment of the dying person's sensory organs with holy oil, accompanied by petitions offered on his or her behalf, and was intended as a last cleansing of sins in preparation for final judgment in the afterlife. Once death had taken place, a funeral mass and burial of the corpse, again in accordance with the church's precisely scripted rituals, was to follow shortly.

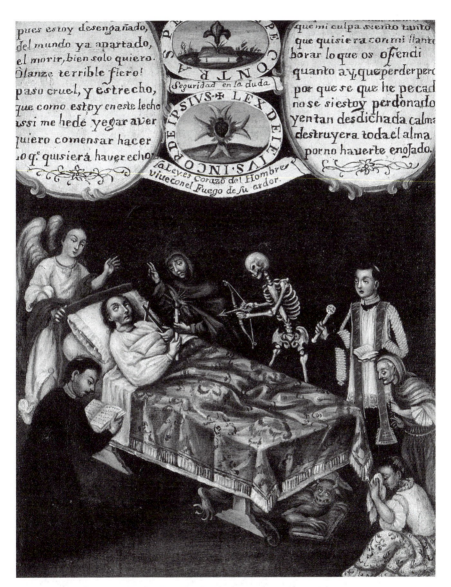

pues estoy desengañado,
del mundo ya apartado,
el morir, bien solo quiero.
Olanze terrible fiero!
pasu cruel, y estrecho,
que como estoy en este lecho
ussi me hede yegar aver
quiero comensar hacer
lo q.e quisiera haver echo.

que mi culpa siento tanto
que quisiera con mi llanto
borar lo que os offendi
quanto ay, que perder perc
por que se que he pecad
no se si estoy perdonado
y en tan desdichada calm[
destruyera toda el alma
por no hauerte enojado.

Seguridad en la duda

IPSIVS ✠ LEX DEI E[
 a Ley, es Corazó del Hombre
 viue con el Fuego de su ardor.

This 18th-century Catholic death-bed manuscript from Mexico reminds
the churchgoer that a sinner cannot enter heaven. Part of the inscription
tells us that the dying man knows he has sinned and does not know if
he is pardoned. "I want to begin to do what I wish I had done," he says.
But it may be too late; notice the devil waiting under the bed for his prey.
(The Granger Collection, New York)

As we have already seen, however, unorthodox practices frequently escaped the efforts of the authorities to control them, sparking both repression of and accommodation to the popular will on the part of ruling sectors interested in maintaining social control as best as they could. Nowhere, perhaps, was this tension more evident than in the beliefs and practices associated with death and dying. All societies have developed powerful ideas about proper disposal of the dead, and most have also assumed the existence of an afterlife and the need to mediate the relationship between the living and the dead in one way or another. The native societies encountered by the Iberians in the New World were no exception, nor were the African ones from which involuntary migrants were forcibly transported to the Americas. The Spanish and Portuguese themselves, especially the majority of commoners, held on to and acted on many notions regarding the dead and the spirit world that were distinctly at odds with Christian doctrine. Sometimes the church was able to suppress such notions, but it was forced to tolerate others more or less openly, seeing them as hopelessly ineradicable remnants of what it characterized as pagan superstition.

Popular Celebrations of the Dead

The present-day Mexican celebration of the Day of the Dead provides one example of the persistence in Latin America of rituals surrounding death and dying that do not conform to the beliefs the church first began imposing five centuries ago. A crucial aspect of the celebration involves treks to the graves of relatives in local cemeteries by families laden with food and drink to be shared with the deceased. The ritual takes place as the Christian calendar is marking All Saints' Day and then All Souls' Day on November 1–2, a clear sign of the church's influence. Nevertheless, many of its primary elements reflect non-Christian understandings of communion with the spirit world.

During the colonial era, Mexican priests regularly took note of the beliefs and practices that continue to inform the Day of the Dead festival, criticizing them but also interpreting them in a manner that made them appear compatible with Christianity, a clear sign of resignation in the face of traditions too strong to be eliminated. The long-standing appeal of All Souls' Day to Mexico's native peoples is indicated in a 1766 guide for priests in the diocese of Puebla. The guide described the preparations made by local Indians as the holiday approached: sweeping the streets and patios of their houses and setting out fruit and bread for the return of deceased relatives. Other unorthodox rituals reported in the guide included the practice of leaving the clothing of deceased individuals at the place of death for a week and burying corpses with sandals. Indeed, the list of items buried with a dead relative might include provisions, money, and even farm implements. While the handbook expressed disapproval of such acts, the priests who read it were encouraged not to view them as fundamentally opposed to the church's teachings, in other words not to concern themselves too greatly with trying to eliminate them.

Rituals of a similar nature were reportedly practiced by people of African origins in Brazil. A bishop visiting Minas Gerais in 1726 described members of the local enslaved population "singing and playing instruments for their dead" and "getting together in stores where they bought various food and drinks, which after they ate they threw into the grave."[7] Once again, practices that proved impossible to root out were accommodated by the church, evident in the fact that some Catholic brotherhoods of the Rosary in Brazil continue to incorporate drumming and songs associated with the rituals of enslaved Africans into burial rites for deceased members. There were, nevertheless, distinct limits to the church's strategy of tolerance, as made clear in the earlier discussion of the campaign to eradicate idolatry in the Andes. Church authorities viewed late-colonial reports that native peoples in a few central Mexican villages were throwing their dead down ravines to be devoured by wild animals as nothing other than proof of their incorrigibly evil natures, not to mention the devil's ongoing efforts to rob the church of the souls its approved rituals were meant to save.

Royal officials, meanwhile, were sometimes alarmed even by the sort of attention paid by the public to properly Catholic observances of death and burial. The Spanish crown issued decrees against extravagance in the purchase of mourning clothes, considered by many Spaniards to be an essential component of their wardrobe and an important gauge of status. The same crown was disturbed by reports of excessive popular enthusiasm for the processions and other rituals that attended a corpse as it was being conducted to its final resting place; therefore, the crown attempted to ban public displays of mourning unless the social status of the deceased individual was sufficiently grand as to warrant it. As with many other aspects of popular culture, the attitudes of the

An 1811 engraving of a funeral rite attributed
to one of the Tupi-Guaraní peoples living
along the Orinoco River in the Amazon basin.
Some indigenous people practiced rites in
which the flesh was removed from the skel-
eton and the bones were used for ritual orna-
ments. (The Art Archive / Bibliothèque des
Arts Décoratifs Paris / Gianni Dagli Orti)

authorities toward the ritualized behaviors surrounding processes
of death and dying seem to have been shaped primarily by the
implications of those behaviors for the maintenance of the prevailing colonial order.

CONCLUSION

In colonial Latin America, both religious and royal authorities
believed they had not only the right but the duty to legislate morality and restrain what they viewed as the excesses of a flourishing
popular culture. Somewhat ironically, the church at the same time
sponsored some of the most important vehicles for those alleged

excesses, such as the cofradía. This seeming contradiction was arguably the logical consequence of the church's efforts to control all forms of cultural expression. Pushed to respond to the spiritual or other enthusiasms of an exploited and potentially restive majority, it sought both to encourage those enthusiasms and to contain them within acceptable boundaries.

At the same time, a major obstacle to the successful transfer of a narrowly Iberian Catholic cultural model to the Americas was the diversity of the populations over which the Spanish and Portuguese ruled. It is not surprising that colonial authorities were unable to impose cultural uniformity with anything approaching complete success on societies that forced together peoples of widely varying indigenous, European, and African backgrounds. The yawning social and economic gap between a tiny elite of wealthy *peninsulares* and creoles, on the one hand, and a poor, largely non-European majority, on the other, also contributed to the persistence of distinctive cultural practices among different sectors of the population. Each of those sectors experienced the profound impact of Iberian Catholic rule in its own way. The next chapter shifts the angle from which to view the significance of that form of rule for colonial daily life, bringing into focus Spanish and Portuguese administrative strategies in the Americas and popular responses to those strategies, both peaceful and violent.

NOTES

In addition to the works cited separately as sources of direct quotations and the authors' own archival research, the following books have been drawn on for specific examples in this chapter: Arnold J. Bauer, *Goods, Power, History*; Joan Cameron Bristol, *Christians, Blasphemers and Witches*; William B. Taylor, *Magistrates of the Sacred*. For full citations and other useful readings, see the annotated bibliography.

1. Thomas Gage, *The English-American his Travail by Sea and Land: Or A New Survey of the West-India's* (London: R. Cotes, 1648), p. 161.
2. Nicole von Germeten, *Black Blood Brothers: Confraternities and Social Mobility for Afro-Mexicans* (Gainesville: University Press of Florida, 2006), p. 23.
3. Quoted in William B. Taylor, *Drinking, Homicide, and Rebellion in Colonial Mexican Villages* (Stanford, Calif.: Stanford University Press, 1979), p. 41.
4. Ibid., p. 37.
5. Quotations from Irving A. Leonard, *Baroque Times in Old Mexico* (Ann Arbor: University of Michigan Press, 1959), pp. 125–26, 128.

6. Quoted in Juan Pedro Viqueira Albán, *Propriety and Permissiveness in Bourbon Mexico*, trans. Sonya Lipsett-Rivera and Sergio Rivera Ayala (Wilmington, Del.: Scholarly Resources, 1999), p. 46.

7. Quoted in Elizabeth W. Kiddy, *Blacks of the Rosary: Memory and History in Minas Gerais, Brazil* (University Park: Pennsylvania State Press, 2005), p. 99.

7

GOVERNMENT, POLITICAL LIFE, AND REBELLION

INTRODUCTION

The imposition of forced labor systems, as well as alien religious and cultural norms, on native peoples and unwilling African migrants in the Americas was accomplished under the umbrella of a royal administrative structure created to manifest the will of the king in the actions of even the most petty local official. Laws rapidly proliferated; when the Spanish crown collected the extensive and sometimes contradictory legislation it had emitted over nearly two centuries in a single publication in 1681, the resulting *Recopilación de leyes de los reynos de las Indias* ran to several thousand regulations. But the relationship between law and daily life was not one-to-one in either Spanish America or Brazil. Royal officials often protected their own vested interests by expressing what they claimed was the king's will in ways that were markedly at odds with the evident intent of the royal decree. Such legal flexibility helps to explain the fact that colonial rule persisted for three long centuries in Latin America. Indeed, overt resistance rarely threatened the colonial system during most of this period, not because conflict was absent but because it was usually contained by some combination of official willingness to accommodate popular grievances and the tendency of marginalized people to "work the system" to their "minimum disadvantage" more or less peacefully, in the formulation of one eminent historian.[1] Nonetheless, the threat of violence on the part of both rulers and ruled was never entirely absent. This chapter examines colonial rule and popular responses to it, up to and including armed revolt and repression.

COMPONENTS OF THE SYSTEM

Spanish American Administrative Networks

Royal Government

The formal outlines of long-term Spanish rule in the Americas began to emerge three decades after Columbus arrived in the Caribbean. Following the conquest of Tenochtitlán, capital of the Aztec Empire, in 1521, the Spanish crown established a Council of the Indies to oversee the affairs of overseas realms that suddenly appeared worthy of sustained attention. The addition of Peru a decade later, followed soon after by the discovery of substantial deposits of silver in both of these new territorial acquisitions, was accompanied by the definitive withdrawal of administrative concessions to *adelantados,* leaders of conquistador bands. Spain's American possessions were now divided into two vast administrative networks known as the viceroyalties of New Spain and Peru, centered, respectively, on Mexico City and Lima. Two more viceroyalties were created in the 18th century, New Granada and La Plata, each representing territories formerly under Lima's control and newly dynamic in an economic sense. Each of these administrative entities was governed by a viceroy sent from Spain to represent the king both practically and symbolically. Smaller administrative regions called *audiencias,* governed by high courts known by the same name, enjoyed a good deal of autonomy from viceregal authority in places like Central America and Chile. Everywhere, nevertheless, power derived ultimately from the king and his Council of the Indies back in Spain.

But distance and extended travel times often left effective decision making in the hands of officials on the ground in the Americas, who might set aside decrees they found inconvenient to enforce. This bureaucratic stonewalling occurred frequently enough to be immortalized in the Spanish phrase *obedezco pero no cumplo* (literally "I obey but I do not fulfill/carry out"), which combined a declaration of ultimate loyalty to the crown with a refusal to implement a particular royal dictate deemed by local authorities to be unworkable and, therefore, contrary to the crown's true interests. Agents of the crown received pitifully low salaries and had to purchase their offices at great cost, an innovation necessitated by the profligate ways of King Philip II (1556–1598), whose government found itself increasingly strapped for cash. It may be understandable therefore that government bureaucrats viewed the procurement of a respectable income as a higher priority than the dispensing of impartial royal justice. The administrative post best exemplifying the conflicts of interest plaguing the system was that of the *corregidor,* a regional administrator who was directly responsible for translating the laws of Spain into the lives of most local people. Designated as "protector" of the native population and upholder of the vast legislation intended to help him in that task, the corregidor generally derived substantial benefits, financial or otherwise, by doing precisely the opposite.

Administering Native Communities

In governing the native population, the corregidor was often assisted by descendants of precolonial nobilities who had managed to sustain their leadership roles, if only at the local level, through accommodation to Spanish rule. Known in New Spain as *caciques,* a term of Caribbean origin, and in Peru as *kurakas,* these native lords, of which there were still more than 2,000 in the Andes alone in 1754, had to balance Spanish demands with the needs of their own people. They were expected above all to ensure the fulfillment of the tribute and labor obligations that were crucial to sustaining the colonial economy. Not surprisingly, members of the colonial-era native nobility were most likely to survive and even prosper in their new role by pleasing their Spanish superiors. In doing so, however, they often became the primary targets of their own communities' complaints. This circumstance was of further benefit to Spaniards, who thereby managed to displace local discontent with colonial rule onto the natives' own representatives. And should these individuals choose instead to resist the dictates of Spanish officials, or simply be too slow to fulfill them, they might be corrected with a public whipping or a stint in the local jail, if not replaced entirely.

Another native political institution that persisted well into the colonial era, although again in modified form, was a local political unit known as the *calpulli* in central Mexico, the *chinamit* in highland Guatemala, and the *ayllu* in the Andes. This unit, the basic building block of precolonial political organization, had its origins in clan-based control over specific lands or other resources wherein loyal clan members were assigned use but not ownership rights over a portion of those resources. While this form of political organization varied in its characteristics and operation from place to place, it continued to provide a strong sense of local community identity in addition to serving as a vehicle for the administration and distribution of privileges and obligations relating to labor, land, and tribute. In general, this clan-oriented sense of political organization posed little threat to the larger colonial order. Groups possessing it were as likely to engage in conflict with neighboring native groups as with Spaniards over, say, access to land or water. In fact, colonial authorities had as much to gain as to fear from native peoples who possessed a strong sense of their own distinctiveness, although only as long as that sense of distinct identity remained locally focused, dividing rather than uniting the larger indigenous population.

Some of the deepest divisions within the native population developed not between different ayllus or calpullis but between *originarios* (original members of local communities) and *forasteros* (outsiders). The latter were individuals who had fled their own villages for good, often out of a desire to escape onerous tribute or labor obligations. They were frequently blamed for all manner of crime or other social problems in the communities where they took up residence. The real threat their existence posed to the traditional social order was both less obvious and more profound. By escaping burdensome obligations in their home villages, they were also cut off from access to village lands and other benefits of communal organization. In order to survive, they had to become wage laborers for Spaniards or in some other way fill new occupational niches created by the economic changes that accompanied colonialism. As such, they embodied the colonial economy's disruption of traditional divisions based on clan, community, or ethnicity.

The Cabildo and Town Planning

A different local political institution, this one of Spanish origins, operated parallel to native-based forms of administration in indigenous villages: the *cabildo* (municipal council). This institution also existed in nonnative towns and cities, where it was generally the key organ of creole participation in colonial government. For Spaniards, urban living was a hallmark of civilization. Every one of the more than 900 towns and cities they founded in the Americas between 1492 and 1809—some, like Lima, from scratch and others, like Mexico City, on the foundations of existing native settlements—

required an orderly government to complement the spatial order imposed on the colonial landscape by means of a new, "checkerboard" form of city planning. That plan saw neighborhoods of decreasing prestige radiating outward from a main square where Spanish power was visibly represented in both a religious and a secular sense by a church and administrative structures of a level of grandeur appropriate to the community's prestige in the larger world.

The cabildos charged with governance of these carefully laid out communities were each staffed by several *regidores* (municipal councillors) and presided over by two *alcaldes* (municipal administrators). In theory, these posts turned over regularly, although they were generally monopolized by local notables, whose houses, in accordance with the colonial urban plan, tended to be located just off the main square. Despite the local prominence of its members, the cabildo was in fact severely limited in its power, not to mention far from democratic. Nevertheless, it was the only form of local political representation available in nonnative communities. An important consequence of this circumstance was that the cabildo became the focal point for creole political ambitions in the early 19th century once Spain's control over its mainland American possessions began to crumble in the wake of Napoleon's 1807 invasion of the Iberian Peninsula. That story is told in the book's conclusion.

Colonial Administration in Brazil

In Brazil, the *engenho* was in many ways a more crucial center of power than the town, at least prior to the 18th-century urban explosion in the mining fields of Minas Gerais. Moreover, as on the peripheries of the Spanish Empire, like northern Mexico or Chile, there was no significant stratum of native villages organized to provide labor and tribute to imperial elites, as in New Spain and Peru. By the early 17th century, as native slavery declined in importance on Brazilian sugar plantations and the Jesuit system of *aldeias* mostly disappeared, the surviving, largely semisedentary native population tended to live beyond the boundaries of Portuguese coastal society. Nevertheless, at the latter's margins, in places like the inland southern settlement of São Paulo, small numbers of people of mixed Portuguese and indigenous ancestry known as *mamelucos* acted effectively to extend European control into the interior. Although their culture was often more native than Iberian in origins, the primary economic activity of the *Paulista* mamelucos was the supply of native slaves to the coast. Despite the early shift to African labor, demand for native slaves never disappeared, and Paulista and other slave-hunting canoemen known as *bandeirantes* pursued them ever farther up Brazil's vast network of inland waterways in great expeditions called *monsoons*. Somewhat ironically, it was these explorers of mixed ancestry who extended the reach of Portuguese colonial administration, and "European discovery," far into the South American interior.

Royal Government in Brazil

As of 1549, Brazil had a formal system of royal government, eventually directed by an Overseas Council in Lisbon, which bore many similarities to the one existing in Spanish America. It was centered for two centuries in Salvador da Bahia before being moved south in 1763 to Rio de Janeiro, coastal outlet for the goldfields of Minas Gerais, another of the fruits of inland exploration by Paulista bandeirantes. Meanwhile, the vast Amazonian region in the north first gained recognition as deserving of special administrative attention with the creation of a separate *Estado do Maranhão*, as opposed to the *Estado do Brasil*, as early as 1621. These administrative regions were subdivided into smaller territories known as captaincies, which technically fell under the jurisdiction of a royal governor, later a viceroy, in Salvador. In practice, they were governed by captains-general, mostly army officers, who often demonstrated a good deal of independence from central control.

Municipal Government in Brazil

At the municipal level, the *senado da câmara* was the rough equivalent of the Spanish American cabildo. It included a couple of distinctive posts: a *juiz de fora*, a professional and presumably disinterested royal magistrate; and a *juiz do povo*, charged with representing the interests of artisans and other common folk. The post of juiz do povo was abolished in the early 18th century, at least in Salvador, where the sugar planters who dominated the city council successfully appealed for its elimination. It seems they had been unable to neutralize opposition to their interests by means of the bribes and other inducements regularly employed by the wealthy and powerful in colonial Latin America in order to secure the cooperation of officials at all levels. An alternative solution, evidently, was to get rid of the post altogether.

NEGOTIATING THE SYSTEM

Law and Community Relations in Spanish America

One way or another, a privileged elite of largely European ancestry held most of the cards in the struggle over the terms of day-to-day existence that unfolded under the umbrella of the administrative systems outlined above. The Iberian monarchies, if sometimes genuinely concerned to protect their subjects in the Americas in accordance with what they took to be their Christian duty, were almost entirely dependent on the colonists of Iberian origins to procure the fruits of empire. This objective tended to overrule all others. Specifically, the drive to enhance royal revenues provided significant leverage to the wealthier and more European sector whose financial assistance was so badly needed. For example, the Spanish crown decided to allow for the regularization of land titles after 1591 through a process known as *composición de tierras*, which enabled Spanish colonists to obtain legal cover for their prior infringement on the communal lands of native villages in return for payment of a fee. Not surprisingly, this process encouraged further encroachment on village lands, despite numerous laws against such actions. The beneficiaries of the first round of composición correctly anticipated that the crown would need their money again, and more rounds soon followed.

Native communities did not simply accept the loss of lands or other resources without responding, however. They fought to preserve as much control as possible over village property, although not in most cases by means of the most obvious form of resistance (i.e., violence). Instead, they tended to rely on the law, quickly adapting to the Spanish legal system and learning to exploit the protections it offered them as best they could, even if the protections that existed on paper often failed to operate in practice. By challenging Spaniards and their descendants in court, native communities placed royal officials under moral pressure to demonstrate the legitimacy and fairness of the Spanish justice system. This course of action was in general not only far safer but also more likely to result in at least partial success than resorting to violence or other extralegal forms of resistance that were certain to provoke a repressive response from colonial authorities.

The experience of an ayllu in the Peruvian village of Acopia, near Cuzco, provides us with an example. In 1718, the ayllu's leaders succeeded in obtaining a legal order for the return of lands taken by the Spanish owner of a neighboring hacienda, doña Ursula

Velásquez. Such decisions were not as unusual as might be imagined. Spaniards often lost legal battles with native communities, in part because the interests at stake did not usually break down quite as neatly along the lines of race or ethnicity as our initial description of the Acopia case would suggest. It turns out that the ayllu's legal victory was assisted by favorable testimony obtained from another local Spaniard, a longtime resident of the area who was evidently willing to appear on the natives' behalf against Velásquez. The fact that many of the region's "Spanish" residents, perhaps including the ayllu's witness, spoke Quechua better than their supposed mother tongue is one indication of the complexity of the contemporary social context.

Social complexity hardly erased the advantages enjoyed by the powerful, however, and native victories in the judicial system were no guarantee against further conflict. Members of the Spanish elite were generally reluctant to comply with orders like the one Velásquez received, exhibiting a dismissive attitude toward their legal obligations that has arguably remained more characteristic of the Latin American experience than nearly any other in the world. As a consequence, native communities were often compelled to return again and again to the judicial authorities in search of a definitive settlement to problems they thought they had already resolved. During the 17th century, the kurakas of Urcos, another village in the vicinity of Cuzco, found themselves engaged in a decades-long struggle to defend the community's pasturelands and livestock from the depredations of a local Spanish family. The Peruvian viceroy himself intervened in favor of the community in 1652, citing the violence employed by one Pedro del Campo in his quest to seize village property. Forty years later, the complaints of lawless behavior had yet to cease, although by then a new Spanish offender had taken Pedro's place: his son, Andrés.

Voting with Their Feet: Escaping Tribute Obligations

Pressures from land-hungry outsiders were not the only ones faced by native villages. Even worse, perhaps, were the incessant demands for tribute and labor imposed by royal authorities in Spanish America. In the 17th century, these fell on village populations that were in many cases still declining as a result of epidemics and other negative consequences of the European invasions. A community reduced to half the size it had been at the time of the most recent assessment found its members staggering under the weight of obligations that not been adjusted downward. As in the cases mentioned above, village responses were often collective appeals for legal justice by community representatives to the crown. But another equally important response occurred at the individual level and outside the law: abandoning one's community of origin forever in order to escape tribute and labor obligations.

In the Andes, where the demands associated with the *mita* made for especially onerous labor commitments, a veritable flood of forasteros were willing to give up local ties and the access they enjoyed to communal lands in their own villages in order to take their chances elsewhere. As of 1690, almost half the inhabitants of the bishopric of Cuzco were forasteros. The figures were similar for the province of Charcas, located to the south in what is now Bolivia. Some of these migrants sought refuge on the margins of other native villages, where as noted earlier only the originarios were subject to community obligations. The downside for the new-comers was their lack of rights to local land, a circumstance that left them scrambling to make a living and frequently embroiled in conflict with locals. Other forasteros entered the employ of Span-iards on rural estates or in towns and cities as either debt peons or wage laborers. In doing so, they established themselves, and especially their children, as members of a social world that was in many respects far removed from the one they had left behind in their villages.

Not Knowing Their Place: Undermining Racial Boundaries

Illicit migration helped make a mockery of 16th-century Spanish political philosophy, which had attempted to divide the society of the new American possessions neatly into two coexisting but sepa-rate realms: the "Republic of the Indians" and the "Republic of the Spaniards." In this ideal world, native peoples would be protected as much as possible from the bad influences of Spaniards other than the clerics and royal officials who were presumed to have their best interests at heart. Laws intended to keep the two "repub-lics" distinct from one another failed miserably, however, as Span-iards and other nonnatives simply ignored restrictions placed on them in the absence of effective enforcement. At the same time, as seen above, intense pressures on native communities drove many of their members into the "Spanish" world. Moreover, the concept of the "two republics" was already largely irrelevant before it was even formulated, given the rapid emergence after 1492 of legally and socially inconvenient groups that did not fit into the scheme. Initially, it was sexual relations between native women and Spanish men, forcible or not, that led to the production of "mixed" children who confounded the abstract neatness of the concept. The decision soon after to transport African laborers across the ocean by the thousands added significantly to the conceptual confusion.

By the 17th century the population of *mestizos, mulatos,* and other *castas* was growing rapidly in Spanish American territory. The forced migration of enslaved Africans to mainland Spanish America was also reaching its peak in the decades just prior to 1640, although it dropped off sharply thereafter (the trend was far different in Brazil, destination for more than four million Africans between 1640 and 1850). None of these nonwhite peoples enjoyed the legal protections offered to the native population in return for fulfilling specific duties, however illusory such protections often were in practice. Instead, nonnatives who did not enjoy Spanish status were defined legally almost solely by *exclusion,* in other words by what they could *not* be or do. Although they were generally viewed as belonging by default to the Republic of Spaniards, they were blocked from access to land, public office, higher education, and many occupations on the grounds of their "impure" ancestry, which was believed, in a manner we would now label as racist, to produce innate character weaknesses. Slaves were uniquely disadvantaged in this regard, but free nonwhites outside of the native population also suffered legal marginalization. African ancestry was particularly debilitating under the law. Mestizos, presumed to be of exclusively Spanish-native descent, suffered fewer restrictions than individuals defined as *mulato,* black, *zambo,* or any of the myriad other terms connoting some degree of African origins. For example, free people of presumed African ancestry, but not mestizos, were required to pay an alternative tribute known as the *laborío* after the crown decreed its collection in the 1570s.

Not surprisingly, in practice colonial authorities in Spanish America were unable to police ancestry as closely as they wished or to enforce consistently the restrictions they placed on people whose skills, or simply bodies, were often in desperately short supply. Castas, banned in theory from infringing on the Indian world, were often hired to supervise gangs of native workers pressed into service on agricultural estates neighboring their villages. Armed horsemen of African origins, some free and others enslaved, roamed the countryside managing the vast herds of leading cattle barons. Market women of Indian or African ancestry exercised substantial control over key aspects of urban food distribution. And both black and native artisans moved steadily into trades long reserved officially for Spaniards, who generally had little interest in working with their hands.

Sometimes people of mixed origins achieved social positions that were strikingly out of keeping with their low legal status, often through the intervention of a powerful father. An example from early 17th century Guatemala involves Antonio Meléndez de Valdés, the *mulato* son of an enslaved woman. Antonio's father, a high-ranking official from Spain, not only freed his illegitimate son at birth but also left him a substantial parcel of land and ordered that he be treated as an *hidalgo,* or minor noble. The Spanish crown frequently expressed exasperation at such flouting of its prohibitions on social mobility for people of non-European ancestry. A 1622 letter to its representatives in Guatemala expressed grave disappointment at news that "persons of little account such as *mulatos* and mestizos" were shamelessly seeking appointment to official posts "without making mention of the said conditions," in at least some cases with the assistance of powerful relatives who belonged to the Spanish elite.[2]

Rattling Their Chains: Slaves and the Law

Far from Antonio Meléndez de Valdés on the social scale were enslaved people of African ancestry who enjoyed no favor whatsoever from their masters. Antonio's own mother, Juana, was one such person; her owner and former sexual partner, Antonio's Spanish father, sold her while their son was still young, evidently separating mother and child forever. While we know nothing else about Juana's life, enslaved individuals like her engaged in a variety of actions aimed at "working the system" to improve their disadvantaged position in whatever way possible. They were quick to call on the legal protections they enjoyed on paper under Spanish rule, whether in an attempt to prevent family breakup, buy freedom with hard-earned wages, or even seek out someone who would be willing to purchase them from a hated owner.

Among the most remarkable of these actions was the use of blasphemy in order to get a hearing from the Inquisition and thereby draw attention to abuses suffered at the hands of their owners. In the early 17th century, a number of enslaved men and women were hauled before Inquisition officials in Mexico after they renounced Christian beliefs while being physically punished. In doing so, these blasphemers took advantage of the church's requirement that they be brought before the Inquisition as soon as possible, a requirement that put a halt to the punishment, at least temporarily, if obeyed by their tormenters. Once in front of the Inquisitors, slaves could attempt to cast their owners in an unfavorable light in hopes of winning sympathy for their situation.

In 1610, a slave named Juan reported that while being whipped "very cruelly" by his owners' sons "he renounced God once, not with intention to offend him but to liberate himself from the punishment and later he repented." Four years later, another slave, Magdalena, went to the Inquisition to denounce herself after her owner refused to stop a beating and report her even after she vocally renounced God twice. A witness, another slave named Isabel, said that prior to blaspheming, Magdalena had first pleaded "for the love of God do not hit me and she asked it and begged many times."[3] Whatever the precise circumstances of such incidents, whose nature was always disputed by the slave owners involved, they represented attempts by slaves who clearly understood Spanish civil and religious law to try to invoke the protections, however minimal, that even they enjoyed in theory. The barriers these slaves were up against are revealed, however, in the fact that the religious authorities took the side of slave owners in most cases of blasphemy, to the extent of ordering further punishment for Juan and several others like him.

Color and Status in a Slave Society

Despite the presence of enslaved Africans in Mexico and other parts of Spanish America, society was not defined there primarily by dependence on African slavery. It was, however, in Brazil, where the relative absence of native society in areas under colonial control and the far greater importance of a plantation economy made slavery the defining feature of the legal and social landscape. For example, many free Bahian artisans of African origins existed in a state relatively close to slavery because significant numbers of slaves were engaged in the same skilled occupations, driving down their status. On the other hand, enslaved cowboys working on the vast cattle ranches that stretched out along the São Francisco river in the *sertão*, the dry backlands of the northeast, led lives that were very different from those of Bahian artisans, whether enslaved or free, let alone field workers on Bahian or Pernambucan sugar plantations. The daily life of this last group, as we saw in an earlier chapter, consisted almost entirely of labor in the harvest for much of the year, with adult life expectancy often just a few years. "A sugar mill is hell," wrote one Bahia-based cleric in 1627, "and all the masters of them are damned."[4]

Enslaved cattle herders, on the other hand, might see their owners no more than a few times a year. In the meantime, they led a threadbare but relatively independent existence in the remote depths of the sertão, where the dominance of the ranching economy was so thorough that even household utensils and window coverings were made of leather. The lifestyle of these enslaved laborers was essentially identical to that of the free *caboclos*, local residents of mostly Portuguese and native descent who often worked alongside them in the tasks associated with ranching. Slaves who did their work and remained loyal to their owners, the local cattle barons who ultimately dominated the lives of everyone who lived on their lands, enjoyed about as much freedom as was available to any poor person living in the harsh environment of the sertão.

Social Mobility and Its Limits

Legal and social discrimination against people with non-European ancestry was no less intense in Brazil than in Spanish America, with grinding poverty and forced labor of one variety or another the lot of most. At the same time, the demographic significance of nonwhite majorities everywhere in Latin America brought opportunities for social mobility even to enslaved individuals when they filled the more advantageous of the economic niches left open by the relative dearth of people of Iberian origins. Cattle ranching provides one obvious example, although the mobility enjoyed by landless ranch hands living a decidedly marginal existence is probably better described as spatial than social. More possibilities for the acquisition of land and other wealth existed in areas of Brazil dominated by the sugar economy, at least below the level of the planter elite. By the 18th century, some 30 percent of Bahia's *lavradores* were said to be nonwhite, although, in a sign of the limits to mobility, no engenho owner was identified thus. During the same century, the burgeoning mining communities of Minas Gerais produced some spectacular examples of individual ascent beyond one's prescribed place in the social order. The most celebrated case was Ouro Preto's great sculptor, Antônio Francisco Lisboa, better known as Aleijadinho. The disabled son of an enslaved woman of African descent and a Portuguese craftsman, he created a life-size series of the 12 apostles and numerous other works now considered to be among the very finest pieces of colonial-era art.

DEFENDING THE SYSTEM

Native Peoples in the Service of Iberian Rule

One of the most striking features of Iberian rule in colonial Latin America is the extent to which it was dependent on majority populations of color, or at least portions of them, for preservation from both foreign and domestic threats. While both the Spanish and the Portuguese tended to distrust the people over whom they ruled in the Americas, both found it necessary to recruit some of those same people to assist in the maintenance of colonial order. During their initial invasions, European newcomers had found native allies among various groups seeking advantage against imperial overlords like the Aztecs and Incas, or other traditional enemies. Some of these allies were eventually used in campaigns aimed at pacifying frontier regions, like the Tlaxcalans of central Mexico who fought alongside the Spaniards to conquer Tenochtitlán and, later, Guatemala. By the end of the 16th century, Tlaxcalans were being settled in the northern Mexican deserts to counter the threat posed by nomadic bands of "wild" native peoples lumped together as *Chichimecas* (a Nahuatl term), who long remained free from outside rule.

In Brazil, the mamelucos of São Paulo and their indigenous relatives acted as the spearhead of Portuguese movements into the South American interior. They and similar native-dominated forces also played a key role in the defeat of the *quilombo* of Palmares and other smaller settlements of escaped slaves that were established at the margins of plantation society, a phenomenon discussed at more length below. In response to the threat posed by escaped slaves, the authorities would commission a *capitão do mato* (bush captain) to assemble a band of fighters, and the bush captain in turn often relied largely on natives who were not only accustomed to the local environment but also possessed the martial techniques best adapted to it. Their skills were attested to in the early 17th century by Frei Vicente do Salvador, often referred to as Brazil's first historian. He wrote that escaped slaves were most afraid "of the Indians who with a Portuguese captain seek them out and return them to their masters."[5]

Despite their evident usefulness as allies in certain situations, natives were rarely inducted en masse into the formal militias that began to be established for purposes of general defense in Latin America during the mid-16th century. Outside of a few key ports, these local militias, rather than regular troops, constituted the sole armed forces in Iberian-ruled territories prior to the mid-18th century. Staffing these militias with conquered peoples was considered to be a dangerous business, especially in Mesoamerica and the Andes, where indigenous populations far outnumbered Spaniards and other nonnatives and were more likely to be perceived as a potential threat to societies that were constructed largely on their backs than a dependable defense force. As a result, militia service was at first restricted to men of European origins. In Spanish America, it was initially confined to elite *encomenderos,* whose obligations included the maintenance of a horse and armor and the duty to fulfill local defense needs.

Militiamen of Color and the Challenge to Racial Hierarchy

In the 17th century, a threat very different from the one posed by suspect indigenous majorities thoroughly undermined the initial Iberian policy of restricting militia service to the small minority of European origins. A spate of attacks on both Spanish and Portuguese territory in the Americas by Dutch, French, and English marauders forced colonial authorities to rethink policies of exclusion that had placed the entire burden of defense on a relatively small elite whose members were in many cases no longer much interested in military adventure. Given that doubts persisted over the wisdom of formally arming large numbers of native peoples, only one realistic alternative presented itself: enlisting castas, notably the free descendants of enslaved Africans. The trick for both Spaniards and Portuguese who wished to preserve their own privileges was to offer sufficient incentives to blunt the dangers of putting weapons in the hands of people they had legally marginalized without at the same time giving them full equality. Such a balancing act required compromises with the people whose bodies were needed, who in turn quickly seized the opportunities opened up to them to alter, although not entirely overturn, existing social relationships.

In truth, Africans and their descendants had participated alongside Spaniards in armed conflict in the Americas since the initial invasions of Mesoamerica and the Andes. Although operating for the most part as slaves or servants during the conquest era, they provided sufficiently important support to Spanish forces in at least a few cases to achieve fame and fortune in their own right. Juan Garrido, born in West Africa and transported at a young age to the Iberian Peninsula, participated in the Spanish invasions of Puerto Rico, Cuba, and Mexico, where he earned a plot for a house and the post of town crier in the new capital, Mexico City, that was established on the ruins of Tenochtitlán. Another man of African ancestry, Juan Valiente, was living as a slave in Puebla, Mexico, when he sought permission from his owner to serve among adventurers heading for Peru in 1533. He later invested as a horseman in Juan de Valdivia's expedition to Chile, rose to the rank of captain, and was eventually rewarded with an estate outside Santiago and a grant of native laborers, all without formally acquiring his freedom!

As exceptional as these two cases may have been, they formed part of a larger pattern of mostly informal military service by Africans and their descendants that continued after the era of major conquests. When northern European harassment of Spain's American possessions picked up during the later 16th century, both slaves and free people of African ancestry participated in repelling coastal attacks. In 1595, for example, a small force made up of "fourteen mounted *mulatos* and some Spaniards" ambushed a French raiding party that landed on the Honduran coast. For their efforts, the 14 *mulatos*, identified further as "freedmen as well as slaves," received a handsome monetary reward from the crown.[6] At the time, royal legislation banned the arming of any person of African origins, especially a slave. The crown's action was further evidence of the gap between the ideal, hierarchical world that Spaniards sought to construct in the Americas and the one that circumstances forced upon them.

As enemy incursions intensified during the early 17th century, colonial authorities eventually took the logical step of formalizing militia service by non-Spaniards. By the 1640s, companies of *gente parda*, yet another term for free people of part-African ancestry, were being mustered throughout Spanish America. Mestizos, however, tended to be inducted into Spanish companies, swelling their ranks and simultaneously reducing the potential for social unrest on the part of a broadly unified, and now armed, casta population. But a policy of unequal treatment of militiamen whose common bond was African ancestry carried its own risks for the ruling elite. It strengthened their sense of sharing a distinct, common identity, as well as a set of shared grievances, at the very same time that they were acquiring additional means with which to challenge subordinate status predicated on supposed group inferiority.

Soon enough, ongoing foreign pressure on Spain's American territories built up to the point of enabling newly powerful militiamen of African ancestry to exact concessions from royal officials by threatening to withhold their increasingly vital military service. As early as 1631, members of free *mulato* militia companies, which had helped Lima stave off a Dutch attack in 1624, obtained relief from the laborío, the alternative tribute payment owed by free people of African ancestry. Over the next few decades, similar developments took place in New Spain, Central America, and the Caribbean. In all of these places, black and *mulato* militiamen exploited the Spanish crown's dependence on their military usefulness to escape tribute obligations, heretofore a key marker of inferiority under the law.

Brazil, too, saw the emergence to prominence of militiamen of African ancestry during this era of increased hostile activity on the part of northern European powers. Among the Portuguese forces that ended a quarter century of Dutch control over the major sugar-producing region of Pernambuco in 1654 was a famed contingent of *preto* (black) troops under the command of Henrique Dias. By the 18th century, militia companies made up of free blacks and *mulatos*, known as *Henriques* to commemorate Dias's feats, were to be found all over colonial Brazil. But since Brazil was a slave society based primarily on the policing of Africans and their descendants, the authorities appear to have made a deliberate effort to mix native militiamen into these companies, probably to offset the perceived dangers of solidarity among armed nonwhites of shared ancestry. Nevertheless, the incentives provided for loyalty to colonial authorities tended to outweigh the ancestral connections that may have linked, say, a Brazilian-born, free *mulato* militiaman and an enslaved, recently arrived Angolan. After all, African roots were no more a guarantee of common interests than the backgrounds shared by the Spanish and the English or the Mexica and the Tlaxcalans. The historical evidence indicates clearly, for example, that most of the "Portuguese captains" described by Frei Vicente do Salvador as commanders of native slave hunters were actually free individuals of African ancestry. They were, quite naturally, well compensated for their work.

CHALLENGING THE SYSTEM

Although the strategies of nonwhite majorities for surviving, sometimes even prospering, in societies in which they were designated as inferior involved accepting the rules imposed by elites, overt and sometimes violent resistance was not at all uncommon. In an important sense, such resistance was simply one more, albeit extreme, negotiating tactic. It rarely threatened the larger colonial order, because its effects generally remained localized owing to the swift measures undertaken in most cases by authorities to prevent the spread of unrest. Indeed, in many cases overt resistance may have achieved fewer permanent gains for marginalized peoples than working within the system, an issue that remains very much open to debate. That such overt resistance occurred regularly in a variety of forms is not, however, in any doubt.

Maroon Communities and Rebel Slaves

An obvious example of violent resistance is provided in the experiences of escaped slaves in Brazil alluded to earlier. Contrary to slave owners' fantasies of happy plantation workers, resistance in one form or another to the brutalities of the slave system was a constant of plantation life, which explains the need for the whip, not to mention more extreme forms of torture devised by some masters for their recalcitrant human property. The Jesuit administrator of one 18th-century Brazilian engenho referred to the slaves under his control as "devils, thieves, and enemies," hardly a description of a docile, contented group.[7] Whether simply dragging their feet in response to orders or stealing sugar from under the nose of an unwary master sugar maker in order to sell it privately, these and other unwilling workers caused no end of frustration to their bosses, who were forced against their wishes to acknowledge the humanity of "devils" whose actions continually escaped the bounds of the role to which their owners wished to confine them.

In some notable cases, slaves responded directly in kind to violence used against them, despite the grave risks of such action. In 1789, some of the 300 or so enslaved workers on the Engenho Santana in Ilhéus, south of Bahia, revolted and murdered their overseer. Fleeing the plantation for the forest, they resisted a number of attempts to recapture them over the next several years before entering into negotiations with their owner, Manoel da Silva Ferreira, over the conditions under which they would agree to return to work. They sought limits on certain tasks as well as guaranteed access to independent garden plots, the produce of which they would fully control. They also made noneconomic demands such as time to "play, relax, and sing without needing permission," insisting on their right to enjoy the full range of human experience.[8] It was perhaps their desire to choose their own overseer that most vexed their owner, however. After pretending to accept their proposals, he shipped them off to a buyer in the Amazon region as soon as they returned to the plantation. In the end, the cards were stacked firmly against these rebels, but both the revolt and subsequent negotiations reveal that they were determined to shape their own fate to the extent possible in the unfavorable circumstances in which they lived.

They were not alone. Escape was a common response to plantation life in Brazil almost from the moment the Portuguese began growing sugar there. A Jesuit cleric's description of the enslaved population of Bahia in 1619 contained the following observation: "this people has the custom of fleeing to the woods and joining in hideouts where they live by attacks on the settlers, stealing livestock and ruining crops and canefields . . . [and] in these attacks they seek to carry off their male and female relatives to live with them like gentiles."[9] The most common English term for an escaped slave living in such a community is *maroon*, from *cimarrón*, a word first applied by Spaniards to wild cattle in the Caribbean and later to their escaped slaves. Meanwhile, the term usually applied to a settlement of escaped slaves in Brazil was *mocambo*, or "hideout" in the Angolan language Kimbundu, spoken by many of the Africans brought to Brazil during the 17th century. Mocambos were generally established in relatively inaccessible and easily defended forest areas, although usually not too far from plantations or towns, given the difficulties of survival in the remote interior for all but the native population. Roughly three dozen mocambos are known to have existed at one time or another in Bahia alone between 1614 and 1826, including at least one with several hundred inhabitants. But few survived more than a year or two. They were weakened by their dependence for supplies and new residents, especially women, on the very plantation world they wished to escape, often returning again and again to raid nearby farms and villages. Give this circumstance, colonial authorities were generally quick to organize an assault force under the command of a *capitão do mato* who could eliminate the threat such a community posed.

Palmares

One settlement of escaped slaves, located northeast of Bahia in the remote interior of Alagoas, stands out from all the rest in terms of size, longevity, and symbolic importance. Palmares, known by the Kimbundu term for "war camp" as a quilombo, was composed of a series of interconnected, fortified villages. It contained at least 10,000 inhabitants at its height. Founded early in the 17th century, it survived for nearly a hundred years, fending off repeated assaults by both Dutch and Portuguese forces. It eventually fell in 1694 to Paulista bandeirantes, those masters of native-style warfare, after a two-year siege. The final battle left roughly a thousand of the remaining defenders either dead or captured. In a last act of defiance, some 200 were reported to have committed suicide rather than give themselves up to the representatives of the colonial state.

While it lasted, the economy of Palmares was based on a combination of agriculture, trading, and raiding, similar to that of the typical mocambo if on a far grander scale. Society was hierarchical, governed by a succession of rulers known as kings who ruled with the assistance of a council of subordinate village headmen. Much of the labor, meanwhile, was done by slaves captured from Portuguese-controlled territory. Palmares thus resembled Portuguese colonial society in many respects, while drawing at the same time on West Central African precedents owing to the preponderance of residents with roots in Angola or the kingdom of Kongo. Life appears to have been strictly regimented, hardly surprising in view of the persistent military threat faced by the inhabitants. Even in defeat, Palmares continued to stand as the most important symbol of African resistance to the Portuguese slave system in Brazil. For at least 50 years after its final destruction, fugitive slaves continued to flee to the site in search of refuge.

Spanish American Maroons

Colonial Spanish America also witnessed the establishment of numerous communities of escaped slaves. These outlaw settlements were often known in Spanish American territory as *cumbes* or *palenques*. Circumstances were especially favorable for the emergence of such settlements during the early colonial era, when forced African migration to the Spanish American mainland was relatively high and Spanish control over the more remote areas to which Spain laid claim was weak or nonexistent. In the Veracruz region near the Gulf Coast of New Spain, fugitive slaves under the leadership of a West African–born ruler, Yanga, maintained their independence for several decades in the late 16th and early 17th centuries before successfully negotiating the transformation of their outlaw settlement into a formally recognized town, San Lorenzo de los Negros, around 1618. Similar communities also rose and fell in marginal areas of Central America, New Granada (Colombia), Ecuador, Venezuela, and the Spanish Caribbean.

Like Yanga's followers, the inhabitants of these communities sometimes achieved freedom and legal status by compelling colonial authorities to make treaties with them. Most of the small number of free black communities formally established in Spanish America during the colonial era had their origins in such treaties. But many Spanish American maroon bands were ultimately unable to resist defeat and destruction. Among the latter were some 20 residents of a small settlement of escaped slaves that survived for about eight years in the Pacific lowlands of Guatemala before falling to militiamen in 1611. These outlaws built a well-ordered community of nine huts and a small storehouse in which to collect the corn, cotton, chiles, plantains, squashes, and sugarcane that they planted and harvested in nearby plots. However, as in many similar cases, their need to trade with outsiders for certain essentials like steel implements made them vulnerable to betrayal, while their success in stealing enslaved women in the interests of achieving gender balance and sustaining the community's African character ensured that slave owners would seek their capture. Their value as property kept them all alive after their return to "civilization," although the individual identified as their captain and another rebel were killed in the militia ambush that led to their defeat. But when one of the band's former members escaped again a year later, he was tracked down and swiftly executed. According to his wife's testimony, he told her they "didn't have to serve anyone," a dangerous sentiment indeed in a hierarchical colonial world.[10]

Slave Rebellion in Mexico

Outright slave rebellion, in which slaves rose up in arms against their owners rather than simply escaping them, was relatively rare. This rarity is largely explained by the savage repression that greeted rebellion; captured leaders invariably earned a painful death. Conspiracies to rebel, suffocated prior to explosion, were apparently more frequent, although the evidence for them must be considered in light of masters' perpetual fears that their slaves were plotting against them. In the 17th century, these conspiracies shared common themes such as the election of a king and queen who were often selected from among the African-born individuals in the slave population, the massacre of Iberian men, and the enslavement of Iberian women. One such conspiracy was uncovered in Mexico City in 1612, when local authorities claimed to have preempted a Holy Week uprising planned by a black *cofradía* whose members had chosen an Angolan couple as their king and queen. The response was decisive: 35 presumed rebels, 28 men and 7 women, were quickly hanged.

The Haitian Revolution and Its Impact

By far, the most important slave rebellion to occur during the colonial era, and one that terrified slave owners throughout the Americas, was the Haitian Revolution (1791–1804). During this epochal event, tens of thousands of slaves rose up against their masters in the world's wealthiest colony, French Saint Domingue, the sugar-producing western third of the island of Hispaniola. Throwing off the shackles of bondage, these rebellious ex-slaves eventually dissuaded French, English, and Spanish troops from their attempts to reimpose control by a European power. This massive and prolonged uprising led to the establishment of Haiti, the second independent republic in the Americas and the first one dominated by a citizenry of African ancestry.

The outbreak of the Haitian revolution was followed by an uptick in rebellions or conspiracies by both slaves and free people of African ancestry in Cuba, Colombia, Louisiana, and Venezuela. The last of these places had seen the arrival of thousands of African laborers during the 18th century as cacao plantations expanded around Caracas, transforming the region into the most important destination for the reduced numbers of slaves landed in mainland Spanish America after 1640. In 1795, free blacks and slaves briefly revolted in the coastal Venezuelan town of Coro in favor of the "French Law," the abolition of slavery by revolutionary France the previous year. That abolition, the first by a European power, was short-lived, as Napoleon Bonaparte soon overturned it in the course of a failed bid to suppress the Haitian rebels and reconstruct the slave-based plantation economy they had destroyed. One of the first acts of an independent Haitian government in 1804 was to abolish slavery once and for all, the first place in the Americas to do so.

An image made during the final phase of the 13-year war for freedom by the ex-slave rebels of Saint Domingue (Haiti), showing Napoleon's French forces under assault by rebel combatants in 1802. (ullstein bild / The Granger Collection, New York)

Meanwhile, the pernicious influence of both French and Haitian revolutionaries was suspected by slave owners well beyond Coro and other centers of unrest around the Caribbean. The 1798 "Tailors' Conspiracy" in Bahia involved demands for a republic based on the ideals of *liberty, equality,* and *fraternity* that French rebels had begun proclaiming in Paris nearly a decade earlier. These principles were strikingly reflected in the composition of the 49 people arrested for participation in the conspiracy. The majority were free *mulatos,* including the leader, João de Deus do Nascimento, but the group included 11 enslaved individuals and 10 whites as well. Evidence of actual planning for an armed revolt was thin, with possession of revolutionary literature translated from the original French being one of the more serious charges. Nevertheless, a number of the alleged rebels were militiamen from local regiments of color. This circumstance was sufficiently alarming to the authorities that 4 of the alleged rebels, including Nascimento, were hanged, drawn, and quartered.

These and other examples of insurrectionary activity frightened members of elite creole minorities in plantation regions everywhere, despite the fact that many had their own grievances against the colonial authorities. The resentment of American-born "Spaniards" toward their overseas rulers had increased particularly sharply during the later 18th century. A wave of Enlightenment-influenced reform began to restrict the freedom with which they had previously flouted unpopular royal legislation, a development that bore similarities to the one experienced by American-born "Englishmen" in the 13 colonies of British North America around the same time. Beginning in the 1750s, Spanish American creoles found themselves increasingly marginalized by a set of economic, administrative, and military reforms aimed at strengthening Spain's control over its colonies and recapturing and expanding the economic benefits of empire. The most unpopular measures were aimed at eliminating smuggling, enforcing the systematic collection of sales and other taxes, and replacing creoles in colonial administrative and judicial posts with presumably more trustworthy peninsulares. These Bourbon reforms, so called for the royal dynasty that replaced the Habsburgs on the throne of Spain after 1700, were echoed in many respects in Portugal's realms by the Pombaline reforms, which were named after the key royal minister who spearheaded their adoption during the later 18th century, the Marquis de Pombal.

Native Uprisings

Despite high levels of dissatisfaction with the Bourbon and Pombaline reforms, the prospect of independence was far less attractive to American-born whites living amidst indigenous or racially mixed majorities in Latin America than it was to the slaveholders of British North America, where whites far outnumbered minorities of African or native ancestry. In fact, the Haitian Revolution and its contribution to unrest among both slaves and free people of color in Latin America's plantation regions ended up dampening the enthusiasm of creole elites for a break with the mother country. Meanwhile, one of the major Spanish American centers of native population, the Peruvian Andes, was just recovering from a different version of the sort of social upheaval that created panic among creoles. In 1780, a colonial system that had long succeeded in deflecting or dispersing native resistance was shaken to its roots by an insurrection initiated by a local kuraka, José Gabriel Condorcanqui, who styled himself a new Inca under the name Túpac Amaru II. Terrified creoles saw themselves transformed into the targets of native insurgents' rage as a massive rebellion swept through large portions of Peru and Bolivia, leaving thousands dead in its wake. The scope of the violence was unprecedented, as we shall see below, although not the act of rebellion itself.

Village Revolts in Mexico

As on sugar plantations, armed revolt was always a last resort in native villages owing to the repressive response it was likely to encourage. Nevertheless, it occurred with surprising frequency. One historian has counted 142 instances of village revolt in central and southern Mexico alone between 1680 and 1811, with at least one-quarter of the revolts led by women. Crucially, though, nearly all of these uprisings broke out more or less spontaneously with the aim of resolving a specific local grievance, whether a boundary dispute or the arrogant and heavy-handed administration of a hated priest or other outside authority. In 1720, for example, local Indians concerned about encroachment on their lands attacked surveyors with rocks not far from the city of Oaxaca, while in 1773 the villagers of Zimatlán revolted against a priest who was trying to keep them from speaking their native tongue, Zapotec. Such unrest often ended with the replacement of an unpopular official along with relatively mild punishment for the rebel leaders. In this manner, through a "calculated blend of punishment and mercy."[11] Spanish officials managed to prevent most such rebellions from spreading beyond the village level or taking on a larger social agenda. And as long as the focus of these revolts remained local, they posed little threat to the overall colonial order.

Túpac Amaru II and Andean Rebellion

In the Andes, the Spanish crown's determination to impose new, revenue-enhancing measures intensified pressures on native communities that were already experiencing difficulties associated with renewed population growth in the 18th century. Under the Bourbons, the *alcabala*, or sales tax, was raised from two to six percent, applied to an expanded range of products including cheap alcohol and coca, and collected more systematically by a larger number of officials appointed explicitly for that purpose. Moreover, the corregidores charged with putting new and unpopular crown policies into effect were compensated with the right to force native communities to purchase bulk quantities of unwanted goods at inflated prices, a process of unequal exchange known as the *reparto de mercancías*. In the 1770s, Antonio de Arriaga, corregidor of the district of Canas y Canchis near Cuzco, imposed three of these *repartos* on the local people. The popular consensus was that he was allowed to do this only once. For these and other perceived abuses, Arriaga was executed in the village square of Tungasuca on November 10, 1780, on the orders of the kuraka who would become known to history as Túpac Amaru II. It was the first act in a grand rebellion that nearly ended Spanish rule in the Andes 40 years before independence finally came.

The name chosen by the rebel leader was highly symbolic. It had belonged to the last ruler of an independent Inca kingdom, a mountain refuge that survived the initial Spanish invasion of the Andes and resisted conquest until 1572. Despite this association, Túpac Amaru II initially proclaimed rebellion against corrupt Spanish colonial officials in the name of the king of Spain. In doing so, he echoed a common theme of popular uprisings in monarchical societies by appealing to a ruler who surely would not approve of his underlings' abusive behavior if he were aware of it. Túpac Amaru also sought support from all social sectors except for Iberian-born Spaniards, including creoles. But most of the latter soon threw themselves into the arms of Spanish troops, shaken by the massive response to the call to arms on the part of an indigenous population that often seemed unable, or unwilling, to distinguish among people of European ancestry. Large creole landowners, after all, were often the most obvious face of an oppressive colonial order. Creole fears were intensified when a nearly simultaneous revolt by Aymara-speaking peoples to the south, in the Chayanta region of what is now Bolivia, made the entire nonnative population the target of its wrath from the outset.

The early elimination of the key rebel leaders did little to stem the tide of insurrection. Túpac Amaru himself was captured six months after his rebellion began and executed in Cuzco's main square along with his wife, Micaela Bastidas, a commander in her own right. The original leaders of the Aymara revolt, the Katari brothers, were dead by then as well. But the massive revolt swept on, its supporters apparently undaunted by the dispersal throughout the viceroyalty of the body parts of their executed leaders for public display, a vivid reminder of royal justice. Not until 1783 were the Spanish troops who had been rushed to the highlands able to suppress the uprising for good.

CONCLUSION: TOWARD OR AWAY
FROM INDEPENDENCE?

Appeals to an Inca or African past, or to a future of liberty and fraternal solidarity, clearly contributed a sense of purpose to many outbreaks of armed resistance against repressive colonial regimes. Bahian planters complained in 1816 that "the spirit of insurrection is seen among all types of slaves, and is fomented principally by the slaves of the city [of Salvador], where the ideas of liberty have been communicated by black sailors coming from Saint Domingue."[12] But demographic and economic pressures, like those building up in the Andes prior to the Túpac Amaru rebellion, often played a vital role in stirring up discontent in the first place. Rising consumer prices and new fiscal demands helped spark opposition to the Bourbon reforms in New Granada (Colombia), where the multiclass Comunero Revolt of 1781 coincided with Túpac Amaru's farther south. The participants in Bahia's "Tailors' Conspiracy" sought pay raises for militiamen and a rollback of manioc prices that had recently climbed by 25 percent. The dangers of urban food shortages had long been evident to colonial officials. A major riot in Mexico City in 1692 was preceded by disastrous crop failures that drove the price of the chief local staple, corn, to its highest level in a century. A hundred years later, distressed residents of Latin America were even more likely to blame a similar worsening in the circumstances of daily life on royal governments whose reforms were correctly suspected of benefiting the economies of Spain and Portugal rather than their own.

Creoles, the sector of the colonial population with the greatest access by far to education and other useful tools of organization, remained ambivalent about the idea of independence in spite of their increasing unhappiness with what they experienced as second-class status. In a world shaken by events like Túpac Amaru's revolt and the Haitian Revolution, what might the true costs of a struggle for independence be? Hearing of the Peruvian events, Venezuelan creoles like don Juan Vicente Bolívar y Ponte, a slaveholding member of the cacao-planting elite of Caracas, expressed their opposition to any movement that might end in the destruction of the social hierarchy in their own region, where free *pardos* made up half the population. During the 1790s, the Caracas city council opposed the creation of new militia units of color for fear such a development would "increase the arrogance of the pardos, and give them organization, chiefs, and arms to facilitate a revolution."[13] Years later, during an initial bid for independence, Simón Bolívar, son of Juan Vicente, encountered Venezuela's mostly nonwhite *llaneros*, horsemen from the cattle-ranching interior, allied with royalist forces *against* him. He only won their support, and became South America's Great Liberator, after he abandoned the creole exclusiveness that marked a first, failed independent government in Venezuela and incorporated soldiers of color on terms of reasonable equality into his own rebel forces.

But the initial spark for the Latin American wars of independence, which finally broke out during the second decade of the 19th century, was not provided by unrest on the part of creoles or anyone else in the Americas. Instead, royal government and the colonial system over which it presided began to collapse in Spanish America as a result of Napoleon's 1807 invasion of the Iberian Peninsula and dethronement of the legitimate monarch of Spain, Ferdinand VII. The same invasion sent the Portuguese ruler to Brazil, preserving monarchy there, although not Portugal's dominance, for most of the 19th century. From Mexico to Chile, the following two decades of independence struggles saw momentous political changes. But the conditions of daily life were to remain harsh for the majority of people in independent Latin America despite a long history of persistent and sometimes violent efforts to improve them.

NOTES

In addition to the works cited separately as sources of direct quotations and the authors' own archival research, the following sources have been drawn on for specific examples in this chapter: Dauril Alden, "Late Colonial Brazil, 1750–1808," in *Colonial Brazil*, ed. Leslie Bethel; Arnold J. Bauer, *Goods, Power, History*; Matthew Restall, *Seven Myths of the Spanish Conquest*; Charles F. Walker, *Smoldering Ashes*. For full citations and other useful readings, see the annotated bibliography.

1. Eric Hobsbawm, quoted in Ward Stavig, *The World of Túpac Amaru: Conflict, Community, and Identity in Colonial Peru* (Lincoln: University of Nebraska Press, 1999), p. xxvi.

2. Archivo General de Centro América (Guatemala City), A1, legajo 4578, expediente 39531, folios 26v-27.

3. Quoted in Joan Cameron Bristol, *Christians, Blasphemers and Witches: Afro-Mexican Ritual Practice in the Seventeenth Century* (Albuquerque: University of New Mexico Press, 2007), pp. 134, 138.

4. Quoted in Stuart B. Schwartz, "Plantations and Peripheries, c. 1580–c. 1750," in *Colonial Brazil*, ed. Leslie Bethel (Cambridge: Cambridge University Press, 1987), p. 67.

5. Quoted in Stuart B. Schwartz and Hal Langfur, "Tapanhuns, Negros da Terra, and Curibocas: Common Cause and Confrontation between Blacks and Natives in Colonial Brazil," in *Beyond Black and Red: African-Native Relations in Colonial Latin America*, ed. Matthew Restall (Albuquerque: University of New Mexico Press, 2005), p. 93.

6. Archivo General de Indias (Seville), Audiencia de Guatemala, 10, R.22, N.164.

7. Quoted in Stuart B. Schwartz, *Sugar Plantations in the Formation of Brazilian Society: Bahia 1550–1835* (Cambridge: Cambridge University Press, 1985), p. 395.

8. Quoted in Stuart B. Schwartz, *Slaves, Peasants, and Rebels: Reconsidering Brazilian Slavery* (Urbana: University of Illinois Press, 1996), p. 54.

9. Quoted in Schwartz, *Slaves, Peasants, and Rebels*, p. 105.

10. Archivo General de Indias (Seville), Patronato, 89, N.4, R.1.

11. William B. Taylor, *Drinking, Homicide, and Rebellion in Colonial Mexican Villages* (Stanford, Calif.: Stanford University Press, 1979), p. 120.

12. Quoted in George Reid Andrews, *Afro-Latin America, 1800–2000* (New York: Oxford University Press, 2004), p. 68.

13. Quoted in Andrews, *Afro-Latin America*, p. 220, note 115.

8

CONCLUSION: INDEPENDENCE AND BEYOND

INDEPENDENCE: CHANGE OR CONTINUITY?

The years from 1808 to 1825 constitute the independence era in Latin American history, when all of mainland Spanish America, along with Brazil, threw off Iberian rule, although the Caribbean islands of Cuba and Puerto Rico remained Spanish possessions until 1898. Thousands of people died in bloody, prolonged fighting in Mexico and Spanish South America, while the lives of tens of thousands of others were disrupted by the more general economic and social chaos that accompanies sustained armed conflict. Grand movements of large numbers of soldiers and just as many camp followers, spouses or other women who accompanied the troops providing both domestic and sexual comforts, swept across vast territories in a manner unlike anything seen in three centuries. Royalist forces looted and burned indiscriminately, and insurgents fought back with equal savagery. Disease, as in most wars, ran rampant. Some of Spain's territories, notably in Central America, managed to escape the horrors of war almost entirely, while Brazil made a relatively peaceful transition to independence under the rule of an emperor, Dom Pedro I, who was the son of Portugal's king. But throughout Latin America, a new political atmosphere raised new questions regarding the nature and practice of self-government. The manner in which "the people" should participate in governing newly independent nations was perhaps the thorniest question of all and one that remains far from clearly resolved even today.

As noted in the preceding chapter, the colonial-era *cabildo*, or municipal council, turned out to be a key institution of political organization in Spanish America after Napoleon deposed Spain's King Ferdinand in 1807. In the absence of a recognized, legitimate monarch, cabildo members, mostly creoles, assumed the right in many places to exercise political power until such time as the king was restored to his throne. This assumption of power by creole cabildo members did not go uncontested by other claimants to royal authority. Nevertheless, cabildo politics provided leading creoles with a key forum in which to debate the possibility of severing ties with Spain. Meanwhile, as they had during the preceding centuries of colonial rule, various sectors of the marginalized, mostly nonwhite majority made their presence felt in other ways.

Revolt in Mexico

In the fall of 1810, a widespread uprising by thousands of natives and *mestizos* under the leadership of a rural creole priest, Miguel Hidalgo, interrupted the political maneuverings of creoles and *gachupines* (a derogatory term for peninsular Spaniards) in Mexico City. Hidalgo's poor and ragged troops declared loyalty to the Virgin of Guadalupe and the deposed Spanish monarch, but death to any gachupines in Mexico. They proceeded to lay waste to the countryside northwest of the capital. In the wealthy mining town of Guanajuato, Hidalgo's forces massacred elite whites whom they held responsible for colonial oppression, terrifying gachupín and creole alike. These two groups, like Andean elites faced with Túpac Amaru's rebellion in the Peruvian highlands three decades earlier, closed ranks to put down the unrest. Creole military officers, including the man who became the first ruler of an independent Mexico a decade later, Agustín de Iturbide, fought alongside Spanish troops to crush the revolt. In an effort to dissuade others from similar actions, royalist forces executed Hidalgo and sent his head to be impaled on a pike outside Guanajuato. Mexican creoles, like their counterparts in the Andes, chose the maintenance of their privileged position within the existing social order over participation in an independence movement involving the lower social elements.

War, though, always threatens the preexisting social order. Men of mixed origins like José María Morelos and Vicente Guerrero soon emerged to replace Hidalgo at the head of the anti-Spanish struggle. Morelos, a rural priest like Hidalgo, raised the quality of the rebels' military leadership and promulgated a revolutionary constitution declaring the equality of all Mexicans regardless of ancestry before he was captured and executed by royalist forces in 1815. And Guerrero, guerrilla leader and former muleteer, forged an alliance between his own rebel forces and conservative creoles just long enough to win independence at last in 1821. He went on to oppose Iturbide's short-lived rule as emperor of Mexico and eventually served briefly as president of the new nation himself during the turbulent years of Liberal-Conservative conflict that followed. Much of that conflict would result from ongoing elite efforts to suppress the ambitions of Guerrero and others of similarly modest social origins.

Revolt in South America

Further south, the creole leader Simón Bolívar used a period of Caribbean exile following his initial defeat at the hands of royalist forces and their *llanero* allies to rethink his strategy for winning independence. On his return to the South American mainland, he regained the upper hand after opening up his patriot armies, including his officer corps, to both free and enslaved men of African origins. This crucial shift in policy sprang in part from military necessity and in part from Bolívar's promise to the Haitian president, Alexandre Pétion, to abolish slavery in return for Pétion's help in renewing the stalled struggle against Spain. When Bolívar offered enslaved men freedom for enlisting, some 5,000 rushed to take up arms under his command in Colombia alone between 1819 and 1821.

Free men of color also began placing their military experience at the service of the independence cause, encouraged by Bolívar's newfound willingness to ignore distinctions based on color. Some of these men ended up rising to the highest levels of the officer corps in the patriot armies. However, Bolívar was never entirely able to overcome his deep distrust of the noncreole majority, a distrust shared by most creoles, and he felt particularly threatened by potential rivals from among the racially mixed groups. In a famous incident, he ordered the execution of one of his army's most prominent officers of color, the pardo general Manuel Píar, for allegedly favoring *pardocracy*, or rule by nonwhites. Of course, in places where the latter were in the majority, as in most of Latin America, *pardocracy* was merely democracy by another name.

The other great leader of South American independence, General José de San Martín, began recruiting slaves in return for the offer of freedom in and around Buenos Aires as early as 1813. At least half of the soldiers who accompanied him on a grueling expedition across the Andes to attack royalist forces in Chile in 1817 are known to have been *libertos,* or ex-slaves. The impact on Buenos Aires' black population of this campaign and a subsequent one to Peru are suggested in census data from the independence era, which reveal a dramatic decline in the ratio of men to women in that population from roughly even in 1810 to just 6 males for every 10 females in 1827. Among whites, the corresponding ratio at the end of the independence era was approximately 9 males for every 10 females. These figures help explain the decreasing demographic weight in subsequent decades of the city's black population, which had represented some 30 percent of all inhabitants at the beginning of the century.

Life During Wartime

The siege of Lima by patriot forces seeking to retake the city from royalist troops in 1823 provides one example of the disastrous impact of the fighting on civilian populations in areas directly affected by the war. In the wake of the royalist victory over San Martín's Peruvian allies, some 10,000 patriot sympathizers fled the city, or were forced from it, into the surrounding countryside. Unfortunately, the independence army they supported had little to offer them and was itself so desperate for supplies that it was in the process of bankrupting nearby landholdings by requisitioning oxen and other supplies. Elite observers made few distinctions between patriot fighters and common criminals in viewing these developments. Those observers, of course, had been on edge over the rebellious potential of the lower orders ever since Túpac Amaru's revolt 40 years before.

Throughout Latin America, troops on both sides, and particularly those from marginalized social sectors, were often motivated by objectives other than those stressed by their leaders. Their violent acts frequently exhibited a clear logic that was not so much criminal in nature (a regular accusation by elites) as deeply threatening to the entire social order, what elites most feared. A contemporary French traveler in what is now Uruguay commented that the slaves who contributed to José Artigas's unsuccessful independence struggle "were fighting for their own freedom," a conclusion that might have been obvious to any intelligent observer. Unlike many other independence leaders, Artigas had in fact made the radical vow that "the most downtrodden shall be the most privileged" in a bid for the support of the less favored members of local society. The "most downtrodden" evidently took him at his word. The same French visitor mentioned above observed that "the rebel soldiers would enter the [ranches] and take whatever they liked. . . . Often a black, a mulatto, [or] an Indian would appoint himself an officer and, together with his band of followers, would rob the landowners."[1]

THE COLONIAL LEGACY

In the short term, formal independence brought little beyond symbolic change to the everyday lives of most Latin Americans. Although laws upholding discrimination based on ancestry were eliminated in Spanish American republics that on paper were constituted of free and equal citizens, a remarkable achievement in comparison with the rest of the world, such discrimination did not end in practice. The struggle for daily survival continued much as before for the impoverished majority, and often in economic circumstances made worse by long years of conflict. In many places, though, governments now came and went seemingly overnight. For good or ill, other than in imperial Brazil, the political stability associated with the long era of colonial administration was a thing of the past.

The sacrifices of slaves and other members of the popular sectors who had fought on the side of independence were generally not well rewarded. For example, even though pressure from ex-slave soldiers helped bring about the establishment of Free Womb laws in many places during the 1820s, granting free birth to the children of enslaved women, the final abolition of slavery did not occur in most of Spanish South America before the mid-1850s. Meanwhile, daily life went on much as before with people carrying on their long-established practices at home, at work, at worship, at play, and in bed. And the common people continued to resist the political structures imposed on them by their social "betters" who hoped to harness their labor to the new national wagon.

DAILY LIFE AFTER INDEPENDENCE

Having arrived at the end of the colonial period, our task now is to sum up daily life in its various manifestations in order to understand the legacy bequeathed to the new independent nations by the societies constructed during the previous 300 years. Politically, all of South and Central America had severed its relationship with Spain and Portugal, but that is not to say these people had a clean slate on which to build their new societies and economies. What they would build was based on what they knew, as well as on which social groups had the skills and the power to design and construct the building.

Independence brought no change at all to gender systems, so life at home in the patriarchal extended family went on undisturbed. Many families were touched by the ravages of war, certainly, and some found their status changed by losses of men and property due to the war effort. The basic institutional structures of marriage and the family survived the independence war intact, however, and would not suffer serious fissures for more than a hundred years. During the Bourbon reforms of the 18th century, the secular state had granted parents more power over their children's choice of a marriage partner, and parents kept a firm grip on this power after independence. Among elite families, marriage continued to be a contract and a tool for maintaining honor and social status, while the common people of the middle sectors of society went on ignoring the authorities, as long as they could get away with it, and practiced cohabitation. The family emerged from the colonial period as an ambivalent institution. On one hand, it functioned as a repressive structure, severely limiting the options of elite women—many of whom were virtually imprisoned in their own homes—and exposing women of all classes to the sometimes violent discipline of fathers and husbands. On the other hand, the family provided almost the only emotional refuge for most people.

Regarding people's work lives, not much changed because of independence. If anything, working people lost what little protection the Iberian crowns provided and found themselves at the mercy of creole landowners and businessmen. Work was an area in which the common people very much needed, indeed demanded, change. The slaves who flocked to join Simón Bolívar's army did so in exchange for a life of freedom that remained elusive in many cases. Workers who had been exploited by the colonial system became the labor force that American elites hoped would build new nations. At times, enslaved workers found themselves freed into a work life that closely imitated their previous status as slaves, except now they competed in a job market that provided no protection against layoffs, unemployment, injury, and old age. And, of course, enslaved workers in Brazil would not be freed for another six decades. Since the independence wars were won with elite leadership, the socio-economic structure was not overturned, and elites managed to hold onto their position at the top of the social ladder. In most cases, they were able to keep the electorate small and defeat any moves toward suffrage for working people, thereby retaining the political power to pass legislation designed to protect their economic position. They did what they could to perpetuate the labor systems that had characterized the past, relying on institutions of the colonial period like debt peonage, slavery, and the mita to provide the basic framework of labor after independence.

The Roman Catholic Church also retained much of its power after independence, although its proper role in society emerged as a major source of political controversy. Advocates of ideas of political and economic liberalism associated with Enlightenment thinking sought to reduce the political and social influence of the church drastically and to convert its property to private use for purposes of economic development. Conservative traditionalists, meanwhile, defended the church's monopoly over both religious practice and education as a key plank in their larger campaign to resist social change.

Conservative leaders often succeeded in rallying support for their program from native peoples and other marginalized members of society because liberal advocates of "progress," much like Spain's "enlightened" Bourbon reformers in the late 18th century, generally made clear their disdain for the supposedly backward aspects of popular culture. Indeed, liberals found their models for independent Latin American societies in England and France, believing ardently in the necessity of ridding their own countries of embarrassing Spanish and Portuguese cultural influences, not to mention anything associated with indigenous or African roots. Moreover, liberal economic doctrine viewed individual property holding as inherently superior, and liberal-oriented administrations produced legislation that threatened not only church wealth but also communal ownership of village land in native communities. What conservative elites wanted to preserve, of course, was hierarchical social and racial organization in the colonial style, all the while protecting their position at the top. Nevertheless, native peoples and other members of a still-excluded majority often preferred the conservative vision to an alternative that appeared to involve massive disruption of their social and cultural lives.

To the despair of reformers, religious organizations like the *cofradía* retained their central importance in the cultural life of many native communities after independence. Moreover, key symbols of popular religion became intimately entwined with the imagery of modern, independent nationhood, notably in Mexico, where the dark-skinned Virgin of Guadalupe, around whose standard Hidalgo's indigenous and mestizo troops had rallied, emerged as an iconic representation of Mexican unity. Nevertheless, church authorities found themselves ever more on the defensive against secularizing tendencies in society. As we have seen, those authorities had never been fully able to control the religious practices of common people even at the height of their power during the colonial era. Now, though, the church was confronted not only with heterodox influences derived in part from competing indigenous and African religious traditions, but also an anticlerical backlash from urban popular sectors in places like Mexico City and Lima, where priests had long been closely identified with the repressive colonial institutions headquartered in those cities.

In the realm of sexuality and love, people's real lives seem to have diverged considerably from the model prescribed by the church, and in a way, the postindependence instability served to lessen the threat to people's private lives posed by the authorities. Not only is there substantial evidence of homosexual activity, but baptismal records show high levels of children born to unmarried parents and appreciable numbers of children who were the product of adulterous relationships. Significant numbers of children were also fathered by priests. The surviving evidence shows that punishments were inflicted on enslaved workers who had sneaked off the plantation to visit a loved one, an outcome they surely could have anticipated but seem to have been willing to risk. The church faced a challenging task as it attempted to apply its moral precepts to the people of the Americas, especially since many people had roots in African or indigenous societies that held views on sexuality that diverged widely from Catholic teachings.

In elite circles, however, the church had better success. As the recognized authority on appropriate behavior both inside and outside the house, the church used its power to set the parameters of acceptable sex. Since elite families had a lot to lose, specifically the family honor and good name, intangibles that carried little significance among the common people, they went to great lengths to create at least the appearance of propriety. In chapter 1 we saw that several couples who seem to have felt a deep commitment to each other were separated, for years or forever, by parents and priests who valued the family's status above the wishes of the young couple. A premarital pregnancy might pose a serious threat to the family

A 1795 image from revolutionary-era Paris, home to the abolitionist Society of Friends of Blacks. The image is accompanied by a poem celebrating the capacity of slaves, "friends of reason," to recognize and enjoy what the poet describes as the social virtues of marriage. (Courtesy of the John Carter Brown Library at Brown University)

honor too, in which case all the family members conspired to hide the evidence of this divergence from the church's moral code.

The culture of sexuality that characterized elite society, obsessed as it was with concerns of family honor and adherence to church guidelines, diverged widely from that of the masses of working people. This suggests that these two widely divergent sexual cultures would leave two distinct legacies to people of the postcolonial period, and this is indeed what happened. Elites struggled to keep up the appearance of propriety after independence, as they had before, while the common people enjoyed greater success in avoiding the authorities, now quite busy with matters of state. Many of the popular classes managed to do as they liked, discretely in most cases, and stay out of sight and out of reach of the law.

As in matters of sexuality, the responses of ordinary people to the efforts of the authorities to control their lives often took the form of quietly pursuing their interests as best they could either within or outside the law, while avoiding direct confrontation with the powerful forces that backed the social order. But confrontation, violent or not, was sometimes unavoidable, since in practice popular resistance was often the only curb on the ambitions of the wealthy and powerful, in whose favor the law tended to operate. The colonial era is full of examples of such resistance, whether in the form of moral challenges to the lawless behavior of elites through a court system that was supposed to protect the weak or in the form of armed unrest. Yet even the wars of independence, in a certain way the greatest example of violent resistance to authority, produced few fundamental changes in societies marked by profound inequalities in the distribution of wealth and power. Simply put, the struggle for daily survival among the poor and mostly nonwhite majority created almost insurmountable difficulties to organizing on the scale necessary to overcome tight-knit elite groups whose ancestors had violently seized control over the vast majority of Latin America's resources.

And yet, there were victories. The Haitian Revolution stands as a remarkable testament to the determination of people to free themselves from oppressive conditions of work and life. The attempt at social revolution by Hidalgo and Morelos in Mexico, although a military failure, nevertheless contributed to the emergence of a republic that with all its postindependence problems elected a full-blooded Indian, the Zapotec Benito Juárez, as president less than 50 years after the end of a colonial regime founded on the subjugation of the native population. Even in Brazil, where African slavery lasted longer than anywhere else in the Western Hemisphere, outbreaks of slave resistance of the sort that had troubled planters since the early colonial era helped bring down the institution at last in 1888. There is no reason to suppose that any of these developments would have occurred had the social hierarchy that the Spanish and Portuguese worked so hard to impose on their colonies in the Americas been accepted without complaint by those who were relegated to its bottom reaches.

A FINAL WORD

Any deep understanding of Latin America rests firmly on a base of colonial life as it was lived by the people of the region over the

300 years from the arrival of Columbus in the Caribbean in 1492 to the surrender of the last Spanish loyalists on the mainland at the port of Callao, Peru, in 1826. The people already living in this hemisphere, the invaders from the Iberian Peninsula, and the people brought from Africa to work came together to talk, to fight, to worship, to eat and drink, to work and play, and to have sex, some willingly and some against their will. They were born, lived their lives, had children, and died, building societies, economies, and political structures that slowly evolved over the period. And they bequeathed to those who came after a legacy that set the terms of the early postindependence period.

Some of the patterns and institutions they established have disappeared, like the old coerced labor systems, but others are still important today. The large estate, the patriarchal extended family, and the social structure based on racial characteristics have lived on over the 200 years since independence and are still very much alive in parts of the region, structuring daily life as it is lived by Latin Americans in the 21st century. In this study, we have tried to get as close as possible to the daily lives of the people of the 17th and 18th centuries and to examine how they lived within or across social boundaries, how the legal apparatus structured their lives or failed to, and how at times they accepted and at other times rejected the world they were born into, or brought into. Latin America today is the result of what they did every day.

NOTES

In addition to the work cited separately as a source of direct quotations, the following source has been drawn on for specific examples in this chapter: Christon Archer, ed., *The Wars of Independence in Spanish America*. For full citation and other useful readings, see the annotated bibliography.

1. Quoted in George Reid Andrews, *Afro-Latin America, 1800–2000* (New York: Oxford University Press, 2004), p. 60.

GLOSSARY

adobe—Housing material of bricks made from mud, usually with a heavy clay component, mixed with straw and dried in the sun.

alcalde—Municipal administrator in Spanish America.

aldeia—Jesuit-run settlement in early colonial Brazil where native peoples were congregated for purposes of Christianization and, in theory, protection from enslavement.

altiplano—Highlands.

arriero—Mule driver.

atol—Porridge or hot drink, usually based on a starch (e.g., maize, plantain).

audiencia—Large Spanish American administrative region governed by a high court of the same name; there were several *audiencias* in each viceroyalty.

bandeirante—Participant in slaving expeditions sent up vast inland waterways into the Brazilian interior from settlements like São Paulo.

barracoon—Large, dormitory-like sleeping quarters on an estate used to house the enslaved population.

cabildo—Spanish American municipal council.

caboclo—Term applied to people of mixed, often Portuguese-native, ancestry in northeastern Brazil.

cachaça—Alcoholic beverage in Brazil that was produced from sugarcane juice.

calidad—Social rank or status.

Carrera de Indias—Spanish fleet system.

casa grande—Main house.

casta—General term applied to all persons of mixed ancestry in Spanish America.

charqui—Meat jerky.

chicha—Andean corn beer; major source of alcohol consumption in the Andes prior to Spanish arrival.

chile—Pepper.

chuño—Freeze-dried potatoes.

cimarrón—Escaped slave, frequently living in an outlaw community with other escapees.

cofradía—A confraternity, or lay religious brotherhood, in Spanish America.

colegio—Private school generally run by a religious order.

comal—Stone griddle for heating corn tortillas in Mexico and Central America.

consanguinidad—State of being related to someone by blood.

corregidor—Regional administrator in Spanish America; duties included the regulation and defense of the native population.

correo mayor—Postmaster general.

criollo/a (Port. crioulo, Eng. creole)—Term originally applied to an enslaved person of African descent born in the Americas or the Iberian Peninsula; later came to mean Spaniard born in the Americas as well.

curandero/-a—Popular healer, often a woman of indigenous or African origin.

debt peon—Individual tied to a rural estate or other economic enterprise by debts originating in advances offered by an owner seeking a resident labor force.

dispensa—Church waiver of an impediment to marriage.

encomienda—Grant to an individual Spaniard of labor and tribute from one or more native villages; most *encomiendas* eventually reverted to the Spanish crown.

engenho—Brazilian sugar mill; often applied in the sense of *plantation* to an entire sugar-producing operation, including canefields.

expediente matrimonial—Marriage document prepared by the priest who interviewed a prospective couple.

farinha—Manioc flour.

forastero—Term applied to outsiders in native villages, often indigenous people who had fled labor and tribute obligations in their own communities.

frijoles—Beans.

garapa—A type of sugarcane alcohol in Brazil.

gaucho (Port. gaúcho)—Ranch hand, cowboy in the Southern Cone of South America.

hidalgo—Member of the minor nobility in Spanish realms.

huipil—Women's top, blouse.

Inquisition—Roman Catholic tribunal charged with rooting out and punishing heretical beliefs, witchcraft, and other thoughts or behavior considered to deviate from religious orthodoxy; jurisdiction in Latin America restricted to the nonnative population.

irmandad—A lay religious brotherhood in Brazil.

kuraka—Local ruler/chieftain among indigenous Andean peoples; often a descendant of precolonial Andean nobility.

laborío—Alternative tribute levied in Spanish America on free people of African ancestry and natives not bound to specific villages by labor and tribute obligations.

lavrador—Category of Brazilian farmer below the level of the sugar-planting elite.

llanero—Venezuelan ranch hand, cowboy; resident of the *llanos* (plains).

mameluco—Individuals of mixed Portuguese and native ancestry in places like São Paulo; their cultural knowledge often made them expert slave hunters (see *bandeirante*).

maroon—See *cimarrón*.

mascarada—Popular entertainment consisting of a lively parade by masked performers representing well-known personages from the realms of myth, history, or well-known literary works.

mazombo—Brazilian-born Portuguese, as opposed to *reinois* from Portugal.

mecapal—Tumpline, leather strap worn across the forehead and tied to a load carried behind the back.

mestizo (Port. mestiço)—Applied originally to individuals of mixed Spanish and indigenous ancestry and often more generally to people of mixed origins.

metate—Grinding stone for preparing the corn flour used to make tortillas in Mexico and Central America.

minga—Wage laborer in Andean silver mines.

mita—Labor draft in the Andes, from a Quechua word; used most famously to provide labor for silver mining at Potosí and mercury mining at Huancavelica; see *repartimiento*.

mitayo—Indigenous worker subject to the *mita*.

mulato/-a—Term originally applied to individuals of mixed African and European ancestry; also used in many parts of Spanish America to describe people of mixed African and indigenous ancestry.

originario—Native-born resident of an indigenous village, generally with long-term ancestral roots in the community; included in assessments of village labor and tribute obligations.

pardo—Literally "brown," applied to people of part-African origins in many parts of Spanish America; less pejorative than *mulato*.

patrón—Large landowner or other elite Spaniard who offered a combination of credit and protection from the law to employees, expecting loyalty and submission in return.

peninsular—Spaniard from the Iberian peninsula, as opposed to a *criollo* (creole), or American-born Spaniard.

petate—Sleeping mat woven of reeds.

pulque—A cloudy, weakly fermented Mexican beverage made from the *maguey* cactus; main alcoholic substance prior to Spanish arrival.

quilombo (Sp. palenque)—Outlaw settlement of *maroons* (escaped slaves).

quinoa—A grain eaten since ancient times in the Andean region of South America.

recogimiento—State of seclusion for women, either in the home or in an institution known as a *casa de recogimiento,* for a variety of reasons ranging from protection to punishment.

regidor—Municipal councilor in Spanish America.

reinois—Portuguese from Portugal (i.e., from the *reino,* or "kingdom," as opposed to Brazilian-born *mazombo*).

repartimiento—Labor draft by which a fixed proportion of a native village's adult male population was sent to work for Spanish employers in mining or agricultural activities for a specified length of time; generally called *mita* in the Andes.

resgate (Sp. rescate)—Slave trade camouflaged as the "rescue" by European Christians of native peoples subjected to enslavement, cannibalism, or, simply, a non-Christian religious atmosphere while under the control of other unconquered indigenous groups.

safra (Sp. zafra)—Period of the sugarcane harvest, lasting as long as nine months in Brazil.

senado da câmara—Rough equivalent in Brazil of Spanish American *cabildo,* or municipal council.

Siete Partidas—Medieval Spanish law code providing some legal protections, at least in theory, to slaves.

tinku—Ritual conflict acted out in Andean native communities during the days immediately preceding the beginning of Lent; rooted in precolonial fertility rites as well as historical animosities both within and between native villages.

tribute—Tax assessed on heads of household in native villages in Spanish America, generally including a mix of cash and in-kind contributions; an alternative tribute, collected less systematically, was levied on free people of African ancestry and natives who had no ties to particular villages (see *laborío*).

vaquero—Spanish American ranch hand, cowboy.

viceroyalty—Largest administrative region in Spanish America, governed by a viceroy; there were two, Peru and New Spain, until the 18th century, when two more, New Granada and La Plata, were carved out of Peru's jurisdiction.

yanacona—Andean natives tied as domestic laborers to individual Spaniards rather than belonging to a tribute-paying village.

zambo—Used in some parts of Spanish America as a designation for individuals of mixed African and indigenous ancestry.

ANNOTATED BIBLIOGRAPHY

Andrews, George Reid. *Afro-Latin America, 1800–2000*. New York: Oxford University Press, 2004.

Survey of the experience of Africans and their descendants in modern Latin America, with introductory chapters on the role of black soldiers in independence armies and the state of Afro-Latin America at the end of the colonial era.

Archer, Christon, ed. *The Wars of Independence in Spanish America*. Wilmington, Del.: Scholarly Resources, 2000.

Collection of essays and primary sources offering a variety of details on daily life during wartime, including the impact of armed violence, troop movements, and disease.

"The Archive of Early American Images." John Carter Brown Library. http://www.brown.edu/Facilities/John_Carter_Brown_Library/pages/ea_hmpg.html.

Online repository of roughly 6,000 images from the colonial era, many from Latin America, drawn from the library's vast collection of rare books and manuscripts reflecting life in the Americas from the late 15th to the early 19th centuries.

"The Aztecs and the Making of Colonial Mexico." Newberry Library. http://www.newberry.org/aztecs/.

Online exhibition of Aztec codices and colonial-era manuscripts, maps, and images, accompanied by scholarly commentary on native peoples' experience under colonial rule.

Bakewell, Peter. *A History of Latin America, c. 1450 to the Present.* 2nd ed. Malden, Mass.: Blackwell, 2004.

General history of Latin America that devotes substantial attention to the colonial era. The author is a leading expert on labor systems and the colonial mining economy in northern New Spain (Zacatecas) and the southern Andes (Potosí).

Bakewell, Peter. *Miners of the Red Mountain: Indian Labor in Potosí, 1545–1650.* Albuquerque: University of New Mexico Press, 1984.

Major study of the origins and development of the *mita* and its role in Andean silver mining.

Bauer, Arnold J. *Goods, Power, History: Latin America's Material Culture.* Cambridge, Cambridge University Press, 2001.

Examination of the central role that food, clothing, and other material goods have played in the development of Latin American social relationships from the pre-Columbian era to the present.

Bethel, Leslie, ed. *Colonial Brazil.* Cambridge: Cambridge University Press, 1987.

Series of essays by distinguished scholars on various aspects of colonial Brazilian history and society, including chapters on the plantation and ranching economies and the gold rush in Minas Gerais.

Bowser, Frederick. *The African Slave in Colonial Peru, 1524–1650.* Stanford, Calif.: Stanford University Press, 1974.

Major study of the lives of Africans and their descendants in Peru during the era when African migration was at its peak, including discussion of occupations, family life, religious practices, and many other topics.

Boyer, Richard. *Lives of the Bigamists: Marriage, Family, and Community in Colonial Mexico.* Albuquerque: University of New Mexico Press, 1995 and 2001.

Examination of many aspects of life in colonial Mexico based on the author's examination of cases of people brought before the Inquisition on bigamy charges.

Boyer, Richard, and Gregory Spurling, eds. *Colonial Lives: Documents on Latin American History, 1550–1850.* New York: Oxford University Press, 2000.

Collection of 23 fascinating primary sources from both Spanish America and Brazil with introduction and analysis by scholars. Representative topics include Indian villagers' use of the court system, religious workers harassing their parishioners, a drunken party at an estate in Quito, charges of homosexual seduction, a trial before the Inquisition, the wills of wealthy black slaveholders in Brazil, and a Spanish viceroy's assessment in 1816 of the rebellion in Mexico that eventually produced independence.

Bristol, Joan Cameron. *Christians, Blasphemers and Witches: Afro-Mexican Ritual Practice in the Seventeenth Century.* Albuquerque: University of New Mexico Press, 2007.

Analysis of the spiritual life of Africans and their descendants in early colonial Mexico, examining both Christian and non-Christian ritual practices. Includes discussion of the African nun Juana Esperanza de San Alberto, healing rituals, and tactics employed by slaves and other people of African origins to exert greater control over their own lives.

Burkholder, Mark A., and Lyman L. Johnson. *Colonial Latin America.* 5th ed. New York: Oxford University Press, 2004.

Comprehensive introductory survey of political and social life in the Spanish and Portuguese colonies in the Americas.

Burns, Kathryn. *Colonial Habits: Convents and the Spiritual Economy of Cuzco, Peru.* Durham, N.C.: Duke University Press, 1999.

Study of several important convents in Cuzco and Arequipa throughout the colonial era and beyond. Key themes include the origins and development of race- and class-based distinctions among nuns and the role of convents in facilitating the circulation of land and capital among the colonial elite.

Chance, John K. *Race and Class in Colonial Oaxaca.* Stanford, Calif.: Stanford University Press, 1978.

Analysis of race and the caste/class system of the city of Oaxaca, Mexico, emphasizing regional divergence from supposed colonial norms with regard to the race-based social structure.

Chant, Silvia, with Nikki Craske. *Gender in Latin America.* New Brunswick, N.J.: Rutgers University Press, 2003.

Two scholars in the fields of geography and politics review work of the past three decades on changing gender dynamics in the region. Topics include politics, poverty, population, health, sexuality, family, work, and migration.

Conrad, Robert Edgar. *Children of God's Fire: A Documentary History of Black Slavery in Brazil.* Princeton, N.J.: Princeton University Press, 1983.

Wide-ranging collection of documentary evidence addressing all aspects of the lives of the enslaved both on and off the sugar plantation.

Cook, Noble David, and W. George Lovell, eds. *"Secret Judgments of God": Old World Disease in Colonial Spanish America.* Norman: University of Oklahoma Press, 1992.

Collection of essays examining the impact of epidemics in colonial Spanish America, including material on the state of medical infrastructure and public health.

Cope, R. Douglas. *The Limits of Racial Domination: Plebeian Society in Colonial Mexico City, 1660–1720*. Madison: University of Wisconsin Press, 1994.

  Examines the Spanish system of racial hierarchy in an era when that system as originally conceived was breaking down. Includes a detailed description of the events surrounding a major food riot in Mexico City in 1692.

Eltis, David, et al. "The Trans-Atlantic Slave Trade Database: Voyages." Emory University. http://www.slavevoyages.org/tast/index.faces.

  Online database providing a variety of information from the records of nearly 35,000 Atlantic slaving voyages to all parts of the Americas, with introductory commentary by experts on diverse aspects of the history and study of the slave trade.

Gage, Thomas. *Travels in the New World*. Edited by J. Eric S. Thompson. Norman: University of Oklahoma Press, 1958.

  Modern edition of the 1648 memoirs of a renegade English Dominican monk who spent 10 years serving as a priest in Mexico and Central America, mostly in Guatemala, before returning to England, turning Protestant, and agitating for an English invasion of mainland Spanish America. Exaggeration and biases aside, an engaging and informative first-person description of 17th-century Spanish American society by an outsider.

Gibson, Charles. *The Aztecs under Spanish Rule: A History of the Indians of the Valley of Mexico, 1519–1810*. Stanford, Calif.: Stanford University Press, 1964.

  Pioneering study of life in central Mexico's indigenous communities after the Spanish arrival.

Gutiérrez, Ramón. *When Jesus Came the Corn Mothers Went Away: Marriage, Sexuality and Power in New Mexico, 1500–1846*. Stanford, Calif.: Stanford University Press, 1991.

  Examination of the encounter between Spaniards and the Pueblo people and the ensuing efforts of both the church and the local Spanish elite to dominate New Mexico's colonial society through control over marriage and sexual practices.

Handler, Jerome S., and Michael L. Tuite Jr. "The Atlantic Slave Trade and Slave Life in the Americas: A Visual Record." Virginia Foundation for the Humanities and University of Virginia. http://hitchcock.itc.virginia.edu/Slavery/index.php.

  Online collection of more than 1,200 paintings and other images of life in both Africa and the Americas during the era of the slave trade, many of them originating in colonial Latin America.

Hecht, Tobias, ed. *Minor Omissions, Children in Latin American History and Society*. Madison: University of Wisconsin Press, 2002.
> Anthology presenting a wide variety of perspectives on childhood in Latin America including history, art history, sociology, religion, fiction, and the testimony of a 23-year-old Brazilian woman who when she wrote this had spent 14 years living on the street.

"Hispanic Reading Room Online Collections.," Library of Congress. http://www.loc.gov/rr/hispanic/onlinecol.html.
> Provides online access to some of the Latin America–related materials held in the Library of Congress, including Aztec codices and colonial-era manuscripts and maps.

Hoberman, Louisa Schell, and Susan Migden Socolow. *Cities & Society in Colonial Latin America*. Albuquerque: University of New Mexico Press, 1986.
> This anthology includes the work of a wide variety of social historians who cover many aspects of urban life in the colonial period, including a chapter on the working people of colonial Brazil during the 18th century.

Hoberman, Louisa Schell, and Susan Migden Socolow. *The Countryside in Colonial Latin America*. Albuquerque: University of New Mexico Press, 1997.
> A companion anthology to the one listed above, with chapters on the rural economy, material life, agricultural societies and their social structures, conflict, religious workers, indigenous people, and people of African descent.

Johnson, Lyman L., and Sonya Lipsett-Rivera, eds. *The Faces of Honor: Sex, Shame and Violence in Colonial Latin America*. Albuquerque: University of New Mexico Press, 1998.
> Collection of essays on the role of honor in colonial Latin American society and its intimate association with ideas about gender, race, and socioeconomic status.

Juan, Jorge, and Antonio de Ulloa. *A Voyage to South America*. Introduction by Irving A. Leonard. Translated by John Adams. Abridged. Tempe: Arizona State University, 1975.
> Famous 18th-century account of travel through Andean South America by a pair of young Spanish naval officers dispatched to the region on a scientific expedition.

Kiddy, Elizabeth W. *Blacks of the Rosary: Memory and History in Minas Gerais, Brazil*. University Park: Pennsylvania State Press, 2005.
> Examination of participation by Africans and their descendants in brotherhoods of the Rosary in Brazil from the early era of the Atlantic slave trade to the recent past.

Klein, Herbert S., and Ben Vinson III. *African Slavery in Latin America and the Caribbean.* 2nd ed. New York: Oxford University Press, 2007.
Concise, recently updated overview of the experience of enslaved Africans throughout Latin America both within and outside the major plantation zones.

Komisaruk, Catherine. "Rape Narratives, Rape Silences: Sexual Violence and Judicial Testimony in Colonial Guatemala." *Biography* 31, no. 3 (2008): 369–96.
Detailed study of a few cases of sexual assault along with a discussion of how colonial authorities viewed women's safety and why rape cases rarely show up in the judicial record.

Landers, Jane G., and Barry M. Robinson, eds. *Slaves, Subjects, and Subversives: Blacks in Colonial Latin America.* Albuquerque: University of New Mexico Press, 2006.
Collection of essays on the experiences of Africans and their descendents during the colonial era, with a chapter on the transformation of a *maroon* community into a recognized black town on the Gulf Coast of Mexico.

Lanning, John Tate Lanning. *The Royal Protomedicato: The Regulation of the Medical Professions in the Spanish Empire.* Edited by John Jay TePaske. Durham, N.C.: Duke University Press, 1985.
Valuable older study of the regulation of medical professions in colonial Spanish America, including material on both formal and informal medical practices as well as medical education.

"Latin American Network Information Center." University of Texas. http://lanic.utexas.edu/.
Online clearinghouse for information on all things Latin American, including hundreds of links to historical and other resources on the region as a whole as well as individual countries within it.

Lavrin, Asunción, ed. *Sexuality and Marriage in Colonial Latin America.* Lincoln: University of Nebraska Press, 1989.
Anthology of work on women, marriage, and sexuality that helped lay the foundation for an explosion of scholarship in these areas during the past two decades.

Leonard, Irving A. *Baroque Times in Old Mexico.* Ann Arbor: University of Michigan Press, 1959.
Entertaining older study of both elite and popular forms of culture in 17th-century Mexico City.

Leonard, Irving A., ed. *Colonial Travelers in Latin America.* New York: Alfred A. Knopf, 1972.
Collection of primary sources containing observations by a series of European visitors about colonial Latin American society.

Lockhart, James. *The Nahuas After the Conquest: A Social and Cultural History of the Indians of Central Mexico, Sixteenth through Eighteenth Centuries.* Stanford, Calif.: Stanford University Press, 1992.

Study of native communities in colonial central Mexico emphasizing continuity rather than change in native society after the Spanish arrival.

Lockhart, James. *Spanish Peru, 1532–1560: A Social History.* 2nd ed. Madison: University of Wisconsin Press, 1994.

Pioneering examination of various social groups and the interaction between them in early colonial society; provides a basis for understanding the later colonial era.

Lockhart, James, and Stuart B. Schwartz. *Early Latin America: A History of Colonial Spanish America and Brazil.* Cambridge: Cambridge University Press, 1983.

General introduction to the colonial era focusing on the role of precolonial indigenous societies in shaping colonial social developments and emphasizing regional distinctions and the wide variety of colonial lifestyles.

MacLeod, Murdo J. *Spanish Central America: A Socioeconomic History, 1520–1720.* Reprinted with a new introduction. Austin: University of Texas Press, 2008.

Key study of the economic and demographic factors that shaped daily life in colonial Central American societies.

Martin, Cheryl E., and Mark Wasserman. *Latin America and Its People.* Vol. 1. New York: Pearson Longman, 2005.

Survey of colonial Latin America with excellent background on pre-Columbian societies. Includes excerpts from primary sources and short discussions of how they are used by scholars to create a picture of the past.

Matthew, Laura E., and Michel R Oudijk, eds. *Indian Conquistadors: Indigenous Allies in the Conquest of Mesoamerica.* Norman: University of Oklahoma Press, 2007.

Collection of essays exploring the role played by the central Mexican native peoples who served as allies of the Spaniards during the early invasions of southern Mexico and northern Central America.

McAlister, Lyle N. *Spain and Portugal in the New World, 1492–1700.* Minneapolis: University of Minnesota Press, 1984.

Part of a series focusing on the European expansion that began in the 15th century. Begins with the reconquest of the Iberian Peninsula and covers the encounter between the Europeans and the native peoples of the Western Hemisphere and the establishment of the Spanish and Portuguese empires in the Americas.

Metcalf, Alida C. *Family and Frontier in Colonial Brazil: Santana de Paraíba, 1580–1822.* Austin: University of Texas Press, 1992, 2005.
  Analysis of family structures that challenges common stereotypes about slave families, demonstrating that some slave owners encouraged formal Catholic marriage among their slaves even if marriage did not necessarily prevent later separation.

Mintz, Sidney W. *Sweetness and Power: The Place of Sugar in Modern History.* New York: Penguin, 1985.
  Insightful analysis of the relationship between the production and consumption of sugar as these shaped both slave-based plantation societies and the larger modern world.

Nesvig, Martin Austin, ed. *Local Religion in Colonial Mexico.* Albuquerque: University of New Mexico Press, 2006.
  Collection of essays on various aspects of religious life at the local level in colonial Mexico, with chapters on black *cofradías* and slave resistance.

Pilcher, Jeffrey. *¡Que vivan los tamales! Food and the Making of Mexican Identity.* Albuquerque: University of New Mexico Press, 1998.
  Examination of food in Mexican history with introductory chapters on precolonial and colonial cuisine and the encounter between the corn-based Mesoamerican and wheat-based Iberian diets.

Premo, Bianca. *Children of the Father King: Youth, Authority, and Legal Minority in Colonial Lima.* Chapel Hill: University of North Carolina Press, 2005.
  Detailed study of children and young people in the seat of the Viceroyalty of Peru with considerable attention to delinquency, institutions that dealt with children, and shifts that followed the reforms in the 18th century.

Price, Richard, ed. *Maroon Societies: Rebel Slave Communities in the Americas,* 3rd ed. Baltimore: The Johns Hopkins University Press, 1996.
  Anthology of documents and scholarly commentary treating the history of communities of escaped slaves throughout the Americas. Brazil and parts of Spanish America receive substantial attention.

Restall, Matthew. *Seven Myths of the Spanish Conquest.* Oxford: Oxford University Press, 2003.
  Thematic discussion of important but often neglected aspects of the conquest era that shaped subsequent social and cultural developments, including the role of people of African ancestry, both en-slaved and free, in the initial Spanish invasions.

Restall, Matthew, ed. *Beyond Black and Red: African-Native Relations in Colonial Latin America*. Albuquerque: University of New Mexico Press, 2005.
Collection of articles exploring relations, ranging from hostile to harmonious, between native peoples and Africans and their descendants in the colonial era.

Schwaller, John F., ed. *The Church in Colonial Latin America*. Wilmington, Del.: Scholarly Resources, 2000.
Collection of essays on a key colonial institution, including a chapter on investigations of idolatry among indigenous peoples in the Andes.

Schwartz, Stuart B. *Slaves, Peasants, and Rebels: Reconsidering Brazilian Slavery*. Urbana: University of Illinois Press, 1996.
Collection of essays on Africans and slavery in Brazil by a renowned scholar of these subjects, discussing various aspects of plantation life as well as settlements of escaped slaves, notably the Angolan-influenced *quilombo* of Palmares.

Schwartz, Stuart B. *Sugar Plantations in the Formation of Brazilian Society: Bahia 1550–1835*. Cambridge: Cambridge University Press, 1985.
Major examination of the culture of sugar and slavery in Bahia, including a wealth of detail on the everyday lives of the working people of the plantations, both enslaved and free.

Sigal, Pete, ed. *Infamous Desire: Male Homosexuality in Colonial Latin America*. Chicago: University of Chicago Press, 2003.
Edited volume with various chapters on the nature and expression of same-sex relationships involving men in a number of regions of colonial Latin America.

Silverblatt, Irene. *Modern Inquisitions: Peru and the Colonial Origins of the Civilized World*. Durham, N.C.: Duke University Press, 2004.
Study of the operation of the Inquisition in mid-17th-century Peru and its legacy for the modern world. Provides extensive detail from the testimony of individuals caught up in the Inquisition's web.

Socolow, Susan. *The Women of Colonial Latin America*. Cambridge: Cambridge University Press, 2000.
Essential study of women's lives in the period with chapters on women of different ethnic groups, social classes, and occupations, but stressing the centrality of gender in defining women's lives in a patriarchal society.

Stavig, Ward. *The World of Túpac Amaru: Conflict, Community, and Identity in Colonial Peru.* Lincoln: University of Nebraska Press, 1999.

   Examination of indigenous society and Indian-Spanish relations in the southern Peruvian highlands from roughly 1600 to the Túpac Amaru rebellion of the late 18th century.

Stein, Stanley J., and Barbara H. Stein. *The Colonial Heritage of Latin America: Essays on Economic Dependence in Perspective.* New York: Oxford University Press, 1970.

   Older but still fundamental study of the colonial roots of Latin American economic dependency and underdevelopment.

Stern, Steve J. *The Secret History of Gender: Women, Men, and Power in Late Colonial Mexico.* Chapel Hill: University of North Carolina Press, 1995.

   Study of gender and power revealing that women of the popular classes helped shape a moral code that was not always defined by men, but contingent on circumstances. Rather than being passive victims of male dominance, women granted, delayed, or withheld their household services in ways that gained them some power over their lives.

Taylor, William B. *Drinking, Homicide, and Rebellion in Colonial Mexican Villages.* Stanford, Calif.: Stanford University Press, 1979.

   Systematic analysis of the three phenomena listed in the title, with numerous examples of their respective manifestations in rural daily life.

Taylor, William B. *Magistrates of the Sacred: Priests and Parishioners in Eighteenth-Century Mexico.* Stanford, Calif.: Stanford University Press, 1996.

   Exhaustive study of the late-colonial church in key Mexican regions, explaining its economic, social, and cultural importance especially in rural communities.

Thornton, John. *Africa and Africans in the Making of the Atlantic World, 1400–1800.* 2nd ed. Cambridge: Cambridge University Press, 1998.

   Examination of the African role in shaping the world of the transatlantic slave trade, emphasizing the continuity of African cultural practices in the Americas.

Twinam, Ann. *Public Lives, Private Secrets: Gender, Honor, Sexuality, and Illegitimacy in Colonial Spanish America.* Stanford, Calif.: Stanford University Press, 1999.

   Study of 144 applications for legitimacy and the struggle for honor and a good name in colonial society.

van Deusen, Nancy E. *Between the Sacred and the Worldly: The Institutional and Cultural Practice of* Recogimiento *in Colonial Lima.* Stanford, Calif.: Stanford University Press, 2001.

Examination of the practice of secluding women either in their homes or in *casas de recogimiento* for both protective and punitive reasons.

Van Oss, Adriaan C. *Catholic Colonialism: A Parish History of Guatemala, 1524–1821*. Cambridge: Cambridge University Press, 1986.
Study of the role of regular and secular clergy in shaping colonial culture.

Vinson, Ben, III. *Bearing Arms for His Majesty: The Free-Colored Militia in Colonial Mexico*. Stanford, Calif.: Stanford University Press, 2001.
Examination of the key role played by free people of African ancestry in staffing colonial Mexican militias and the larger social place of these militiamen from the early 17th through late 18th centuries.

Viqueira Albán, Juan Pedro. *Propriety and Permissiveness in Bourbon Mexico*. Translated by Sonya Lipsett-Rivera and Sergio Rivera Ayala. Wilmington, Del.: Scholarly Resources, 1999.
Study of popular culture in 18th-century Mexico City and Enlightenment-oriented efforts to repress it as part of the Bourbon reforms.

von Germeten, Nicole. *Black Blood Brothers: Confraternities and Social Mobility for Afro-Mexicans*. Gainesville: University Press of Florida, 2006.
Examination of changes over time in the nature of participation by Africans and their descendants in colonial Mexican *cofradías*, emphasizing adaptation to Spanish cultural norms.

Walker, Charles F. *Smoldering Ashes: Cuzco and the Creation of Republican Peru, 1780–1840*. Durham, N.C.: Duke University Press, 1999.
Analysis of the Túpac Amaru rebellion and its political and social legacy for highland Peru.

Webre, Stephen. "Water and Society in a Spanish American City: Santiago de Guatemala, 1555–1773." *Hispanic American Historical Review* 70, no. 1 (1990): 57–84.
Rare study of the development of infrastructure for water delivery to a colonial city and the social context that shaped its impact.

INDEX

About the Authors

ANN JEFFERSON has a PhD in history with a focus on Latin America from the University of Massachusetts at Amherst and is a lecturer in the History Department at the University of Tennessee at Knoxville. Her work focuses on resistance and rebellion in Latin America. The central players in her dissertation are the *mulatos libres* of eastern Guatemala at the end of the colonial period.

PAUL LOKKEN has a PhD in Latin American history from the University of Florida and is Associate Professor of History at Bryant University in Smithfield, Rhode Island. He has published a number of journal articles and book chapters on the African experience in colonial Central America.